WITHDRAWN

International Political
Risk Management
The Brave New World

WITHDRAWN
UTSA LIBRARIES

International Political Risk Management

The Brave New World

Theodore H. Moran, Editor

The World Bank
Washington, D.C.

© 2004 The International Bank for Reconstruction and Development / The World
Bank
1818 H Street, NW
Washington, DC 20433
Telephone 202-473-1000
Internet www.worldbank.org
E-mail feedback@worldbank.org

All rights reserved.

1 2 3 4 07 06 05 04

The findings, interpretations, and conclusions expressed herein are those of the
author(s) and do not necessarily reflect the views of the Board of Executive Directors of the World Bank or the governments they represent.

The World Bank does not guarantee the accuracy of the data included in this
work. The boundaries, colors, denominations, and other information shown on any
map in this work do not imply any judgment on the part of the World Bank concerning the legal status of any territory or the endorsement or acceptance of such
boundaries.

Rights and Permissions

The material in this work is copyrighted. Copying and/or transmitting portions
or all of this work without permission may be a violation of applicable law. The
World Bank encourages dissemination of its work and will normally grant permission promptly.

For permission to photocopy or reprint any part of this work, please send a
request with complete information to the Copyright Clearance Center, Inc., 222 Rose-
wood Drive, Danvers, MA 01923, USA, telephone 978-750-8400, fax 978-750-4470,
www.copyright.com.

All other queries on rights and licenses, including subsidiary rights, should be
addressed to the Office of the Publisher, World Bank, 1818 H Street NW, Washington, DC 20433, USA, fax 202-522-2422, e-mail pubrights@worldbank.org.

ISBN 0-8213-5649-6

Library of Congress Cataloging-in-Publication Data has been applied for.

Library
University of Texas
at San Antonio

Contents

Preface

International Political Risk Management: The Brave New World is the second in a series of volumes based on the MIGA–Georgetown University Symposium on International Political Risk Management. Like its predecessor, this volume offers leading-edge assessments of needs and capabilities in the international political risk insurance industry. These assessments come from senior practitioners from the investor, financial, insurance, broker, and analytical communities who attended the Symposium at Georgetown University on October 25, 2002.

The volume leads off with the perspective from the "supply side" of how the political risk insurance market has reacted to the events of September 11, 2001, the Argentine economic crisis, and other corporate upheavals. It then turns to "demand side" concerns of investors and lenders, in particular those involved in large infrastructure projects in emerging markets. It concludes with an assessment of "finding common ground or uncommon solutions" in the face of currency crises, and new challenges to the definitions of expropriation, breach of contract, and political force majeure. The uncertain and unsettled nature of the arguments contained here makes the use of the subtitle "The Brave New World" particularly appropriate. But the diverse and detailed arguments in this volume come together in a somewhat surprising consensus that change, contraction, and even losses will prove beneficial for all participants in the industry, leading in the future, as in the past, to new creativity in managing exposures to international political risk.

MIGA's objective is to facilitate the flow of foreign direct investment to developing countries by alleviating investors' concerns about noncommercial risks. MIGA has always pursued this objective in a variety of ways. In addition to providing political risk insurance to investors and offering assistance in investment promotion to host countries, MIGA has selectively sponsored research on the challenges of assessing and managing political risk. This volume is a part of these larger endeavors.

The Karl F. Landegger Program in International Business Diplomacy at the School of Foreign Service, Georgetown University, conducts teaching and research at the intersection of international corporate strategy, public policy, and the conduct of business-government relations. The Landegger Program has active teaching and research programs devoted to political risk management techniques that might be useful to international investors and host governments alike.

To assist the reader, the editor of this volume, Dr. Theodore H. Moran, has provided a brief overview on each of the volume's three major sections.

Our shared objective is to promote productive foreign direct investment that can enhance the growth and welfare of developing countries. Our common hope is that readers will find that this volume contributes to reaching that objective.

Gerald T. West
Multilateral Investment
Guarantee Agency
The World Bank Group

Keith Martin
Multilateral Investment
Guarantee Agency
The World Bank Group

Theodore H. Moran
School of Foreign Service
Georgetown University

List of Acronyms

ADB	Asian Development Bank
AIG	American International Group
AIU	American International Underwriters
BOO	Build-Own-Operate
BOT	Build-Operate-Transfer
CCP	Chance-constrained programming
CEN	Confiscation, Expropriation, Nationalization
CESCE	Compañia Española de Seguros de Credito a la Exportación (Spain)
CEZ	Confederacion de Empresarios de Zaragoza (Spain)
COFACE	Compagnie Francaise Pour L'Assurance Du Commerce Exterieur (France)
COTUNACE	Compagnie Tunisienne Pour L'Assurance Du Commerce Exterieur (Tunisia)
CUP	Cooperative Underwriting Program
DFC	Development Finance Corporation of Belize
ECAs	Export credit agencies
ECGD	Export Credits Guarantee Department
EDC	Export Development Corporation of Canada
EBRD	European Bank for Reconstruction and Development
Ex-Im	U.S. Export-Import Bank
EU	European Union
FDI	Foreign Direct Investment
FFIEC	Federal Financial Institutions Examination Council of the United States
FMO	Financierings-Maatschappij voor Ontwikkelings-landen, N.V. (Netherlands)
GAREAT	Gestion Assurance / Réassurance des Risques Attentats & Actes de Terrorisme (France)
GIEK	Garanti-Instituttet for Eksportkreditt (Norway)
GSM	Global System for Mobile Communications
IBRD	International Bank for Reconstruction and Development

IDB	InterAmerican Development Bank
IFC	International Finance Corporation
IFTRIC	Israel Foreign Trade Risks Insurance Corporation, Ltd.
IMF	International Monetary Fund
IPP	Independent power project
IRA	Irish Republican Army
MDB	Multilateral development banks
MIGA	Multilateral Investment Guarantee Agency
MITI	Ministry of International Trade and Industry of Japan (part of METI as of 2001)
MOTC	Ministry of Transportation and Communication of Taiwan
MOU	Memorandum of understanding
MVM	Magyar Villamos Művek (Hungary)
M/LT	Medium/long term
NEXI	Nippon Export and Investment Insurance
OECD	Organisation for Economic Co-operation and Development
OeKB	Oesterreichische Kontrollbank Aktiengellschaft (Austria)
OII	Overseas Investment Insurance
OPIC	Overseas Private Investment Corporation
PPA	Power purchase agreements
PRI	Political Risk Insurance
RMS	Risk Management Solutions
SACE	Istituto per i Servizi Assicurativi del Commercio Estero (Italy)
SARS	Severe Acute Respiratory Syndrome
SASRIA	South African Special Risks Insurance Associations
SEC	Slovene Export Corporation
SIMEST	Societa Italiana Per Le Imprese All'Estero (Italy)
SME	Small- and medium-size enterprises
SRIR	Special Risk Insurance and Reinsurance Luxembourg, S.A.
S&P	Standard and Poors
TPSA	Telekomunikacja Polska (Poland)
TRIA	Terrorism Risk Insurance Act of 2002
UNCTAD	United Nations Committee on Trade and Development
WTO	World Trade Organization
ZEMS	Zurich Emerging Markets Solutions

Introduction

Motomichi Ikawa
Executive Vice President
Multilateral Investment Guarantee Agency

It is my distinct pleasure to introduce this second volume, *International Political Risk Management: The Brave New World*. The following papers and commentary grow out of the 2002 MIGA–Georgetown University Symposium on International Political Risk Management, held in October 2002. This third biennial symposium was held at a critical moment in the development of the political risk insurance (PRI) industry, given global and regional political and economic developments that had occurred since the previous symposium in 2000.

The symposium itself—both through the papers and commentary, and in the discussions with the audience—highlighted the challenges facing the PRI industry at this critical juncture. Readers of this volume will doubtlessly be able to appreciate the fact that our industry remains in flux—contradictions and unanswered questions abound, and it remains unclear how the expectations of host countries, investors, and insurers can all be met. Nonetheless, it is extremely important to highlight both the areas of agreement and of disagreement (or questioning) in order to move forward and bridge the gaps.

In this context, I would like to highlight some recent developments. Compared with April 2000, when the previous symposium was held, the world is a different place. As the contributors to this volume highlight, there has been a decrease in both PRI demand and supply—as well as some fundamental changes in the industry itself.

On the demand side, foreign direct investment (FDI) flows to developing countries have fallen—and they remain concentrated in a handful of countries. Furthermore, risks associated with FDI in emerging economies are higher—both in their scope (from civil unrest and war to economic crisis) and geographic dispersion. However, many of the risks faced by investors now blur the line between commercial and political acts, leading some investors to question the value of PRI. On the supply side, events in Argentina, the September 11th attacks, and instability in many corners of the world have also had a profound effect on the PRI industry, reducing many providers' capacity and tenor for projects in developing countries and making them more risk-adverse. Additionally, terrorism and sabotage, long included in standard property coverage, is now routinely carved out by property insurance providers, leading investors either to self-insure for those risks, or to seek coverage with PRI providers.

Complicating matters for investors and insurers is the fact that the nature of certain underlying risks has changed in recent years. Historically, PRI has covered risks associated with events readily identifiable as being political—such as war and civil disturbance, currency inconvertibility, and traditional expropriation. As highlighted by several contributors, who have reviewed recent claims and near-claims, however, it has become more relevant to analyze whether the host government was in a position to avoid causing a claim to arise in the first place. Economic crises appear to be pushing traditionally pro-FDI governments into taking a course that may cause expropriation, inconvertibility, or breach of contract/contract frustration claims. Examples include the actions of Indonesia with respect to the cancellation of power plants and Argentina's imposition of currency controls. In this sense, political risks are becoming more economic events rather than purely concerned with the political will of the host country.

Another factor that makes the lives of investors and PRI providers more difficult is that increasingly, privatization and decentralization are blurring the line between commercial and noncommercial risks, when a public entity acts in a commercial capacity (e.g., as a recipient or a supplier of goods and services). A growing number of projects (especially involving FDI) either include a role for these parastatals or for subsovereign entities, such as municipal and provincial governments. Increasingly, sponsors are worried about the ability—or willingness—of central governments to enforce contracts that involve parastatals and subsovereigns. Beyond this, though, investors are also concerned about whether the political risk insurance coverage they have been purchasing is adequate to cover them for contract frustration on the part of these entities, particularly when an argument can be made that they were acting in a commercial capacity.

Part of the reason for the growing number of conflicts between investors and various host country authorities (including parastatals and subsovereigns), particularly in infrastructure privatizations, lies in the often unrealistic expectations of both sides at the onset. This is highlighted by several authors in this volume. The problems are compounded by the fact that the legal and regulatory frameworks in many countries are not yet sufficiently mature to ensure adequate, equal protection for FDI—or to enable the host countries to adequately bargain with foreign investors at the outset. When faced with economic difficulties and public concern over sudden, large increases in tariffs (e.g., the result of an external shock to a domestic economy that leads to a rapid depreciation of the local currency), many governments—especially at the local and state levels—are tempted to try to change arrangements that have been made with foreign investors.

As a result of these often bitter experiences, privatization is no longer considered to be a panacea by the public in many developing countries. MIGA has increasingly witnessed examples of this in recent years, especially in the power sector, where attempts to renegotiate power purchase agreements have become commonplace (e.g., in the context of a rapid devaluation of the local currency in relation to the dollar or euro). I want to emphasize, however, that with a strong commitment on their respective parts, host governments and investors can avoid conflicts resulting in a claim. In one recent example, we were able to successfully mediate a dispute between a power company and the government of Jiangsu Province in China regarding a project MIGA had guaranteed. With the support of the government of China, we were able to find a solution that took into account the interests of both sides. Nonetheless, this case is still an exception; many other investment disputes are pending in developing countries around the world. Both sides must focus on their long-term interests, rather than on possibilities for short-term economic or political gain, in order to find mutually acceptable solutions when extenuating circumstances arise.

One cumulative effect of these developments is that lenders have become reluctant to take on emerging market risks at all. We have seen the closing of project finance departments at some major banks; other banks have been withdrawing capacity from developing countries and emerging markets, especially in Latin America. The lenders no longer see PRI as a sufficient risk mitigant on its own, given the fact that some of the major risks may lie outside of the scope of traditional political risk coverages, as several authors point out. For their part, equity sponsors of projects are increasingly turning to other sources of financing—including local financing in the developing countries—and to innovative public-private partnerships. These sponsors are also asking for new risk mitigation tools that take into account the changing political risks of today's marketplace, such as coverage in local currency and expanded contract frustration coverage.

Not all of the news in the PRI marketplace, or in emerging economies, is negative. Since investment insurance is not an actuarial science, it relies on both providers and purchasers to learn from events, and to fashion a stronger product. One example is that many clients, particularly lenders, are reviewing their PRI coverages more carefully in the wake of pesification in Argentina. Given that pesification did not fall into the definition of events for which banks had traditionally purchased coverage (transfer/inconvertibility and expropriation of funds), banks are now increasingly interested in purchasing full expropriation coverage. Insurers, too, are learning lessons from these events, and efforts to increase FDI flows to developing countries will hinge, in part, on the industry's willingness to provide the necessary coverage, even in markets that may be perceived to be risky.

Another positive development is that most governments around the world have been proactively facilitating private foreign direct investment, as they come to the realization that FDI is vital for economic development and poverty reduction. Very rarely do governments these days engage in outright nationalization without compensation, or impose long-lasting transfer or convertibility restrictions. What has changed in recent years, in a good number of cases, is the *form* of foreign involvement. Many of the large-scale privatizations of the 1990s are completed, and developing countries have learned a variety of lessons from them. One is the increased emphasis—especially in sensitive sectors like water and sanitation—on private-public partnerships that involve an explicit role for public authorities in the project. These investments offer new challenges for investment insurers, particularly in the area of breach of contract coverage, as they may not operate on a fully commercial basis (continuing, for example, explicit subsidies for the poor).

Given the increased risks, the changing nature of FDI into developing countries, and the transformation of political risks themselves, how can we sustain and increase FDI flows into emerging economies and developing countries?

First, we will need a new vision of our industry, and even of the meaning of political risks. In particular, many investors have questioned whether their political risk insurance is really effective against the risks they are actually facing now. These investors have increasingly requested more comprehensive coverage of their investments—including some portion of commercial risks. In the PRI market, breach of contract/contract frustration coverage has become more commonplace compared with three years ago. As several contributors point out, a new distribution of risks among those who are best positioned to shoulder them is critical for sustaining and increasing FDI flows into developing countries.

Second, redistributing the risks will call for enhanced partnerships and collaboration among insurers and other risk mitigation entities. MIGA already has extensive experience in this area; we have forged strong relationships with private and public insurers, reinsurers, and brokers that are standing up well in the current difficult PRI market. As we look forward to strengthening existing relationships, we need to recognize that the changing nature of risk will require new partnerships with other players in the risk mitigation marketplace. Given the difficult environment, it is equally imperative that insurers and banks adequately address ongoing issues, such as pledge of shares and Basel II. For public insurers, such as MIGA, it may also require reviewing some of the restrictions imposed on them by their constituent authorities, preventing them from fully playing the constructive, pro-development role they could play.

Third, the host countries themselves need to step up their efforts to promote FDI and to minimize the risks to investors. This is especially true for investments in infrastructure projects and privatizations of state-owned enterprises. Those are two areas where host governments, through their regulatory agencies, traditionally have significant control with respect to tariffs and other potential issues that may be of concern to investors. Hence, if the host government can control and significantly reduce the risks to such projects, then the country can better ensure a continuous FDI flow into these sectors. This will not happen overnight—but it can be done through new, effective public-private partnerships, and through more effective legal, judicial, and regulatory frameworks. MIGA, together with the rest of the World Bank Group and other development institutions, can and must play an important role in this respect. On a larger scale, however, building an effective pro-investment climate should involve all parties that have a stake in the outcome: international financial institutions and development agencies; host governments (including the regulatory agencies and provincial or municipal governments); donor countries; industrial associations and chambers of commerce in the host countries; as well as foreign investors, lenders, and political risk insurers. This type of new partnership and effective dialogue is needed in order to forge a better, more predictable investment climate.

At the end of the day, change brings with it both risk and opportunity for all of us. Rethinking how risks—and particularly political risks—are managed, and what part investors, insurers, and host countries need to play, is not easy. We must stay focused on the fact that the potential returns for investors are significant, and that there continue to be vast numbers of good business opportunities in developing countries. There must be an emphasis from investors and host countries alike on flexibility, innovation, and long-term returns. A deal is a good deal if it benefits both sides, and this is just as true in developing economies as it is in developed ones. Through the kind of dialogue between practitioners (investors, insurers, brokers, and academics) that is highlighted in this volume, it is my hope that we can take some important steps toward finding ways to improve the risk profile of projects in developing countries—and thereby stimulate increased FDI flows. Finally, though, in a time of such fundamental changes in the process of globalization, and of so much need for effective poverty reduction, we must realize that the price of standing still—for all of us—is much higher than that of taking calculated risks. Those who do not adapt to the new risks and opportunities will become dinosaurs.

Political Risk Insurance Providers: In the Aftermath of the September 11 Attacks and Argentine Crisis

Overview

Theodore H. Moran, Editor

Part One provides a first look from the "supply side" at the reaction of the political risk insurance market to September 11, 2001, the Argentine economic crisis, and other recent corporate upheavals. This section starts off with the public provider's perspective, provided by Vivian Brown, Chief Executive of the U.K.'s Export Credits Guarantee Department (ECGD) and President of the Berne Union. The private market perspective is offered by David James, Senior Underwriter at Ascot Underwriting Limited (London), and John Salinger, President, AIG Global Trade and Political Risk (New York). Finally, the role of reinsurance in shaping the new marketplace for political risk insurance is discussed by Brian Duperreault, Chairman and Chief Executive Officer, ACE Limited, and Julie Martin, Vice President, MMC Enterprise Risk.

The impact of the September 11 attacks and the Argentine crisis "has dented the confidence of the private insurance market," argues Vivian Brown. Public providers of political risk insurance (PRI), meanwhile, are taking a more long-term view and are providing continuity in the marketplace, he says. On both the supply and demand side, the PRI industry is a very cyclical business.

September 11 alone resulted in the largest insurance loss ever recorded—estimates range from $40 billion to $100 billion in claims across multiple classes of coverage, including property, casualty, automobile, life, worker's compensation, and business interruption. However, Brown points out that statistics on worldwide economic activity and trade reveal the slowdown in foreign direct investment (FDI)—and the consequent decrease in demand for PRI—derive initially from the weakening global economy in 2001–02, and cannot therefore be attributed simply to specific events such as September 11, the Argentine crisis, or corporate scandals and failures.

Prior to September 11 and the Argentine crisis, Lloyd's of London represented approximately two-thirds of the market capacity, the remainder being split among public and other private providers. Following these events, however, the decrease in demand for PRI and the even sharper decline in the supply of coverage by Lloyd's and other providers has resulted in the maximum coverage available for any single transaction being decreased by half (to $1 billion); tenors being shortened from 10 years to 7 years, 7 years to 5 years, and 5 years to 3 years; and prices and premium rates being increased. Consequently, Lloyd's now supplies only one-third of the market, and export credit agencies (ECAs), multilateral agencies, and non-Lloyd's private insurers account for the remainder. Reinsurers have become especially cautious where risks are difficult to measure.

In Brown's view, September 11 and the Argentine crisis may represent a watershed for the evolution of the PRI industry, and for the interaction between public and private providers, including reinsurers.

Reinsurers have emerged as a key determinant of the evolution of the PRI industry, according to Brown. The ability of private insurers to provide the capacity and tenor required by investors depends directly upon the availability of reinsurance. However, World Trade Center losses alone reduced reinsurance capital by some $100 billion, and, while it is estimated that approximately $30 billion in new capital may flow in to replenish the reinsurance industry, it is not clear whether reinsurers will want to devote this capital to political risk coverage. In this environment, public insurers can complement private insurers by filling the gap in longer-term coverage.

The increase in demand for "pure terrorism" coverage—and the reluctance of the private sector to supply it—has also heightened the role of public sector providers. A number of ECAs previously included terrorism in their PRI cover without extra charge; after September 11, 2001, they have begun to charge a premium for it. The U.K. government has widened the scope of its terrorism coverage, by acting as insurer of last resort, for commercial property in the domestic market.

Brown notes that public providers of PRI have an advantage over private insurers, because public sector coverage allows investors to turn to their government for help with foreign host authorities. For example, following the change of government in Indonesia in 1998, ECGD had the U.K. embassy in Jakarta provided advocacy on behalf of U.K. investors, leading to successful continuation of their insured project.

It would be unfortunate, in Brown's view, if a split developed between public and private providers. Public agencies—most certainly ECGD—would like to encourage the private sector to respond to investors' needs. The Berne Union is a vehicle for encouraging cooperation between public and private insurers, and promotes the synergies between public and private sector coverage, instead of crowding out private suppliers.

The Argentine crisis raises questions of whether the resulting defaults arose from commercial or political events ("can't pay" versus "won't pay"). If claims are not paid, the credibility of political risk coverage could suffer. It is hoped, concludes Brown, that September 11 and Argentina enable the insurance industry to demonstrate how business risks can be covered by PRI, rather than indicating that such cover is illusory.

In contrast to the paralysis in other segments of the insurance industry, created by the uncertainty about future terrorist acts, political risk insurers have responded well to the challenge, argues David James.

September 11 represents the largest single claims event to which the insurance market has had to respond. It is difficult to accurately state the ultimate magnitude of the losses, as the majority of the losses result from life and liability coverage. However, when an estimated $40 billion to $100 billion is lost from a given industry, it would inevitably have a significant impact on the future functioning of that industry and would cast doubts on the solvency of the principal insurers. For example, Lloyd's has been downgraded by the rating agencies, even though it has never defaulted on a claim payment.

Underwriters have been forced to rebuild their balance sheets and reassess their risk models. Insurers have had to sell stocks during a period of depressed stock markets, to maintain liquidity. Further, the complacency toward the possibility of terrorism in developed countries that had marked risk modeling has suddenly shattered, James asserts.

Under normal circumstances, Argentina would have occupied the focus of attention for the political risk insurance industry. The Argentine crisis has, however, been overshadowed by preoccupation with global terrorism. The Argentine experience, in James's view, will question some of the central assumptions of insurers and bankers: Will the exclusion of insolvency and devaluation, upon which insurers rely, prevail? What caused a given loss—the insolvency of the borrower or the confiscation of funds? How are these different from inconvertibility? What is the value of an extended waiting period? Whom does the extended waiting period benefit—the insurer or the insured? Are equity holders better positioned to claim hard currency than lenders? Does the legal jurisdiction of the insurance policy make a difference?

It is an "unfortunate truth," James points out, "that only when loss occurs is the product truly tested." At the end of the day, he predicts, many clients will be glad they purchased coverage. The main preoccupation of political risk underwriters is not that claims have to be paid, but that the collapse of the Argentine economy has no end in sight. It is important to find a restructuring plan that provides a long-term solution to the country's plight. In this context, the wording in political risk insurance contracts that prevents the acceleration of loan repayments could be a blessing in disguise, as it provides time for a more fundamental resolution of the Argentine crisis.

Corporate scandals, such as those involving Enron and WorldCom, argues James, may benefit the quality of future foreign direct investment projects. These scandals will likely inspire greater scrutiny of complex financial structures and greater transparency on the part of investors. This will ultimately be helpful for firms that provide coverage against various kinds of investment risks.

John Salinger underscores the cyclical nature of the political risk insurance industry He argues that the post-September 11 market contraction may benefit all participants.

There was extraordinary growth in the private political risk insurance market during the 1990s, Salinger points out. Coverage capacity for a single risk grew from $250 million in 1992 to much more than $1 billion in 2000, and tenors lengthened from 3 years to 15 years. For the first time, private insurers could virtually match the offerings of governmental insurers. On the demand side, there was an explosive growth of FDI in emerging markets, encouraged by large-scale privatization in host countries around the world.

Although the attacks of September 11 did not directly cause a single loss in the political risk or trade credit markets, Salinger points out, the shock to the reinsurance industry spilled over, resulting in a shrinkage of political risk coverage to approximately $300 million per project. Insurance syndicates depleted their reinsurance protection, without being able to renew their coverage. The simultaneous arrival of recession, scandal, and the heightened perception of vulnerability, led to a crisis in business confidence for international investors and lenders, causing both to dramatically cut back their activities. Although insurance rates for property coverage, and for officers' and directors' liability coverage, have increased, weaker demand may hinder similar increases for political risk insurance and prevent new capital from replenishing the industry.

Salinger argues that the shrinkage of the private sector political risk insurance market following September 11 can be viewed as a positive development—a needed correction—since the industry had grown too large. Like Vivian Brown, John Salinger concludes that the optimal outcome would be a renewed impetus for public-private sector cooperation through co-insurance or reinsurance, a direction that OPIC has chosen. The Berne Union could facilitate such collaboration. A less desirable outcome would be for government insurers to compete more vigorously against their private sector counterparts.

It is clearly the case, continues Brian Duperreault, that the public and private political risk insurance markets are much more interdependent today than ever before. The ACE Group is unique among reinsurers in that its companies collaborate with multilateral banks, ECAs, and private underwriters to support transactions around the world.

Since September 11, 2001, political risk insurers have altered their view of risk. For the ACE Group of Companies alone, losses associated with this single event exceeded $550 million. Few—if any—companies are now willing to cover terrorism risk as part of a general property policy. What had previously been viewed as a seemingly minor risk by the political risk industry is now seen as too large and too unpredictable to be taken on as an unlimited liability. Terrorism risk insurance has been transformed into a catastrophe product, with strict limits of loss aggregation and geographic segmentation, shrinking the potential exposure for property losses associated with terrorism from trillions of dollars of nominal exposure to a few billion dollars. Governments in the industrialized world now have to fill the need for an insurer of last resort for terrorism.

It is possible that the economic meltdown in Argentina—and in other developing countries—may come to be known, according to Duperreault, as the "September 11 for Emerging Markets." More than the Latin debt crisis of the 1980s, the subsequent Mexican "tequila crisis" in the early 1990s, or the "Asian flu" of 1997–98, Argentina is proving to be a test case for the effectiveness of political risk insurance when an entire economy implodes. Whichever way the Argentine crisis concludes, it is certain that, in the future, policy wordings will be tighter and less ambiguous making it more difficult and onerous to close transactions.

Amidst more general retrenchment, the relationship between the ACE Group of Companies and MIGA could prove significant. Since 1997, ACE has allied with MIGA as an all-encompassing treaty reinsurance partner. ACE also participates with MIGA as a direct insurer through its 50 percent ownership position in Sovereign Risk Insurance Ltd., and through ACE Global Markets, the ACE Lloyd's syndicate. ACE has found considerable value, concludes Duperreault, in the extra protection and risk mitigation capabilities that multilateral bank guarantee facilities, bilateral insurers, and ECAs provide.

The September 11 losses, forecasts Julie Martin, will be twice or three times as much as the second largest catastrophic loss in recent U.S. history, namely, Hurricane Andrew in 1992, which caused $20 billion in losses.

To put terrorism coverage into perspective, approximately 80 percent of terrorist attacks against American interests over the past 30 years have been directed against American businesses. It would be a mistake to believe, however, that the risk of a future terrorist attack against American interests is likely to be concentrated on U.S. soil. The most recent State Department appraisals identify Latin America, Asia, Africa, and the Middle East as areas in which most anti-U.S. attacks have taken place. Unlike natural disasters, terrorism risk cannot be modeled satisfactorily. Countries that have experienced terrorist attacks have depended upon the government to assume the role of insurer of last resort, such as in Israel, South Africa, Spain, and the United Kingdom. In the United States, the Terrorism Risk Insurance Act of 2002 (TRIA) now provides a federal backstop for the terrorism market, subject to certain qualifications, as Martin identifies in her commentary.

Turning to other parts of the political risk insurance market, Martin agrees it is important that political risk claims are paid in Argentina, otherwise purchasers will discredit PRI as a product of little value. Many companies and lenders have concluded that it is preferable to self-insure, or buy comprehensive cover, rather than take the risk of purchasing PRI only to discover it does not cover a particular event after it has occurred.

Some recent wordings in PRI include economic viability as a test of whether a government's actions trigger expropriation coverage. The argument in the Argentine case is that the "pesification" of local obligations by the government, which results in the economic nonviability of a given entity, should be covered under this provision, even if it's not covered under the broader expropriation language. An interesting development is that Berne Union members are excluded from the requirement of getting Central Bank approval for conversion of local currency into dollars. In the end, however, Argentina may prove to be an exception in the broader realm of countries facing a currency crisis, because of its unusual inflexible peg to the dollar.

The transformation of traditional inconvertibility coverage for banks into a product for capital markets is destined to be limited to specific conditions. This product will depend upon identifying a strong underlying project in a sub-investment-grade country, where there are few alternatives for raising capital and where spreads are wide enough to cover the cost of the insurance (Kenneth Hansen's commentary in Part Two provides further details).

OPIC is working on a modified expropriation coverage for capital markets when there is a sovereign guaranty, Martin observes, but the success of this product will depend upon the existence of a well-functioning dispute resolution mechanism. However, the possible creation of new multilateral financial structures, as proposed by the International Monetary Fund (IMF), which allow sovereign countries to restructure their finances similar to bankruptcy proceedings, may have a significant impact upon such a product.

Regulatory risk has replaced conventional concerns about expropriation by decree. Infrastructure has been opened over the course of the 1990s to the private sector, without the earlier requirement of certain legal, financial, and regulatory regimes being in place.

Reflecting upon the experience of MidAmerican Energy Holdings Company and its private and public insurers in Indonesia,[1] it has become clear that the private participants would not have received any compensation if it had not been for the presence of OPIC and its claims management. While OPIC was not able to deter the claim from being triggered amidst the economic collapse in the host economy, the corporation played a critical role in the salvage efforts.

Note

1. Martin, Julie A. 2001. "OPIC Modified Expropriation Coverage Case Study: MidAmerica's Projects in Indonesia—Dieng and Patuha." In Theodore H. Moran, (ed.), *International Political Risk Management: Exploring New Frontiers*. Washington, DC: The World Bank.

Political Risk Insurance after September 11 and the Argentine Crisis: A Public Provider's Perspective

Vivian Brown
Chief Executive, ECGD
President, Berne Union

Overview

Investing abroad can be a risky business, but political risk insurance (PRI) provides valuable cover to investors for the main political events of expropriation, war (political violence), restrictions on remittances (currency transfer and inconvertibility), and where appropriate, breach of government undertakings (breach of contract). The impact of September 11, 2001, and the Argentine crisis in 2002, dented the confidence of the private insurance market, as the climate for global investment became depressed and investors began to move to "quality and safer" markets. Public providers of PRI have not experienced an increase in demand for cover since September 11 and the Argentine crisis. Nevertheless, the public provider has an important role to play in providing PRI, by offering continuity, stability, and leadership during these volatile times.

Trends in Foreign Direct Investment

Since the early 1990s, foreign direct investment (FDI) has grown substantially for both low- and middle-income countries. There are several reasons for this. Firms from industrialized countries have been looking to relocate production to markets with cheaper labor costs. Thanks to better and cheaper communications and transportation, they can now more easily locate to developing countries. Further,

FIGURE 1.1 NET FDI AND PORTFOLIO INVESTMENT IN EMERGING MARKETS

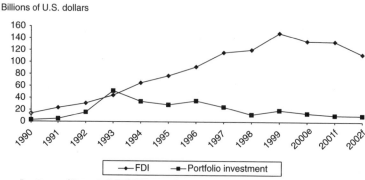

Billions of U.S. dollars

Source: Institute of International Finance data.

developing country privatization programs increasingly encourage investment from the developed world.

The rise in FDI to developing countries, while still apparent, is not as dramatic when FDI to China and Brazil are excluded from the figures. FDI is not evenly distributed between the emerging markets, and countries such as China receive the major portion. In 2001, China received net inflows of $40 billion, almost 30 percent of the total, while sub-Saharan Africa still struggles to attract any FDI. Throughout the 1990s, the top 10 recipients of FDI (China, Brazil, Mexico, Argentina, Poland, Chile, Malaysia, South Korea, Thailand, and Venezuela) accounted for 64 percent of all FDI to emerging markets.

The graph above illustrates the growth in net FDI flows and the path of net portfolio investment flows to emerging markets over the last decade. In 2002, FDI flows fell, but this is partly cyclical. The worldwide economic slowdown made emerging market governments more reluctant to pursue structural reforms, resulting in a reduction of privatization activity and a maintenance of barriers to foreign investment. The current weakness in the technology and telecommunications sectors has also contributed to reducing FDI. There appears to be little impact on FDI as a result of September 11 and, while the crisis in Argentina has rapidly reduced FDI there, it does not appear to have had a more widespread impact. A fall in FDI to Brazil (the second largest recipient of FDI) has been due to a reduction in privatization activity and political uncertainty over the outcome of the 2002 elections.

FDI is likely to remain strong in the future, but growth rates may not be as high as in the past as privatization activity tails off. In addition, we may see a change in the direction of FDI to different economies (e.g., Central Asia, India, and Vietnam) and also a change in the type of FDI. The substantial growth in "brownfield" investments (investments in existing industries, or perhaps state entities which were subsequently privatized) may not continue, due to the one-off nature of privatization and relocation of production. Instead, we may see more "greenfield" investments, with investment in new facilities that are majority-owned by the investor.

Trends in Portfolio Investment

Figure 1.1 also shows that portfolio investment (PI) has been considerably lower than FDI. The late 1990s witnessed a fall in net PI flows, due to the crises in the Asian and other emerging markets. However, there is reason to believe these flows will rise again, as they did in the early 1990s. The relaxation of regulations governing cross-border capital flows led to many pension funds and institutional investors diversifying into emerging markets. As private pension provision becomes more important in the United Kingdom and other developed markets, we can expect larger volumes of PI seeking higher returns. Indeed, this type of investment can and does move around faster as it responds very rapidly to changes in the business environment.

In 2002, PI in emerging markets increased early in the year, due to the poor performance of developed economies and their stock markets and the relatively stronger performance of emerging markets, especially in Southeast Asia. Later in 2002, corporate governance concerns in the United States, among other factors, led to a shift to safer investments, such as government bonds.

September 11 in itself did not have a significant impact on PI flows. Moreover, although the Argentina crisis resulted in a fall in PI flows in Latin America, its impact has not been pervasive abroad. Concerns about corporate governance in emerging markets (particularly Asia) remain, so countries will need to continue to reform in order to retain investor confidence.

Trends in Political Risk Insurance

As Figures 1.2 and 1.3 show, PRI is on the rise, while export credits seem to be declining. PRI business for Berne Union ECAs has increased considerably since the early 1990s, reaching more than $17 billion in new business in 2001. The rise reflects the significant increase in FDI during the same period, as well as the widening membership of the Berne Union to include a number of private insurers. On average, between 10 to 15 percent of FDI is covered by

FIGURE 1.2 NEW M/LT EXPORT CREDITS AND PRI FROM ALL BERNE
            UNION ECAS

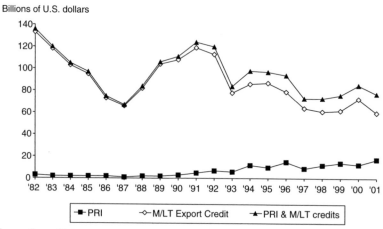

Billions of U.S. dollars

Source: Berne Union.

FIGURE 1.3 NEW INVESTMENT INSURANCE BUSINESS BY BERNE UNION
            MEMBERS

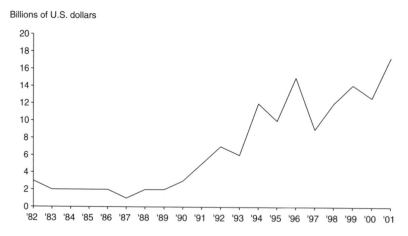

Billions of U.S. dollars

Source: Berne Union.

PRI from ECAs. As emerging markets open up to foreign investment and private capital flows, we can expect the shift away from export credits to continue while PRI continues to rise. This trend would reflect developments like the privatization of utilities and an increase in build-operate-transfer/Project Finance deals without sovereign guarantees.

Impact of September 11 and Argentina on Investment

As already mentioned, FDI is cyclical and the decline during 2002 is due more to a global economic slowdown that was already in effect, than due to specific events such as September 11 or the Argentine crisis. The general turmoil in the financial markets affected investment intentions. Investment levels dropped and investors took flight to "quality and safer" markets in Europe, the United States, and parts of Asia (e.g., China, Malaysia, and the Philippines), rather than investing in "risky" markets such as Argentina and Brazil.

The corporate accounting scandals of Enron and WorldCom have also highlighted concerns over the leverage and liquidity of major international companies, their accounting policies and trading practices, and the lack of transparency in their structured finances. Directors, accountants, advisers, and auditors have to play their role in restoring trust in financial reporting in order to contribute to the stabilization of the capital markets. Investors need assurance that they are dealing in fair and transparent markets where prices are unaffected by fraudulent activities. Failure to protect markets from such malpractice not only damages the reputation of the market but also drives up the cost of capital and reduces liquidity, as investors transfer capital to "cleaner" markets. Investors also need to assess their credit risk more accurately. Lenders desire watertight security, but this increases the costs of insurance. Indeed, many banks will not lend money to projects without PRI, either because of their own internal risk management concerns or because they have reached their lending limits for the market concerned.

The impact of September 11 and the Argentine crisis has dented the confidence of the private insurance market. On the other hand, public providers of PRI have taken a more long-term view and provide continuity in the marketplace. As a result, once overseas investment recovers and demand for PRI increases due to these events, public providers can expect to see more business while private providers remain reluctant to take on risks. PRI from public providers is particularly important in rehabilitation markets such as Africa, the former Yugoslav republics, and others, where the risk is too high to allow export credits. PRI cover for FDI allows foreign investment to take place, and thus helps the market.

PRI cover since September 11, 2001

Investors are still considering PRI cover but are either not buying insurance because they are comfortable with the risk themselves or are investing in "safer" markets. Some investors are buying reduced levels of cover to fit what they can afford. They are also concentrating on keeping their existing investments insured rather than making new investments, thus limiting new demand for PRI. Several brokers have informed ECGD that demand for cover has reduced by as much as 50 percent since 2001; this reduction has hit the market for ECGD and Lloyd's particularly hard.

After September 11, demand for terrorist cover has increased significantly, and it has created demand for "pure terrorism" cover. There is limited provision of this type of cover from private and public insurers. Reinsurers do not provide terrorism cover as a free-standing product in emerging markets, but as an add-on to PRI cover.

Some ECAs used to include terrorism cover in the standard PRI contract and did not charge extra for it. However, since September 11, they have either started to charge for this cover or have stopped providing it altogether. The British government has widened the scope of terrorism insurance for commercial property in the United Kingdom to include contamination from nuclear and biological attacks. It has done this by extending the permit of Pool Re (the mutual set up in 1993 after IRA terrorism caused commercial insurers to abandon the market), for which the U.K. Treasury acts as reinsurer of last resort.

September 11 has raised issues about what PRI actually covers, and whether such terrorist activity can be, or is, covered. All ECAs have been closely monitoring political and economic developments in the markets (particularly in Latin America) and, since September 11, most ECAs have begun to re-examine the political violence wording in their contracts. A heightened awareness of the potential for terrorist events has already affected the nature and cost of the political violence coverage available to investors, especially in the private market, with much more emphasis on (and higher pricing of) separate terrorism coverage.

PRI since the Argentine Crisis

As of the end of 2002, the private market has had no appetite for new business in Argentina. Investors are concentrating on renewing existing portfolios, as they expect business in Argentina to get even tougher in 2003. ECAs are also taking a more cautious stance in Argentina, and are not as forthcoming in their provision of PRI cover for investments into the country.

Prior to September 11 and the Argentine crisis, Lloyd's accounted for approximately two-thirds of the PRI market capacity, and the remainder was split among public and private providers worldwide. While there has been a significant drop in the demand for PRI as a result of the slowdown in FDI in emerging markets, there has been an even bigger downward shift in the willingness of Lloyd's and other private providers to support new business. As a result, the maximum cover available for any individual transaction has halved to $1 billion; horizons of risk have shortened (Lloyd's has reduced its horizons of risk from 10 years to 7 years, 7 years to 5 years, and 5 years to 3 years), and the prices and rates of cover have risen significantly. Lloyd's now only accounts for one-third of the market, and ECAs and other private providers hold the remainder. However, ECAs have not witnessed any overall increase in demand for PRI cover since September 11.

Claims and Near Claims Experience

ECGD has not experienced any PRI claims or near claims since September 11 or the Argentine crisis for investments insured under its Overseas Investment Insurance (OII) scheme. Apart from OPIC, which has received many notices of potential claims in Argentina, not all of which will result in actual claims, other ECAs have reported no claims or near claims under their PRI schemes arising out of September 11 or following the crisis in Argentina.

The experience of the private market has been similar to that of the ECAs with respect to claims resulting from September 11. As for Argentina, several lenders have experienced problems with inconvertibility, resulting in potential claims. American and Bermudan companies, in particular, are facing higher claims than Lloyd's, as the latter is not a major credit underwriter. It has yet to be established whether the Argentine defaults are the result of commercial or political events (i.e., "can't pay / won't pay"). How private market claims are settled by insurers is likely to be significant. If claims are not paid, the credibility of the PRI market could be badly affected.

Reinsurance Market

The reverberations of the events of September 11 are still being felt by the markets, which makes the long-term impact difficult to assess. Some estimates suggest, as of late 2002, reinsurers' capital has been reduced by $100 billion as a result of the World Trade Center losses and the decline in stock and bond values. It is also estimated that approximately $30 billion in new capital is likely to enter the market. This new money is said to be hunting around for business to support; so, despite the net capital outflow, it is unclear whether the markets are now undercapitalized.

This dramatic hardening of capacity among reinsurers has been a significant factor in the reduced capacity in the private market and has driven down the level of available insurance. As previously mentioned, reinsurers have shortened the horizon of risk, and premium rates have risen to ensure profits. In addition, reinsurers can get all the business they need from more profitable avenues than PRI.

If there is sufficient capital in the market, what could this mean for PRI and the opportunity for ECAs to transfer risks to the private market? In theory, increasing involvement in PRI by reinsurers may offer them diversification benefits. For example, reinsurers could view PRI as a different kind of catastrophe cover to add to the spectrum of risk they would normally cover. On the other hand, there may be a tendency to retrench and focus on traditional business, which can now be priced to provide greater returns.

In ECGD's experience, September 11 has not only had an impact on pricing and capacity, but has also made reinsurers wary of new ideas which involve risks that are difficult to measure. As a result, market conditions have made it more difficult for ECAs to transfer medium-term political risks to the private market. While it is possible to package ECA risks to make them more digestible to the market, it would undoubtedly be easier to achieve this in a more expansive environment, rather than in the current market's hesitancy towards longer-term political risks.

Several ECAs regard reinsurance as playing an increasingly important role in shaping the marketplace for political risk, as government and public alternatives are scaled back. Their experience is that political risk appetite has remained fairly stable, but the conditions have become stricter and more expensive. Indeed, reinsured transactions are currently very few and of modest size. The availability of reinsurance will be critical to the ability of the private market to respond to the needs of investors and to continue providing ample capacity and tenors. For the public market, the focus will be on stability, availability, and leadership as they are crucial to stabilizing the market during these volatile times. Indeed, the current problems of the private market graphically illustrate the need for public providers to continue to complement the private market and bridge the gap in availability (especially in tenor) during troubled times.

Conclusion

All PRI providers, public and private, face challenging times ahead. While investors and lenders will continue to want the option of PRI cover, buying it will depend on the cost and the risk involved. We believe there is an appetite for political risk, but investors are being cautious. The political environment, in the wake of September 11, continues to represent a negative factor. Investors are nervous about the prospect of a further terrorist attack, or action against other perceived "rogue states."

Although Argentina remains on the verge of total economic collapse, the contagion is limited so far. Improvements in country surveillance and data dissemination, as a result of IMF-led policy initiatives, have enabled investors to discriminate between the credit status of different emerging markets. They are, therefore, less likely to "rush to the exit." Indeed, many investors have been able to re-balance their portfolios in advance of the crisis, strengthen their balance sheets, and increase their provisions as a buffer to the eventual shock.

In view of these recent events, public and private political risk insurers have reviewed their cover policies for markets such as Argentina, and have either come "off cover" or are not taking on any new business until the market improves. In general, the insurance market has not had to pay out political risk claims on Argentina. Some ECAs have also been re-examining their political violence contract wording, in light of September 11, and now offer "pure terrorism" as separate from the standard PRI cover.

Public PRI providers are looking at ways to generate new business and to work more closely with private insurers. For example, ECGD has embarked on a marketing drive, visiting key customers, talking to brokers, and seeking out potential new customers, by outlining the type of support ECGD can provide. Obviously, the terms and scope of cover vary from market to market. ECGD can provide a fixed premium rate on a market, and the private sector can offer a variable rate that may be cheaper, depending on the risk involved. Using China as an example, the private market rate for the three standard risks of Expropriation, Political Violence, and Transfer and Inconvertibility could vary from 0.40 percent to 1.00 percent, compared to ECGD's current rate of 0.70 percent.

One of the advantages that the public provider enjoys over the private insurer is that its policyholders can depend on their respective governments to resolve specific problems with the host government. If a political event interferes with the business of an overseas enterprise, the public provider has the ability to resolve the matter before the investor has to make a claim, thus ensuring minimum disruption of business. For example, following the change of the Indonesian government in 1998, ECGD called on the British Embassy in Jakarta to assist one of its client investors in ensuring that their project was not cancelled. This timely intervention resulted in the successful continuation of the investment.

Investors, therefore, have the choice of seeking PRI cover with the public or private market. While some investors have taken flight to "safety" and assumed the risk themselves, others have bought reduced levels of cover depending on what they can afford. Undoubtedly, political factors are important. Political stability and strong democracies are more likely to attract investors, while political and civil unrest and financial crises deter investors.

September 11 and the Argentine crisis may come to be regarded as a watershed in the development of the PRI market and for the interaction between public and private providers, including reinsurers. Investors will have seen the private market almost closing shop after September 11, cover horizons being drastically reduced, and premium costs being dramatically increased. This seems to apply to business around the world, not just in certain affected areas. Reinsurers have not stepped in, nor have they seen the PRI market as offering new or growing opportunities for profitable business to support private insurers.

Since late 2002, investors' perception of the PRI market has weakened. The way that perception changes henceforth will depend on future events, in particular, how claims are settled in Argentina. Banks and investors will want to see the value of the PRI cover that they purchased. Unless they are reassured that the cover was worth buying, the PRI market may decline and opportunities for it to develop into other areas will diminish.

Meanwhile, public providers have largely kept their nerve, although they have come off cover in individual markets, such as Argentina. But this is to be expected.

It would be unfortunate if these events led to a divide between public and private providers. Most government-backed agencies, such as ECGD, want to encourage the private sector to develop the market and the business. Collaboration on particular deals and through forums like the Berne Union, are ways of building the market and encouraging a transition from the public to the private side. It would be very detrimental to crowd out the private market.

A careful watch will have to be kept on future trends—on investors looking for opportunities in emerging markets, and the appetite of private insurers and reinsurers to meet this demand and develop the market to cover other areas of risk.

In short, September 11 and the crisis in Argentina can take the PRI market in two different directions: they can help it to grow by practical demonstration of the nature of the risks that can be covered by insurance, or they can cause the market to decline if the value of PRI cover is seen to be illusory. Public and private providers of PRI will have to work together to achieve the first of these two outcomes.

Political Risk Insurance after September 11 and the Argentine Crisis: An Underwriter's View from London

David James
Senior Underwriter
Ascot Underwriting Limited

Introduction

The months following September 11, 2001, have produced the most spectacular underwriting conditions across all classes of business since 1992. Ascot Underwriting Limited, a new managing agency in London, has been presented with unique challenges and opportunities. The purpose of this chapter is to provide a London underwriter's view on the immediate and medium- term effects of the two major events of the September 11 attacks and the crisis in Argentina. The arguments presented here constitute a personal view, not that of either AIG (which provides capital to Ascot) or of the Lloyd's market in general.

As an underwriter for a new syndicate, I hope to give a balanced reflection on the unique market conditions Ascot has faced, especially the market conditions that affect political risk insurance. Ascot was formed in 2001 to take advantage of an improving market—before the tragic events of September 11 and the economic collapse in Argentina. The combination of these two events threw down the gauntlet to all underwriters participating in the political risk market. These challenges had a dramatic effect on the availability of capital and reinsurance for Lloyd's syndicates. While the key drivers of the market (namely, risk capacity and appetite) combined with the high level of uncertainty caused by the potential for future terrorist actions, paralyzed large sections of the insurance community, the political risk market responded well to the challenge.

One Day in September

September 11, 2001, has probably had more written or said about it than any other day in my lifetime. It has changed many things. It has altered our perception of personal safety and financial security. It has made us think differently about what we do in a fundamental sense. It almost seems trite to try and discuss these events in an objective business sense—but that is what we must do.

Political risk, by definition, engenders a perverse element. The political risk market only comes into focus when humanity acts at its most extreme: for example, war, aviation atrocities, and coups d'etats. The fact is, the largest single variable in a political risk account will be a malicious human event. A classic example is the Gulf War—like all the best examples of political risk events, it combines unpredictability with huge financial risk. Such conditions produce excellent underwriting opportunities. However, no single day has so dramatically altered our perspectives, as individuals and as underwriters, as September 11.

Effects on the Industry as a Whole

It would be wrong, with respect to September 11 , to look at the political risk market in isolation. Political risk insurance is a class of business in a global *industry*—an increasingly complex and professional industry. The most obvious element about September 11 is that it will result in the single largest insured event and consequential claims that the market has ever experienced (whether this constitutes one event or two for reinsurers). Current estimates record between $40 billion and $100 billion in potential claims. One of the reasons for the wide variation in loss estimates is because the majority of the losses come from life and liability coverage. The remainder will be made up of physical damage and business interruption claims from properties directly affected by the collapse of the World Trade Center buildings. The removal of large amounts of cash from the financial system will inevitably have a major impact. The market's solvency is challenged—prospective clients begin to look more closely at whom they are buying insurance from, and examine the presumptions of rating agencies that assess and grade them. Lloyd's is among the many businesses that have been downgraded, even though

Lloyd's maintains an exemplary record of never having knowingly defaulted on a valid claim. Rating agencies did not have a good year in 2002. Like everyone else, they too failed to quantify and calculate the effects of the various financial shocks to the international financial system caused by Argentina, September 11, and the scandals that hit corporate America. Perhaps reliance on such agencies will be more tenuous in the future.

Lloyd's, like many other businesses, has had to make great efforts to enhance its own financial security, drawing a levy from its members, and bolstering its balance sheet. Aside from the direct losses of September 11, two effects were felt at the corporate level for many underwriters—rebuilding of balance sheets and reassessment of underwriter's models.

Rebuilding Balance Sheets: Rating and Investment

In the aftermath of September 11, many insurers had to sell major stock positions on a stock market already very nervous with declining prices. The legislative and regulatory demands on insurers to maintain liquidity forced many, particularly life insurance companies, to sell their positions, achieving much less than they would have hoped and expected. This in itself has added to further negative pressure on an already stressed stock market. It greatly influenced the demands placed on insurers in all sectors to rebuild their balance sheets. Ultimately, it will take several years for the industry to regain sufficient capital to replace what has been exhausted. The main driver of higher prices in all markets is the necessity of re-establishing financial strength and the premium base.

A New Era for Risk Modeling

September 11 made underwriters worldwide realize that their "professional" underwriting, based upon risk modeling and aggregation tools for natural events (fire, storm, wind), were suddenly insufficient for 'all risk' perils. The modelers had always allowed for the subtleties of nature, but the malicious element of the terrorist was previously unrecognized. The terrorist's ability to seek out the weakest areas of defense, and the maximum impact, is unlike the "dumb" impact of a natural disaster. The events of September 11 represented a classic political risk—human, subjective, severe, and unpredictable. Yet, September 11 caused no single direct loss to a political risk book of business.

Business practice until September 11 was to provide "all risk" policies. Only in the emerging markets was it felt necessary to look at excluding human means of shock loss, such as terrorism, from the "all risk" property book. The developed world was seen as predictable, and the risk of terrorism was so confined to nationalist movements that it was not a general risk. The insurance industry had not factored in the unpredictable human element in the developed world. The complacency, even on hindsight, seems unbelievable. Market forces dictated broad coverage, yet underwriters (direct and reinsurance) did not factor in human shock loss. War risk losses suffered in Spain in the 1930s demonstrated that unless financial exposures to human risk are properly aggregated, they must be excluded wherever possible. It is for this very reason that war coverage was not written in the London market until aggregate tools were developed to cope with it. In the 1990s, these tools had to be sharpened again to allow the risk community to model and control terrorism exposures in the United Kingdom, when losses caused by IRA attacks forced a radical restructuring of terrorism underwriting. Since September 11, the London market has had to swiftly develop aggregation tools to respond to a new intense demand for terrorism coverage. Through trial and error, the market has finally settled on a 500-mile radius as a terrorism footprint for aggregation. Accompanying this, most syndicates have developed electronic aggregation systems for their exposures in the United States, in particular.

Nevertheless, September 11 should demonstrate to us that no model is ever beyond question. Underwriters need to do more than think in straight lines, and should be prepared to consider the unthinkable, whatever their class.

It should be mentioned that September 11 has had a great impact on governmental involvement in terrorism insurance. Most significantly, the U.S. government has implemented a three-year terrorism backstop, which obliges all insurers to offer insureds with exposure in the U.S. terrorism coverage (from international terrorism only), to the limit of their "all risks" policies. Other countries, including Australia, France, Germany, and even Switzerland, are considering implementation of terrorism pools (or have already done so), while the United Kingdom has increased the insured perils under Pool Re.

Argentina

At any other time, Argentina would undoubtedly have been the primary focus of political risk insurers. Arguably, part of the reason

Argentina has remained in such a difficult position has a lot to do with the change of international political focus. That said, Argentina was already badly affected before the September 11 attacks, but a prolonged and sustained crisis was unthinkable at that time. Argentina was a Latin American "powerhouse," central to United States policy in the region. When Argentina suffered its crisis, most commentators expected significant U.S. and multilateral involvement/intervention. September 11 changed the focus of politicians and financiers, especially in the United States. The global debate shifted toward "the war against terror." We have all become accustomed to the new phraseology of "an axis of evil" and "pre-emptive action," when talking about regime change. The world suddenly became a lot less interested in Latin American economic change or the potential currency crisis there. Outwardly, September 11 had nothing to do with Argentina, but it remains a matter of conjecture whether the current Argentine position would have been allowed to develop to the extent it has, had it not been for September 11. The main concern for political risk underwriters, in the context of the Argentine crisis, should not be that claims must be paid, but rather for how long they will have to keep paying them. Most underwriters today must hope that a long-term viable solution is found for the Argentine economy to allow restructuring and rescue plans to have an effect.

Lessons Learned

Argentina is, undoubtedly, the political risk market's largest test case to date. It will establish, once and for all, whether many of the presumptions of insurers and bankers actually work.

Insurers' reliance upon insolvency and devaluation exclusions will be tested. What caused the loss—the insolvency of the borrower or the confiscation of funds? How does this differ from inconvertibility? What is the value of an extended waiting period—does 240 days really bring that much benefit over a 90-day waiting period? Does the share pledge issue make any difference? Is equity better placed to extract currency than debt? Who benefits from a long-term policy period—the insured or the insurer? Does the law and jurisdiction of the insurance policy make that much difference?

Many of these questions have been discussed at great length between insurers, clients, and their lawyers since September 11. A better understanding of risk and risk transfer will, doubtless, come out of this process. It is an unfortunate truth that it is only when loss occurs that the insurance product is truly tested. This is true for all lines of insurance business. Ultimately, many insured investors will be delighted they purchased cover.

I believe that insurers who insisted on longer waiting periods will benefit in the medium term. However, longer policy periods protect both the insurer (who will maintain a good spread of business across many countries) and the insured in an emerging market suffering shocks. Ultimately, the accumulation of inconvertibility risk will become a major factor in writing and controlling exposures forwarding the future. Underwriters will have to take a long, hard look at the diversification of their portfolios. This balance of risk is often overridden by the desire to accumulate market share in what is perceived to be profitable business for reinsurers and underwriters. A major test of the insurer's own risk assessment lies ahead.

A good result for the market would be a neutral one, with undisputed claim payments, no major impact on the marketplace, and excellent recoveries. Unfortunately, the first claims, which are starting to come out of the crisis, are only the beginning of the long-term effect of this catastrophic event. To date, the emphasis has been on restructuring and managing financial exposures. Such schemes will only work if Argentina finds a way out of the current crisis. The longer the uncertainty about the future of Argentina continues, the greater the likelihood is for such restructuring schemes to fail and for losses to accumulate. The most exposed areas in any portfolio will be sovereign and subsovereign debts. Bankers and underwriters will benefit from the security provided by the insureds, but the true worth of insurance will not be known in the short term. Ultimate losses will run into billions of dollars, and will represent a good return for those who bought political risk products. The most effective protection of the market may well prove to be its insistence on preventing the acceleration of loans in most policy wordings, giving time for a resolution of the crisis in Argentina.

Direct Impact on Political Risk

Rating

In most lines of business, the normal rules of supply and demand operate very effectively. The first 12 months after September 11 witnessed a dramatic decrease in capacity for most insurers, as they looked to control their exposures and sought to rebuild their bal-

ance sheets, driving premium rates up. Policy conditions and attach-
ment points also moved significantly in favor of underwriters. The
underwriting cycle has turned once again.

Interestingly, the smallest movements have occurred in the mainstream political risk product lines. Rating on most standard confiscation and contract frustration coverage is largely unchanged
since September 11. There has been change only in the capacity
risks, and those with exposure in regions of greatest instability. An
underwriter in the property or energy sector would probably indi-
cate that the average rate increase is more than 200 percent. In the
political risk market, rating has not noticeably changed for the simple reason that PRI is generally not considered a "must have" product and buyers will not tolerate a rate hike. Other reasons can be
identified, but the basic rationale for political risk remains—if the
price is too high, the client will find a different way to manage the
risk or not take it at all. The buyer of property insurance, on the
other hand, has much less room to maneuver. Further, a trader or
banker enjoys an array of options to manage political risk. Finally,
the other less reliable, but equally valuable, rule in political risk
underwriting is: if the rate is too high, a loss is almost guaranteed.
The hard market has not entirely eradicated the taste of some
underwriters for the more extreme risks, but the appetite for it has
certainly diminished.

Supply

It is worth taking a few moments to dwell on the reduction in the
PRI market. Market estimates vary, but mainstream political risk
capacity has undoubtedly declined. Simple statements on political
risk capacity do not tell the whole tale, but it is clear that two major
changes have occurred. First, gone are the days of the underwriter
quoting a risk and taking a 100 percent share of it, or routinely quoting a maximum line. This makes all discussions on theoretical
capacity exactly that—theory. Capacity in London has been reduced
by 50 percent in real terms, with market placements of four or more
underwriters becoming the norm on most risks. This reflects two
things—a natural caution by the underwriting community to
achieve a spread of risk and a desire to maximize significantly
reduced country lines. The country line factor is often forgotten in
broker surveys. Most underwriters will operate with two primary
controls on their underwriting capabilities: (a) the risk line, which
is the insurer's ability to take a financial position on an exposure of

a given project or investment, and, more importantly, (b) the country line, which dictates the maximum exposure the underwriter can take in any given geographical country, for the blend of exposures in his political risk book (i.e., his "event" control). Some underwriters may define the parameters of this "book" of exposures differently, but the same primary control mechanism for a country line remains for all. Underwriters work on the presumption that their worst-case event is the complete collapse of a country, resulting in total losses across all policies written with defined financial exposures. The most difficult areas of country capacity are Brazil, China, and Russia.

Reinsurers dramatically reduced their support for the political risk class of insurance after September 11. The most notable effect has been felt in the country lines of underwriters. Underwriters who operate using their balance sheet only, rather than reinsurance, will likewise have come under dramatic pressure from their own management to reduce their political risk exposure. In this hard market, there is pressure on underwriters to reduce their country lines. The focus of capital providers and reinsurers, with conditions as exceptional as they are today, is on obtaining a maximum return from property and casualty lines.

Demand

Foreign direct investment flows offer as good an indicator of market demand as any other measure. Flows of FDI for 2002 have fallen dramatically. Estimates show a 50 percent decline from the highs of 2000, and a further decline is expected in 2003.[1] While this decline has been felt most dramatically in the industrialized world, it is a worldwide issue with few notable exceptions. Major inflows of capital in emerging markets continued last year in China, Mexico, and South Africa. Generally, lending and investment have fallen. Corporate companies are refocusing their domestic bottom line to deal with the shocks of late 2001–02, in the larger corporate governance area, as well as their own balance sheets, before looking for new opportunities overseas. The impact of the WorldCom/Enron corporate governance issue may yet have a significant role to play in establishing the quality of FDI forwarding the future. The days of "clever" tax structures and off-balance sheet financing are in the past, and we are likely to see an increase in financial due diligence and transparency on all projects. This will benefit all investment risk-takers.

The Market

The global downturn in investments, and the consequential reduction in the mainstream political risk business since 2000, has been more than supplemented by other opportunities.

Some underwriters have returned to their core products. Within Lloyd's, ACE and Liberty Mutual have done a great job of continuing to lead much of the traditional trader or contract frustration (CF) business, providing nonpayment and nondelivery type coverage. Ascot has focused on equity risk, contractors' plant and machinery (covering mobile assets), and opportunities in the energy sector. Its main involvement with lenders has been in developing its hedge product for extractive resources. Ascot has been able to write a strong book of core political risk that marries well-spread, well-managed risks with long-term buyers.

In a normal year, 80 percent of the agency's income originated from confiscation (CEN) business; the remainder was produced by its political violence/war book. The exceptional environment prior to September 11 presented many opportunities to develop an excellent political violence book. These percentages have been reversed in the past 12 months. Ascot's major focus has been on managing and underwriting terrorism, particularly in the developed OECD countries. Ascot has now found a new application for an established political risk product. Essentially, it is underwriting a one-peril property-based policy, created to fill the gap in the "all risk" coverage.

The terrorism insurance market, immediately after September 11, was both opportunistic and nervous. The last couple of months of 2001 were a period of great uncertainty and very little confidence. The impression that al-Qaeda was an organization able and willing to strike at will against American interests created the feeling that terrorism was uninsurable. On several occasions, informed commentators and industry experts have stated that terrorism risk cannot be underwritten. Within the broad range of risks that insurers underwrite, there are a number of notable classes of insurance in which it is extremely difficult to underwrite terrorism coverage. Underwriters like Ascot, who are able to take on stand-alone terrorism exposure, have done so in a very clear and defined manner.

Underwriters, especially at Lloyd's, have overcome the technical and emotional hurdle of underwriting terrorism risk. The main providers of terrorism risk insurance today are AIG, Lloyd's, and insurers in Bermuda.

The major technical challenges of terrorism risk are in controlling and modeling the exposure, and managing the "event" model to formulate an underwriting philosophy. The premium underwritten worldwide for stand-alone terrorism in 2002 was estimated to exceed $750 million—a huge number by any standard—and reflects the continuing risk and potential accumulation issues faced by the insured and insurers, respectively.

Ascot's standard model for terrorism is not the World Trade Center, as some might expect, but rather an event along like Oklahoma, Bishopsgate, or the St-Mary-Axe bombings in London. This analysis is supported by the excellent deterministic modeling in this field, carried out by Risk Management Solutions, Inc. (RMS), and partly reflects the 500-mile blast zone formula previously mentioned. It is interesting to note that political risk has generally avoided industry modeling—until now. Past efforts to create models of political risk exposures, particularly investment risks, have not generally been supported by the underwriting community. Models can be useful underwriting tools, but not means of controlling aggregate exposure. A model can be a useful balance for the application of the underwriting philosophy of a particular underwriter.

Terrorism remains a core part of Ascot's political risk book. It falls within the core principles of malicious human risk inspired by ideology. Ascot has sought to bring the political risk underwriting discipline to the field of terrorism risk, by focusing on coverage and aggregation control, whether such exposures are in Pakistan or in New York.

The approach is to blend an understanding of Ascot's products with the political risk mainstream of the terrorism market, which has developed since September 11. For example, Ascot has blended the boilerplate of a traditional political risk lender's policy with coverage of the specialist terrorism form. This has plugged the gap for this type of insurance in the marketplace. When focusing upon the lender's need, we eliminated the need for negotiating specific lender's clauses on what is deemed a physical damage policy, which is not geared to the debt. Until now, the lender has been the last party considered by the client buying, or the broker placing, terrorism coverage. The lender has his own concerns: non-visciation, acceleration of loans, erosion of security, and the basis of indemnity. The terrorism lender's form is designed to meet all these challenges. Essentially, the lender's form provides a double trigger policy protecting against nonpayment of loan or impairment of security, following a terrorism loss at a scheduled location.

Traditional Political Risk Business in London

Ascot is among many underwriters in the diverse London market-place. Risk capacity may be significantly reduced, but the cyclical nature of the political risk market is well established, and a change in capacity and appetite is only likely when the reinsurance market softens and capital rushes back into the insurance sector. Estimates show that capacity will remain tight in 2003–04. This may sound bleak to the risk manager, who is currently looking at major rate increases on property insurance in the next two years. However, this does not take into account how cheap insurance had become.

Today, most risks seen by the political risk underwriters are generally between $30 million and $50 million, with scarce country capacity in Brazil, China, and Russia. Projects in all other countries that come to the political risk market today are likely to be well-received, albeit on a syndicated placement. A major placement may require over 10 lines to finish the slip, with underwriters from Bermuda, London, and the United States. Yet, few major new placements have come to the market since September 11. Some underwriters have reported that their political risk income has fallen by as much as 40 percent from what they expected in the last three years.

For Ascot, the main areas of demand have been:

1. *Confiscation protection.* The form of confiscation coverage previously provided in energy all risk placements (CEN) is increasingly being excluded, or rated separately, from the all risk elements.
2. *Trade risks.* There is increased demand for short-term contract frustration on nondelivery and nonpayment, particularly for oil, cotton, tobacco, and other primary crops.
3. *Country risk protection.* Long-term buyers of country risk protection want to insure against erosion of their balance sheets, especially for projects in the leisure industry, manufacturing, and utilities. The major sector to suffer a backlash from underwriters is the power sector. Underwriters are of the opinion that potential buyers of PRI regard the insurance as a back-up to sovereign guarantees on long-term power contracts, and this use of political risk policies is unsustainable, given the loss record in this sector.
4. *Banks.* The amount and value of bank business is significantly reduced. Nonetheless, there continues to be strong demand for letter-of-credit facilities, bond portfolios, and

creditor guarantee coverage. Lender's interest rate products remain on hold while the market awaits the return of large-scale FDI.

5. *Mobile plant and equipment*. The multi-line CCP product is very much a London market catchphrase. These products have been particularly successful for lessors of equipment, the energy sector, and large-scale project contractors.

Looking Ahead

Dramatic changes have marked 2002, and 2003 has been equally challenging. The Gulf is the focus of American and European government attention. The continuing search for "hard targets" and the American doctrine of "pre-emptive action" is cause for concern for investors and underwriters. This will only prolong the uncertainty on commodity prices and regional investments. It is likely that tensions will remain in a various areas, not only in the Middle East. Terrorism-related tensions may have a direct impact on the political risk business. With al-Qaeda being a "vanguard" of change, and inspiring attacks against American interests worldwide, a regime change may have a greater effect on the broader "Western" interests. Al-Qaeda is the first truly transnational terrorist organization. It recruits from 47 different countries, and its presence in an estimated 98 different states spanning the Middle East, Asia, and the West, holds the potential for significant new attacks against American interests, subsequent counter-measures, and government responses to them. American interests will increasingly come under the microscope, particularly in the emerging markets of Southeast Asia. The changing focus of American international relations may yet produce a loss in the political risk market.

Against this background, I expect to see terrorism commanding the focus of the underwriter's attention. Stand alone terrorism coverage and macro-country risk protection will remain important in the future.

Banks and developers will need to integrate a rational model and methodology to deal with their exposures. Likewise, when investing overseas, prospective foreign investors will have to consider the changing environment in which they operate and purchase the appropriate coverage. I do not expect to see rapid or dramatic changes in rating or market conditions. Policy periods are likely to remain generally capped in the three to five year range, as the market refocuses its attention on its core business.

The challenge for underwriters in 2003 and beyond will be to adapt their risk management tools in the most effective way possible, to fit the changing political environment. The political risk community faces interesting times ahead.

Note

1. UNCTAD (U.N. Conference on Trade and Development). *World Investment Report 2002: Trans National Corporations and Export Competitiveness.* www.unctad.org.

The Impact of September 11 on Trade Credit and Political Risk Insurance: A Private Insurer's Perspective from New York

John J. Salinger
President
AIG Global Trade & Political Risk Insurance Company

The attacks of September 11, 2001, did not directly cause a single loss in the political risk or trade credit insurance markets. Nevertheless, the ripple effects of that day have affected so many aspects of our lives, and have seriously affected the political risk and trade credit insurance markets as well.

As a consequence, political risk capacity in the private sector has shrunk. There is less capacity per risk, less capacity per country, and in the case of trade credit insurance, less capacity per obligor. Time horizons, which had lengthened to as long as 15 years, have been shortened.

It may be surprising to regard these effects as a positive development, but the private insurance market had grown too large, and a correction was necessary. As private sector capacity drops, it will be interesting to follow the reactions of government underwriters. The optimal reaction would be a renewed effort to work with the private sector to underwrite more transactions on a coinsurance or reinsurance basis. OPIC of the United States has taken steps in that direction and, hopefully, others will follow their lead. The suboptimal reaction would be a renewed effort by government underwriters to compete against their private counterparts. In any event, the cyclical waning of private sector capacity underscores the long-term need for government-backed underwriters.

Concurrently, a sharp drop in demand has accompanied the reduction in capacity. The United Nations published figures projecting that final FDI data will show a reduction of 27 percent in 2002, following a similar drop in 2001. The drop will be even more precipitous in the poorest countries. FDI in Africa will drop to $6 billion, down from $17 billion in 2001.[1] Most underwriters are also reporting a reduction in business and deal flow.

The effect of September 11 on the political risk and trade credit markets can be assessed in two ways. First, it had a direct technical impact on the markets. Second, it affected the global risk environment, which in turn affects the trade credit and political risk insurance markets.

The dramatic expansion of the private sector in trade credit and political risk insurance must be seen in the context of the general insurance market. The property/casualty insurance industry experienced a steady decline in premium rates during the 1990s. The general industry is always concerned about exposure to large natural catastrophes that can threaten the survival of a company. Insurers and reinsurers in a "soft market" look for additional sources of income that do not add exposure to losses due to earthquakes in California or hurricanes in Florida. During the 1990s, underwriters seeking reinsurance support for political risk or export credit programs were welcomed.

Concurrent with the growing interest for specialty risk programs in the reinsurance market, government underwriters began to withdraw from some segments of the market. ECGD in the United Kingdom led the way in 1991, with the privatization of its short-term export credit business. Exim Bank of the United States quickly followed suit. By 2000, the private sector had virtually replaced government underwriters as the primary provider of short-term export credit insurance, in most countries.

In the political risk (or investment insurance) markets, growth in the private sector was spectacular. By 1998, the historical time horizon had stretched from the traditional three years to 15 years. Capacity in the market to cover a single risk grew from $250 million in 1992 to well over $1 billion in 2000. For the first time, private capacity was on a virtual par with the government sector.

This new capacity arrived in the market at the same time as many emerging market governments adopted aspects of the "Washington consensus," to privatize large sectors of the economy previously served solely by the government. Along with privatization came moves to liberalize foreign exchange controls. "Globalization" was viewed as the way to address issues of poverty and development in emerging markets. New capacity, combined with flexibility and responsiveness, allowed the private sector to equal, if not surpass, the government as the primary provider of investment insurance.

This explosive growth, which reached its peak in 2000, began to level off in early 2001, as rates in the property/casualty market started to harden.

Then came September 11. Primarily, Lloyd's of London felt the immediate technical impact. Many Lloyd's syndicates relied on "whole account" reinsurance on an excess-of-loss basis. This type of reinsurance allows an underwriting syndicate to write multiple classes of risk (i.e. property, casualty, marine, political risk, etc.). Reinsurance is a fixed price and covers larger losses that pierce the per-risk deductible. Most programs allow the reinsurance limit to be "reinstated" after a loss, for an additional premium. A syndicate could have two or three reinstatements during the year.

This reinsurance structure did not withstand the extraordinary insurance losses imposed on the insurance industry by the events of September 11. The loss, estimated at more than $40 billion, is the largest insurance loss incurred in history. There has never been a single event that caused such a large loss in so many classes of insurance, namely, property, business interruption, casualty, worker's compensation, automobile, and life.

Syndicates that thought they were well protected on September 10 exhausted their reinsurance protection, and all their reinstatements, 24 hours later. Even worse, they were left with an existing portfolio of risks completely unprotected in a market where it was difficult, if not impossible, to buy new protection.

Without reinsurance, many syndicates stopped writing new business. This instantly took an estimated $300 million in per-risk capacity out of the investment insurance market.

The second technical adjustment came a few months later when most private sector underwriters faced renewal of their annual reinsurance programs, most of which had to be completed on January 1. The 2002 renewal season reduced investment insurance capacity by an additional $200 million, some of it long-term capacity. These trends will continue in the 2003 renewal season, and capacity will drop further.

Insurance is a cyclical industry. When it is profitable, it attracts capital. Capital creates capacity. Increased capacity creates downward pressure on rates. Eventually, inadequate rates lead to losses, which erodes capacity and capital until rates increase and the cycle continues. After a decade of eroding profits, general insurance rates began to climb in 2000. September 11 had a dramatic impact on rates. Property rates soared 30 to 60 percent. Liability rates for Directors and Officers increased by 200 to 300 percent. In this environment, reinsurers elect to put more capital behind businesses with rising rates.

Special insurance classes, like political risk, are countercyclical to the general insurance markets because they do not include exposure to large natural catastrophes. While professional private sector underwriters of credit and investment insurance produced attractive long-term returns, they cannot promise significant rate increases to match those of general insurance.

Against the backdrop of September 11, the general level of economic and political risk had been increasing. First, there was a global credit risk crisis. Second, there was a growing backlash to the globalization formula being touted as the prescription to address poverty and underdevelopment in emerging markets. September 11 did not cause these situations—both were already under way—but September 11 made them worse.

The political risk insurance market flourished in the 1990s due to the confluence of several factors. Insurers were interested in this class of insurance, and there was ample reinsurance capacity. Globalization, especially privatization in emerging markets, created strong demand. Multinational companies, who were enjoying the benefits of the strong American economy and booming equity markets, were interested in emerging market investments.

There were some hiccups along the way, such as the East Asia liquidity crisis of 1997 and the collapse of the Russian ruble in 1998. Countries such as Indonesia have yet to recover from this crisis. But, for the most part, countries corrected themselves sufficiently to return to growth. Confidence was so high that bad news was completely ignored.

However, by the second half of 2000, growth in the American economy had come to an end. Europe was locked in a low/no growth mode. Japan was mired in a long recession. With no growth in these three great global economic engines, growth in emerging markets was difficult. Some of the bubbles burst along the way. The dot.com euphoria vanished. Telecom dreams soured. Financial markets were stunned by the collapse of Enron, WorldCom, and Adelphia.

September 11 had no connection to these events, apart from timing. But timing is important. All of these events, related or unrelated in terms of causation, had the effect of undermining confidence. September 11 and the collapse of Enron by themselves would have had the effect of undermining confidence. All the others coming together, along with other macro- and micro-economic events, created a crisis in confidence not seen since the oil price shocks of the 1970s, if not before. The result of a crisis in confidence is a credit crisis. Bankruptcies in the United States and Europe are at an all-time high. Countries like Argentina have gone into default. Lenders have stopped lending. Capital markets have shut down.

Further, there is a growing backlash to globalization. One of Osama bin Laden's primary objectives is to force Western troops and investment out of Saudi Arabia and the Middle East.

We see evidence of this in a recent book by Joseph Stiglitz, the former chief economist of the World Bank. We see it in the relative success of countries, such as China and Malaysia, neither of whom fully subscribed to the "Washington Consensus" formula.

Foreign direct investors in the power and telecommunications sector in Indonesia have forced the government to international arbitration and have caused a major investment insurance loss. Interestingly, a government agency coinsured that loss with the private sector. The unfortunate saga of the Dabhol power project in India has been well- publicized. FDI has created a surfeit of power in parts of China that caused losses for those investors.

So, what is the impact of these events on PRI? First, private markets for political risk insurance will shrink. In 2003, it will be difficult for the private sector to cover more than $300 to $400 million on a project, a dramatic decrease from over $1 billion in 2000. It will also be very difficult to arrange coverage beyond a ten-year horizon.

Normally, this would cause rates to increase. Arguably, the risk environment demands rate increases. That probably will not happen because the demand for coverage will remain soft as long as "gloom and doom" is the pervasive mood.

The optimistic outlook is for the government export credit and investment insurance agencies to increasingly collaborate with each other. There are now three new private sector members of the Berne Union (AIG, Zurich, and Sovereign); this type of organization facilitates cooperation.

With a smaller private sector, project sponsors and financiers will be forced to use government capacity, even if this involves surmounting additional barriers. Government agencies will understand the benefits of sharing losses in places like Indonesia and Argentina.

Collaboration can be used to moderate rates if the official agency is prepared to accept differentiated pricing. Longer-term covers can be achieved with asymmetric tenors.

Finally, "gloom and doom" is the mood of the day, but this will change. A few years ago, markets refused to believe bad news. Today, the view is completely reversed— good news is not believed. This, too, shall pass, and there will be better days ahead!

Note

1. U.N. 2002. United Nations Conference on Trade and Development, October 24, 2002. Press release.

In the Aftermath of September 11 and the Argentine Crisis: A Private Reinsurer's Perspective

Brian Duperreault
Chairman & CEO, ACE Limited

I am pleased to contribute to this MIGA-Georgetown volume with my comments on the status of the reinsurance market and its impact on the availability of political risk insurance capacity. ACE Limited has been MIGA's reinsurance partner since 1997. This type of cooperation between private insurance providers and multilateral and public agencies is particularly important in today's challenging market environment. The public-private partnership has proven to be a very efficient business model—it has enabled public agencies to leverage their own resources, and private companies to underwrite in markets where they would otherwise not offer coverage.

In addition to its reinsurance treaty with MIGA, ACE plays an active role in the political risk market through its 50-percent ownership position in Sovereign Risk Insurance Ltd., and through its Lloyd's syndicate—ACE Global Markets.

ACE has become one of the world's largest providers of PRI capacity in the last five years. ACE is unique among reinsurers because it works with, and provides capacity for, transactions written by public and private underwriters through its joint venture partner, XL Capital. ACE collaborates with three main groups of insurers: (a) multilaterals; (b) bilateral Export Credit Agencies (ECAs), and (c) private underwriters:

Multilaterals: These include the Asian Development Bank (ADB), the InterAmerican Development Bank (IDB), and MIGA. With MIGA, as mentioned above, ACE has an all-encompassing treaty, whereby it reinsures a substantial portion of MIGA's global exposure. ACE supports the political risk guarantees activities of the ADB and IDB through Sovereign.

Export Credit Agencies: ACE attaches great importance to its relationship with ECAs. We believe Sovereign's election to the Berne Union in 2001 provides further opportunities for cooperation. Over the past five years, ACE has provided 10 different bilateral ECAs with treaty and facultative reinsurance support.

Private Underwriters: In addition to its 50-percent ownership of Sovereign Risk Insurance Ltd., ACE writes political risk insurance through its Lloyd's syndicate, namely, Ace Global Markets (previously, the Charman Syndicate), which is one of the leading PRI underwriters in the Lloyd's market.

These three sources of PRI are complementary, and provide the ACE Group with an excellent spread in the PRI business.

ACE Group of Companies: A Brief Background

The ACE Group of Companies is one of the world's leading providers of insurance and reinsurance. Set up in 1985, it has its headquarters in Bermuda. ACE provides its clients with a diverse range of products and services to manage risk, including natural catastrophes, property and casualty liability, and political risk, in 50 countries around the world. The combined assets of the Group totaled $38 billion at the end of 2001. ACE is listed on the Bermuda and New York stock exchanges. It is rated A+ with Standard and Poors (S&P) and AM Best, and is included in the S&P 500 list of companies.

ACE has a strong capital base and substantial human and financial resources to underwrite and provide coverage for its clients. ACE has grown to become one of the world's largest providers of reinsurance in several lines of business in which it operates. Hopefully, this will assure nervous investors and bankers, who think that the effect of September 11, combined with recent corporate accounting scandals in the United States, and the weak global economy in general, will result in a void of insurance coverage, particularly for political risk. ACE is a long-term player in the insurance markets in which it operates, and remains committed to supporting its clients' various business operations throughout the world.

Recent Developments in the PRI Market:
Impact on Insurance Capacity

Overall, 2001 was a watershed year for the insurance industry and for business in general. The tragic events of September 11 have changed the way we live and the way we do business forever. Facing a landscape of increased peril, business leaders turned to their traditional source of protection—insurance—and have begun to question whether they had adequate cover. The reexamination of exposure has led to an unprecedented demand for comprehensive insurance coverage.

At the same time, insurers also have an altered view of risk. On September 11, 2001, the industry suffered its largest aggregate loss in history. For the ACE Group, in 2001, losses for this event alone exceeded $550 million, and as a result the year ended with a loss of $150 million, compared to a profit of $550 million in 2000. Major losses like these have an obvious impact on capacity. While a fairly substantial amount of additional capital flowed into the industry subsequently, the net impact of the event to date has been a significant reduction in the capacity of the industry to accept risk.

Insurance against terrorism deserves specific mention in this regard. Terrorism insurance, which was included in most property insurance and reinsurance policies in the United States, is now excluded. As September 11 demonstrated, the accumulation of risk (or clash of coverages) went far beyond anyone's worst-case scenarios.

Terrorism is now being written on a stand-alone basis, like a catastrophe product, or even like a political risk product. Strict limits of loss aggregation and geographical diversification are being observed. Consequently, the world market for property terrorism coverage has shrunk from infinite trillions of dollars of nominal exposure to mere billions. The impact of this shortage of coverage is being felt most severely by the real estate and the construction industries. Most governments in the industrialized world have faced up to the fact that they must act as the reinsurer-of-last-resort for these unpredictable events, and have created various terrorism reinsurance schemes or pools.

This book is aptly subtitled *"The Brave New World."* It is a good description of our world today. We are operating in a new environment, and insurers have had to be much more precise about the perils they are actually prepared to cover. In the softer markets of earlier years, policy language had become increasingly broad and general. Post-September 11, insurers tightened their terms and conditions and now cover only named perils. For example, few insurers—if any—are prepared to cover terrorism risk as part of the general property policy, as was the practice prior to September 11. While terrorism risk before September 11 seemed minor, it is now widely viewed within the industry as too large, random, and incalculable to be insurable as an unlimited liability.

What effect has September 11 had on contract language? My comments regarding the effect on wording and policy terms are made in the context of all the different lines of business in which ACE operates. I expect to see similar changes in the PRI industry. In addition, the PRI market also suffers from another crisis—the unprecedented economic meltdown in Argentina, which may have a further impact on both contract language and capacity for years to come.

What effect has September 11 had on the availability of capacity and on premium levels? My observations, again, are true for all lines of insurance, and apply to the PRI market as well, for the simple reason that, specialized as it may be, PRI is still dependent on the general insurance market. Indeed, the more successful we are in fostering the private-public partnership, the more affected are the multilaterals and bilateral ECAs by what happens in the general insurance industry. While most agencies five years ago would not necessarily worry about what went on in the insurance market outside the political risk field, the private and public PRI markets are much more interdependent today.

Having recognized the magnitude of their exposure, most insurers have re-evaluated how much risk they are able and willing to accept in the future. Some companies have withdrawn from particular risk classes altogether and, spurred by a sharp tightening in the reinsurance market, they have dramatically reduced their limits in other classes—PRI is one of the markets that is certainly beginning to feel the effect of this tightening.

Credit and debt rating agencies have reacted to the turmoil in the financial and corporate debt markets, and to the sudden and dramatic accounting problems for giant, global companies by becoming negatively biased against ratings. That is, these agencies are now more likely to downgrade, rather than upgrade, ratings. This discourages new investment, particularly if such new investment increases corporate leverage.

Even the world's premier reinsurers, such as Munich Re and Swiss Re, have been downgraded by various rating agencies. While this will probably not slow them down in this hard market, such rating actions drive home the urgent need for insurers to return to profitable risk underwriting. It is less likely that giant "national" companies will be able or willing to subsidize their own domestic markets in the future—through inadequate rates—as they had in the past.

Insurance premiums had been hardening even before September 11, but they climbed much more steeply thereafter—especially in lines such as aviation, property, and energy. To earn a reasonable return on capital and protect shareholders against excessive volatility, insurers have had to raise premiums. Post-September 11, businesses can no longer view insurance as a low-cost commodity. Board members and senior executives now involve themselves directly in insurance purchasing decisions. Increasingly, they want to work with insurers that have high ratings and a robust capital base to draw on should a large loss occur.

The year following September 11, 2001, added other challenges that have had, and will continue to have, a substantial impact on business. The corporate scandals in the United States, involving Enron, Kmart, and WorldCom, and reports about accounting irregularities in other large companies, accompanied by the general weakness of the global economy, has further affected the availability of insurance and reinsurance capacity, albeit in less direct ways. The current market conditions are very different from what they were prior to September 11. Obviously, for the PRI market, the event that most directly affects capacity is the economic meltdown in Argentina, an event often referred to as the "September 11 of Emerging Markets." As the ongoing political and financial crisis in Argentina demonstrates, financing and FDI in emerging markets can be unpredictable, and even extremely risky. It is the inherently unpredictable nature of emerging markets and the increased volume of financing and investment in these markets that has driven the rapid growth in the PRI market over the last few years.

Consider current events in three of the major emerging market economies:

Argentina has experienced an unprecedented economic meltdown. Even in the Latin debt crisis of the 1980s, the Mexican "tequila crisis" of the early 1990s, and the "Asian flu" of 1997–98, an implosion of this magnitude has never occurred in a major emerging economy. Argentina will be viewed as a test case for the effectiveness of PRI when an entire economy collapses. It will deliver costly lessons for providers and users of PRI, and while it is still too early to predict the final outcome of the Argentine crisis, underwriters will have to pay claims. In fact, ACE has already paid several claims for policies covering political risks in Argentina.

Brazil went through political developments, leading up to the country's October 2002 presidential elections, which have had profound economic effects. Politics will continue to drive the bond spreads in the country, and continued volatility is likely in the near future. This climate does little to increase capacity in a market where PRI availability is already severely constrained.

Turkey also experienced political uncertainty surrounding elections, which drove Turkish spreads to a high of over 1,100 basis points in early July. As a secular and democratic Islamic nation, a NATO member, a key U.S. ally in the region, and with pending EU membership, Turkey can be expected to receive the international support it needs to overcome its chronic economic weakness. In Turkey's case, like other large emerging market nations, however, everything hinges on politics and market perceptions.

Increased globalization also means that even if a country develops sound economic and political fundamentals, it may be penalized by global investors' loss of confidence in geographically far away markets that have a different economic outlook—or, because investors lose patience with the performances and falling bond prices in emerging markets in general. The same phenomenon is true, although perhaps to a lesser degree, in the PRI reinsurance industry, where reinsurers may come and go depending on market perception.

Depending on its ultimate outcome, the crisis in Argentina could prove to be a watershed event for private sector PRI insurers/reinsurers and major ECAs. For most large PRI underwriters and agencies, Argentina is among the top five countries in their risk portfolio, and in many cases, it is the country with the second- or third-largest exposure (usually behind Brazil). Even if we cannot predict today the ultimate outcome in Argentina, it is likely that, as a consequence, capacity will decrease, contract wording will be tightened, and it will be more difficult to close transactions. On the positive side, we can expect that policy wordings will likely be made clearer and less ambiguous in the future.

Following past crises in emerging markets, the PRI industry has moved quickly to offer new capacity and fill the demand for new political and economic risk mitigation products. ACE's entry into PRI in 1997, when Sovereign was formed during the Asian financial crisis, was largely driven by commercial banks and ECAs' increased need for a new source of stable and highly rated PRI capacity. The question today is, therefore, what effect will the current crisis in Argentina have on the ability of the PRI market to respond to increasing coverage needs among financial institutions and investors in the future?

PRI providers who rely on reinsurance have already indicated that reinsurance capacity will be hard to come by in the near term, and that the amounts and tenors previously available in the market are likely to experience a significant reduction. This retrenchment would result from potential PRI losses in Argentina and elsewhere, as well as higher rates in other, more traditional, lines of insurance, which would, in turn, decrease the amount of reinsurance available for political risks. Reinsurance capacity may thus prove to be a constraint on the further development of the PRI market in the next few years.

Conclusion

It is clear there will be a fairly significant decrease in the availability of reinsurance capacity for PRI in the near-term. This will, in all likelihood, manifest itself in a decrease in the overall capacity and shortening tenors of coverage, as underwriters are traditionally more conservative with longer-term tenors of coverage. To a certain extent, the significant slowdown in FDI flows to emerging markets contributes to easing the demand for PRI capacity. Nonetheless, it is fair to expect that financial institutions and sponsors of large infrastructure projects may experience increasing difficulty in finding adequate long-term PRI coverage in the near term.

This decrease in available capacity is likely to affect rates as well. So far, the PRI market has not been subject to major price increases, in contrast to a number of other lines of insurance. However, as capacity becomes scarce, in order to lure capacity for PRI risks into the market and away from other classes of insurance, higher rates may result in the future.

Another consequence of the major events in the global economy is that underwriters will be more selective with regard to contract wordings, the insurability of certain projects, and risks in certain emerging markets.

ACE, however, views its participation in the market as a long-term player. ACE manages risk and is prepared to accept risks from clients, because we believe in our technical underwriting skills. ACE values its relationship with MIGA and the other multilaterals and bilaterals that it supports, and recognizes the value of the extra protection and risk mitigation capabilities that these alliances afford.

ACE's disciplined underwriting and professional approach to risk management assures stability, reliability, and longevity. Sovereign is structured as a net underwriting joint venture between ACE and XL, and will, therefore, not be affected by the general retrenchment in the reinsurance sector. ACE's cooperation with MIGA will also not be affected.

Finally, I confirm ACE's commitment to the PRI business, as a treaty reinsurer of MIGA, a direct owner of Sovereign, and through its Lloyd's operations. ACE views PRI as an essential component of emerging market finance and investment, and we take great pride in our extensive involvement in this specialized form of insurance.

Commentary on Political Risk Insurance Providers in the Aftermath of September 11 and the Argentine Crisis

Julie A. Martin
Vice President
MMC Enterprise Risk*

General Market Conditions

The 1990s and the Soft Market

The commercial insurance market operates in "hard" and "soft" cycles. These cycles are spawned by the capacity available in the market, loss experience, particularly catastrophic losses resulting from one common cause; investment returns; and the cost of reinsurance cover. During the 1990s, the insurance market remained soft due to the following influences:

- Excess underwriting capacity (supply exceeded demand) kept insurance premium levels low.
- Insurers reduced premium levels to retain their market share and fought to retain current business and gain new business.
- Investment gains from favorable interest rates and performance of the worldwide stock markets enabled insurers to subsidize their underwriting losses.

MMC Enterprise Risk, a unit of *Marsh*, provides consulting services including financial risk solutions, such as credit-risk transfers, asset-value guarantees, revenue guarantees, trade credit insurance, and the financing or transfer of mass tort liabilities. The company has offices in Atlanta, Chicago, London, New York, Paris, and San Francisco.

■ Loss history remained at an acceptable level for most of the 1990s, except when Hurricane Andrew struck the United States in 1992. This was the single most expensive insured event of the decade.

■ Inexpensive reinsurance cover allowed insurers to transfer risk at a relatively low cost.

During the 1990s, insurance buyers benefited considerably from the soft insurance market, obtaining broad cover with low deductibles at low premium levels.

The Return of the Hard Market

During 2001–02, the insurance market hardened considerably. As a result, insurers increased premiums and deductibles, and applied several restrictions on coverage. This occurred worldwide, and for all types of commercial insurance, especially property, business interruption, professional liability, and surety.

■ With stock markets and interest rates falling worldwide, insurers could no longer subsidize their underwriting losses through investment gains. (See figure 1 on the decline of net income.)

■ The focus for insurers moved from maintaining market share to achieving an underwriting profit. Profitability became the

FIGURE 1 CONSOLIDATED PROPERTY/CASUALTY INDUSTRY NET INCOME

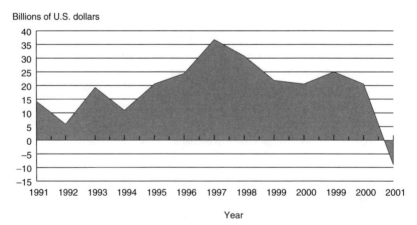

Data Source: A.M. Best Company.

top priority. In the near future, insurers will continue to seek premium increases to achieve greater profitability.

■ Insurers have faced claims from newly emerging risks, arising from modern technology—for example, computer technology (computer viruses) and new power technologies (combined cycle gas turbines using prototypical technology).

Finally, the events of September 11, 2001, exacerbated the already hard market significantly. Insurers worldwide began to impose major limitations on the commercial risk coverage they offer. Losses facing the insurance market from this event are estimated to be at least $50 billion. Latest estimates put property damage and business interruption losses in excess of $20 billion. September 11 is the biggest single loss event that the insurance market has faced in history. To highlight this, figure 2 compares the top 10 catastrophes in the United States.

Impact of the Hard Market

The hardening market has had a major impact on insurance for new projects and renewal terms for existing projects. In general, the impact can be categorized as follows:

FIGURE 2 TOP INSURANCE LOSSES IN THE UNITED STATES

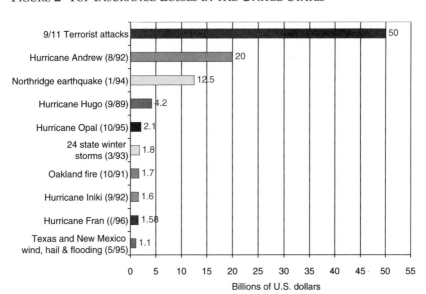

Data Source: Marsh estimates.

- Premiums have increased by almost 100 percent for risks with a good loss history; they have increased by more than 100 percent for risks with medium/ poor loss history.
- Individual insurers have reduced their participation in each risk, as they now have less reinsurance protection. This requires more insurers to participate for complete coverage of risks, and this often means acceptance of loss limits.
- Reinsurers have begun to impose terms and conditions on the reinsurance they provide; and insurers, in turn, pass on these restrictions to investors in the coverage they offer.

Changes in the Political Risk Insurance Market

Impact of September 11

Available capacity in the private market decreased by about 30 percent, per project, after September 11. Most of this decline occurred in the Lloyd's market. Only one public provider, OPIC, increased its per-project limit, and there has been only one new entrant in the market, namely, AXIS Specialty Limited, which is based in Bermuda, and offers both political risk and terrorism coverage. There is still significant capacity for "good" risks in most countries. Virtually all underwriters have little or no capacity in Brazil, and are limiting cover in the Dominican Republic, Turkey and, perhaps, Mexico. Most insurers are off-cover in Argentina, though some are now willing to consider a limited range of projects there.

Pricing has increased somewhat, averaging 10 to 20 percent, but not as much as in other insurance markets. Many purchasers had already considered political risk expensive, and the market did not have the capability to withstand substantial increases. Instead, underwriters seem to be taking a more cautious approach and are less likely to offer broad coverage or innovative products. Most markets are more cautious on all types of coverage, especially for political violence and business interruption. In addition to shrinking capacity and higher pricing, tenors have also been reduced.

Impact of the Argentine Crisis

Argentina could have a profound effect on the market, although it is still too early to know this with certainty. By the end of 2002, some trade credit claims were paid and a few political risk claims had been settled. Most underwriters had received notification of potential claims, and many were in the discovery process. Insurance buyers are closely watching the resolution of these claims as an indicator of the effectiveness of coverage under such unpredictable and unforeseen circumstances.

Recent developments in Argentina include the exclusion of Berne Union members (which now includes several private market participants) from Communication A3537 of the Central Bank, which stipulates the need for Central Bank approval of conversion of local currency to dollars. Loans exempt from this approval must be paid on time if the borrower has sufficient local currency.

Another recent development has been a change in the expropriation language of PRI policies: economic viability has been included as a potential test of whether government actions are expropriatory. As with all new contract language, only a claims situation will truly test the meaning and objective of the language.

Some argue that the "pesification" of local obligations by the government, which led to the economic nonviability of various entities, should be covered under this provision—if not under the broader expropriation language. Meanwhile, some investors are pursuing remedies against the government under the Bilateral Investment Treaties (BIT). The BIT language is often broader than that of PRI policies, which leads some companies to believe that a BIT treaty offers a better chance of recovery.

The Power Sector

PRI for power projects has hardened considerably, following the increase of investment disputes and potential claims losses that have recently emerged. OPIC paid its largest claim for a power project in Indonesia. Private market participants also suffered claims losses in this project. Another major power project—Dabhol in India—has been halted and the pending issues remain unresolved.

There have also been several claims or investment disputes involving the power sector in China. Resolution 34 in Colombia, combined with the terrorist attacks on transmission lines, has resulted in the filing of claims for projects in that country. There are potential claims in Argentina and Venezuela as well. While underwriters continue to consider insurance for power projects, these events have made them more cautious, and the old approaches will probably be revised.

Terrorism Market

Stand-alone Terrorism

In the aftermath of September 11, 2001, a market for stand-alone terrorism risk developed, as most property underwriters began to exclude terrorism risk from the general insurance contract. Terrorism risk coverage had previously been included, essentially at no cost. Some underwriters are the same as those in the PRI market, but others are different. Submissions for stand-alone coverage are for projects in U.S. domestic locations or for worldwide programs in industrialized and developing countries. In a few instances, to meet lender requirements, coverage for terrorism has been purchased for emerging market projects. Terrorism risks and property terrorism insurance are of major concern for the business community, as well as the insurance industry.

Rates

- Rates for stand-alone terrorism coverage stabilized in the second quarter of 2002. However, as the number of clients buying cover increased, some underwriters developed aggregation problems in certain metropolitan areas, such as midtown Manhattan. When available, the cost of the limited capacity for these locations increased.
- Primarily based on the location and occupancy of risk, as well as declared exposures and limits sought, rates generally range from 0.03 percent to 0.25 percent of the total insured value (equivalent to between 0.4 percent and 3 percent of the limit). Rates are higher for properties that are considered high profile or target risks, or for clients who seek low-loss limits with significant exposures.

Capacity

- For most risks, available stand-alone capacity is typically between $100 million to $300 million. Limits are provided on a "per occurrence" and "annual aggregate" basis. Higher limits can be purchased at significantly higher prices, stretching the market supply to its maximum (approximately $500 million). In some cases, even larger limits have been structured; however, as the size of the limit purchased increases, the pricing becomes excessive.

- Key stand-alone terrorism markets include AIG, ACE USA (for Canada and the United States), AXIS Specialty, Berkshire Hathaway, Lloyd's, AEGIS (for its power/utility members), and Special Risk Insurance & Reinsurance Luxembourg (SRIR).

Coverage

- All stand-alone markets offer coverage for physical damage and business interruption / extra expense directly caused by acts of terrorism. None of the markets currently offer any contingent business interruption or other time element coverages.

Terrorism Risk Insurance Act of 2002

In mid-November 2002, the House of Representatives and the Senate passed the Terrorism Risk Insurance Act of 2002 (TRIA). The Act provides a federal backstop for the terrorism market. It is too early to tell what effect the Act will have on pricing and availability of terrorism coverage, but it is known that the Act does not cover domestic terrorism (i.e., acts not committed by, or on behalf of, a foreign person or interest), and it does not extend to properties outside the United States, except U.S. vessels, aircraft, and missions.

Additionally:

- The Act will be administered by the Department of Treasury, and it terminates at the end of 2005. The program is capped at $100 billion.
- To qualify for reimbursement under the Act, the Secretaries of State and Treasury, and the Attorney General, must certify the event. The loss must exceed $5 million.
- Upon enactment, all exclusions relating to terrorism will be null and void. In other words, insurers will essentially offer terrorism coverage at no cost, until the insured client either declines the coverage at the price offered by insurers or fails to pay the premium 30 days after notice.
- The Act backs insurers for certain losses arising from terrorism (property, casualty, surety, and workers' compensation) but extends the program to war for workers' compensation only.
- Insurers will be required to meet a certain deductible or retention, which increases from 7 percent of the previous year's premium for the class of business in 2003, to 15 percent in 2005. Above this level, compensation will be 90 percent by the U.S. government and 10 percent by the insurance company.

■   The federal government is required to surcharge a policy-
    holder's premium at not more than 3 percent of the premium,
    to recoup losses below a certain threshold.

The goal of the program is to allow insurers to resume offering
terrorism coverage over time and to facilitate economic growth.
Some of the decline in the GDP growth of the United States, and the
slowdown in new construction, has been attributed to the lack of
affordable terrorism coverage.

In early 2003, some property insurers extended terrorism cover to
their clients' foreign properties, with coverage under global programs. However, many foreign locations may continue to turn to
the political risk or terrorism risk market for coverage.

Terrorism Risk

Over the last thirty years, 80 percent of terrorist attacks against
American interests have been against American businesses. It is
apparent that U.S. corporations will continue to be the target of terrorist attacks and, therefore, operate in an environment of heightened risk and uncertainty.

Yet, it would be dangerous to believe that the risk of future attacks
is limited to targets on U.S. soil. The U.S. State Department report,
"Patterns of Global Terrorism 2001," released in May 2002
(http://www.state.gov/s/ct/rls/pgtrpt/2001/), reveals that there
were 348 international attacks in the following regions:

Africa	33	
Asia	68	
Eurasia	3	
Latin America	194	(of which 178 were in Colombia)
Middle East	29	
North America	4	
Western Europe	17	

Additional information from the report included:

■   Types of attack: bombing (253, or 73 percent), armed attacks
    (41, or 12 percent), kidnapping (36, or 10 percent), arson,
    vandalism, hijacking, firebombing, assault, and others.

■   Total number of U.S. targets: 228, of which 204 (89 percent)
    were businesses.

■   Total number of facilities struck: 531, of which 397 (74 per-
    cent) were business facilities. This was an increase over the
    383 (68 percent) strikes against business facilities in 2000.

- Total number of casualties (4,655), based on an (unofficial) estimate of 3,000 persons killed in the September 11, 2001, attacks.

Nature of Terrorism Organizations

While various government agencies continue to gather intelligence on where and when the next terrorist attack could occur, in reality there is no way to precisely predict terrorist acts. This is reflected in the fact that there are more than 49 known terrorist organizations associated with some 29 countries around the world.

Terrorism Risk Modeling

Due to the need to incorporate human intent as a factor, terrorism risk models cannot be developed from the same methodologies used to predict earthquakes, hurricanes, and other catastrophes. Consequently, terrorism risk modeling is likely to remain elusive. To be effective, such models will need to be based upon:

- where and when the attacks may occur;
- the nature of the attack (a bomb; use of airplanes, motor, or other vehicles; a biological, chemical, or radiological weapon);
- the probability of a particular type of attack occurring at a specific location; and
- what damages may be inflicted at the location.

This is an extremely complex problem—particularly because history has shown that terrorists generally do the unexpected.

In the past, countries that have suffered terrorist attacks have relied on governments to be the insurer of last resort. Examples of these programs include Pool Re of the United Kingdom, Consorcio of Spain, and SASRIA of South Africa. Israel also has a program. Since September 11, France has developed the GAREAT pool, and insurers, reinsurers, and the government are discussing the creation of a similar program in Germany.

Issues Confronting the PRI Market

Background

The period between 1996 and 2001 saw unprecedented growth, choice, and innovation in the political risk insurance market. AIG lengthened tenors and reduced other terms and conditions. Chubb reentered the market. Sovereign and then Zurich quickly became major players. Several Regional Development Banks and some public agencies developed political risk programs for debt.

Events, such as September 11, resulted in a "hardening" of the PRI market, effecting a return to more conservative underwriting, a retrenchment of the general insurance market, and an increase in the number of potential claims

In addition to these developments in the PRI market, the worldwide economy has entered a recession, many companies have merged or gone out of business, and corporate scandals have plagued several business sectors. The decline in the stock market has caused many companies to sell their overseas assets, in an attempt to bolster revenue. Substantial increases in other insurance costs have dramatically affected insurance budgets, including available funds for political risk coverage.

Many companies consider political risk a discretionary, rather than a nondiscretionary form of insurance. This leads to adverse selection, with negative implications for underwriters and, more importantly, it leaves many companies exposed to potentially catastrophic losses. The PRI industry needs to improve its ability to develop "best practices," and to analyze and quantify potential loss implications.

Changing Perception of Risk

The changing perception of risk and the demands of the current global economy have thrust the political risk market into a new stage of evolution, if not turmoil. In a world of free-floating exchange rates, companies are more concerned about devaluation/depreciation than with inconvertibility. Companies are now concerned about risks such as economic meltdown, which is not covered by traditional political risk insurance.

In many regions, the opening up of infrastructure to private sector development, in the 1990s, without the establishment of the requisite associated legal, regulatory, financial, and physical infrastructure, resulted in the need for a restructuring process for many companies and countries. Regulatory risk has now replaced the old-fashioned version of expropriation by decree as a primary concern among many investors.

New Products

The PRI market took initial steps toward developing new products (such as the limited devaluation product utilized by OPIC in a

Brazil transaction) to address the risk of economic nonviability. These developments may be stunted by the changes in the insurance market since September 11. Further, it is becoming increasingly difficult to obtain adequate PRI for certain infrastructure projects, particularly those squeezed between government providers, suppliers, and offtakers.

In some instances, these initiatives are undergoing review and restructuring by investors, lenders, and underwriters. Often, by the time some power projects go live after several years of development, the surrounding environment in the world is completely changed. Many projects experience a realignment of interest and increased friction among the parties involved. This is evident in the number of claims notifications related to power projects. However, unless the PRI market develops products that respond to the changing business and economic climate in the world, demand for political risk insurance will decline. Already, many companies and banks prefer to self-insure or buy comprehensive cover, than take the risk that PRI will not respond to the type of event that occurs.

Capital Markets

During the past several years, the market has transformed its traditional inconvertibility coverage for banks into a product for capital markets. It is important to pose the question as to why so few capital markets transactions have been closed. One reason may be that the insurance product was not a panacea for bringing the capital markets to emerging markets. It did, however, have a niche role, when the right circumstances were present—namely, a strong underlying credit in a below–investment grade country, with few other alternatives to raise capital, when spreads were sufficiently wide to absorb the cost of insurance.

Since a number of transactions were done in Argentina, it will be interesting to see how the rating-agency approach works in the long term. It appears that most of the transactions were affected more by the devaluation, and the inability to make payments even in local currency, than by inconvertibility. While it may still be too early to tell, given the long waiting periods, the debt service reserve accounts and efforts by the government of Argentina to restore convertibility will certainly offer lessons to be learned.

The next frontier appears to be development of expropriation coverage for the capital markets. The Belize mortgage project insured by Zurich, using its nonhonoring coverage, was a first step in this development. OPIC is working on development of expropriation for the capital markets, but its approach relies on the use of an expedited dispute resolution mechanism. These approaches should be useful for projects that are developed with a government guaranty and are a welcome addition to the list of structures available to facilitate capital flows. However, the proposed new international architecture, which allows sovereigns to go into bankruptcy, must be analyzed by underwriters and capital markets lenders in this context.

Public-Private Cooperation

OPIC has recently become much more flexible in its ability to cooperate with the private market. It has even reinsured private market participants, which it had never done before. It has also been willing to share its salvage or recoveries on a pro rata basis, with no fee or similar charge. These developments should enhance cooperation among OPIC and the other markets. Among Berne Union members, there has been willingness to cooperate. EDC of Canada is a leader among public agencies in syndicated risk to the private sector. A number of public agencies have, in turn, obtained treaty reinsurance from the private sector.

While the private market remains the most flexible option for many projects, infrastructure and other highly visible projects will certainly benefit from the presence of an official entity. In the preceding volume of the MIGA–Georgetown Symposium, I discussed a claim in Indonesia that involved both private and public insurance.[1] During the course of the settlement negotiations, it became clear that the private market would not have received any recoveries had it not been for OPIC's presence and its management of the claims process. While official agencies can deter the actions of the host government toward a project, they may be unable to do anything in the event of overall economic collapse in the respective country. However, there is clearly value in their claims recovery capabilities.

Conclusion

The political risk market is at a crossroads. The crisis in Argentina, and a number of claims in other areas, are testing it. The market has to respond expeditiously to all valid claims if it is to be perceived as being valuable to investors. For the PRI market to remain relevant, especially in these volatile times, it will need to consider how to address the risks that have emerged as the world economic and political order evolves. There is always push and pull as new products are developed and underwriters learn about various coverages through the test of claims. These unsettling times should not be a deterrent to growth, but should serve as a reminder for prudence in innovation.

Note

1. Martin, Julie A. 2001. "OPIC Modified Expropriation Coverage Case Study: MidAmerica's Projects in Indonesia—Dieng and Patuha." In Theodore H. Moran, (ed.), *International Political Risk Management: Exploring New Frontiers*. Washington, DC: The World Bank.

PART TWO

Political Risk Insurance in the Aftermath of September 11 and the Argentina Crisis: Demand Side Issues

Overview

Theodore H. Moran, Editor

Part Two explores the reactions of investors and lenders to the recent upheavals in the global economy. It pays particular attention to the problems confronting large infrastructure projects, in which purchase agreements are guaranteed by the host country, and revenues are denominated in local currency. It examines how political risk insurance can help lenders to return to financing infrastructure development in emerging markets, and asks to what extent investors and lenders need new products or new kinds of coverage to deal with currency crises.

This section comprises discussions by Kenneth Hansen (Partner in the Project Finance Group of Chadbourne & Parke), and Anne Predieri (Managing Director, Banc of America Securities LLC, assisted by Audrey Zuck), and commentaries provided by Daniel Riordan, (Executive Vice President, Zurich Emerging Markets Solutions) and James Alford (Vice President, Citibank).

The history of the political risk insurance industry—including OPIC, MIGA, and private providers—is filled with dynamic innovation and adjustment to changing circumstances, according to Ken Hansen. He identifies two areas that pose especially daunting challenges today.

The first challenge lies in dealing with the mismatch between inconvertibility insurance and protection against devaluation, first confronted by the PRI industry in the 1997 Asian financial crisis. While chaos swept the economies of Asia, currency markets did not close and currencies themselves did not become inconvertible. Power project investors, whose revenues accrued in local currencies, but whose debts required payment in dollars, had negotiated contracts that imposed exchange risk on the host country power purchaser (or on the financial authorities where the power purchaser was located). Host regulatory authorities found it infeasible to pass on to consumers the price increases required to service the foreign currency loans. In subsequent restructurings, lawsuits, and PRI claims in Asia, inconvertibility coverage provided little comfort to project sponsors or their creditors.

Political risk insurers have traditionally been unable to provide devaluation coverage because forward currency markets and swap arrangements are not long term enough to meet the debt-service needs of major infrastructure investors. In 2001, however, OPIC—along with AES and Banc of America Securities—designed a pilot product that could partially meet the needs of infrastructure investors. As Hansen explains in some detail, this pilot product (of which he was one of the principal architects), was a kind of standby foreign exchange liquidity facility, based on the assumption that foreign currency values would track local currency values with, at most, a temporary lag. A financially sound local project, therefore, whose host country revenues were indexed for local inflation, should need coverage only to cover the lag until the two currency values became realigned. The project could draw on the OPIC liquidity facility to keep its dollar debt service payments current, replenishing the facility as local currency revenues caught up. This innovative OPIC product appears to meet investors' needs in the Tiete project in Brazil, and Sovereign Risk Insurance Ltd. has begun to offer a similar product (described later in the commentary by Dan Riordan).

A second area that requires attention, according to Hansen, is the need for enhanced expropriation coverage to mitigate the risk of host government breach of contract. Expropriation coverage has traditionally been designed, Hansen points out, to address the vulnerability of foreign investors to having their projects taken over, or actively interfered with, by host authorities. Expropriation coverage does not guarantee that host authorities will meet promises made to the investor, such as purchasing a projects' output or ensuring payment by a state agency that contracted the output. This distinction has been reinforced by the fact that expropriation without compensation constitutes a violation of international law, whereas under many circumstances sovereign breach of contract does not (a distinction highlighted by Charles Berry of Berry Palmer & Lyle, in Section III).

Hansen also shows how the principal public sector providers have been innovative in helping investors deal with the risk of government breach of contract. OPIC and MIGA have designed a product that covers one particular clause of an investment contract (the arbitration clause), if the host government has ratified the New York Convention on the Recognition and Enforcement of Arbitral Awards. In OPIC's case, the insurer covers the loss if the host government refuses to participate in the arbitration, or prevents the arbitration from moving forward, or loses and then refuses to pay the arbitral award. In MIGA's case, however, the insurer will not pay the claim if the host government frustrates the arbitration.

Private sector insurers have gone one step further with this coverage. They offer "non-honoring of guarantee" insurance, in which a claim will be paid if both payment default and guarantee payment default occur, without requiring the investor to go through arbitration.

Another initiative to deal with the risk of sovereign breach of contracts, Hansen points out, has come through "partial risk guaranties" offered by multilateral development banks, led by the World Bank. Although the World Bank cannot lend to projects sponsored by private investors and lenders, it can guarantee commercial loans to the project against the specific risk that the host government might fail to perform its contractual commitments to the project, provided the World Bank has a back-up agreement with the host government assuring reimbursement for any resulting payments. The Inter-American Development Bank, the European Bank for Reconstruction and Development, and the Asian Development Bank have moved in the same direction. The use of "partial risk guarantees" has been slowed, however, by the determination that the full guaranty amount is counted against the country's overall borrowing limit, generating a high opportunity cost for signatory authorities, as a country approaches its maximum borrowing level.

Hansen concludes that the record of forced renegotiation of infrastructure investment agreements suggests that investors and lenders are likely to be much more cautious in the future than they had been during the developmental euphoria of the 1990s.

Anne Predieri and Audrey Zuck extend the argument that the PRI industry requires continuous innovation to respond to constantly changing circumstances. Political risk insurance is like penicillin, they suggest — it was a useful means of treating many ailments in the early years of investment in developing country markets, but now the traditional forms of political risk insurance, like penicillin, are limited in their ability to combat the new afflictions of today. Specialized medicines will have to supplement them. In short, PRI has proven to be a medication that must be continuously modified to deal with new complaints and disorders.

In responding to new needs, private political risk insurers are not hampered by the public policy constraints relating to developmental benefits, environmental concerns, and human rights and worker's rights issues, that govern public agencies, such as MIGA and OPIC. This allows private insurers to respond more quickly, argue Predieri and Zuck, and to issue coverage in a shorter period of time. It also affords them more flexibility, such as the ability to offer global rather than project-by-project coverage.

Public providers, in contrast, have exceptionally strong credit ratings because they are endowed with governmental backing and often enjoy unique salvage advantages vis-à-vis the host countries. Public providers, however, suffer from a perception among users, according to Predieri and Zuck, that their willingness to provide coverage or pay claims may be subject to political considerations. At the same time public providers do not have to worry about the impact of claims payment on their profitability or credit rating and, therefore, assert Predieri and Zuck, they may be more willing to pay claims than their private sector counterparts. Their record of making payments is more open to public scrutiny than private insurers' payment performance. As a result, rating agencies appear to take comfort in public sector coverage, even when the coverage is subject to exclusions or allows the insurer to terminate the policy, in contrast to private sector coverage.

The new forms of "antibiotics," highlighted by Predieri and Zuck — developed by private and public providers — include arbitral award default coverage; convertibility/transfer coverage for capital markets; and liquidity facilities, like the coverage described by Hansen, to cover divergences between foreign currency values and inflation-indexed local currency revenue streams. These new products have expanded the participation of bondholders in emerging market projects.

Of particular importance to lenders is "enhanced inconvertibility coverage" (including coverage for expropriation of funds), which has enabled some projects to access U.S. capital markets at their local currency rating, rather than at their foreign currency rating, improving the transaction rating by as much as six gradations on the scale of the rating agencies, sometimes reaching a level above sovereign lending. In the process, rating agency assessments have per force become more important, as they determine whether to confer ratings upgrades or not. But enhanced inconvertibility coverage often requires proof that international law has been violated, which is more complicated than demonstrating the presence of currency controls. This may involve arbitration procedures, possibly delaying payment beyond the original schedule.

In the past, argue Predieri and Zuck, many lenders purchased PRI simply to allow themselves to "check the box" to meet syndication requirements, or to obtain credit authorization. Now, for the first time, they have to provide detailed proof that possible future losses are covered under the terms of the policies they hold. At the same time, investors, lenders, and insurers must make complicated, overlapping decisions about how to manage ongoing projects that are in trouble, balancing conflicting interests about the consequences of these decisions with respect to their legal status.

The trials of the contemporary period show conflicts of interest between debt- and equity-holders, and between PRI-

covered lenders and lenders without coverage, that are as complex as the pledge of shares issue, which was the focus of the
previous Georgetown-MIGA volume on International Political Risk Management.[1] Lenders and investors today are more
preoccupied with devaluation than with currency controls, and
with overall credit deterioration than with individual hostile
political actions. Regulatory risk has been accorded higher priority than traditional breach of contract, with the added complexity—as indicated in Hansen's earlier analysis, and treated
more thoroughly by Berry in Section III of this book—that host
country regulatory responsibilities have an inherent legitimacy
that simple contract frustration may lack.

Daniel Riordan takes issue with the contention of Predieri
and Zuck that public agencies, such as OPIC, have a "public
policy incentive to pay claims," whereas private insurers have
the opposite perspective. Public agency claims directors, he
asserts, are professionals who base their determinations on
what constitutes the validity of the claim, not on public policy
or political considerations. Private insurer claims directors,
likewise, provide high quality service to customers, based on
in-depth evaluations of the validity of a claim.

It is also incorrect to suggest, according to Riordan, that rating agencies are more comfortable with loan syndications and
bond offerings backed by public agency political risk insurance. S&P, Moody's, and Fitch have rated capital market transactions that have been covered exclusively by private sector
insurers. The total number of emerging market bond issues
insured by private companies that have been rated, he argues,
exceeds those backed by public agencies.

The demand for PRI from most major customers declined
by approximately 50 percent in 2002, compared to 2001, with
the expectation of further reductions in 2003, says Riordan.
However, there has been growing interest in specialized coverages, including comprehensive political risk-and-credit coverage for banks and exporters, and coverage of sovereign
guaranties.

An innovation in the coverage of sovereign guaranties can
be found in Zurich's securitization of mortgages issued by the
Development Finance Corporation (DFC) of Belize. In this
transaction, the payment of principal and interest of the ten-

year, $45 million bond issue in U.S. dollars, is guaranteed by the DFC, and backed by the unconditional and irrevocable faith and credit of the Government of Belize. Zurich's coverage, described in more detail by Riordan, provides compensation for up to 90 percent of any failed payment on the part of the Belize government. This "Non-Honoring of Sovereign Guaranty" product allowed the bond issue to receive an "A" rating from Fitch and an "A3" rating from Moody's.

Riordan agrees that the crisis in Argentina is proving to be a real test of how products work, and of whether customers understand what they are purchasing. The possibility that losses in Argentina will not result in valid claims is likely to lead to tough questions about the value of political risk policies, in his opinion. This will put pressure on underwriters to develop new types of coverage, or to provide higher levels of comprehensive coverage. The Argentine situation will demonstrate once again, Riordan argues, that it is preferable to resolve possible conflicts about the interpretation of policy wording at the time of writing the policy, rather than later when a claim is being made.

As the private sector PRI industry evolves , public insurers will continue to offer additional capacity for large projects and serve small businesses and high-risk markets, which do not appeal to private companies. Public agencies fulfill their public policy role best, in Riordan's view, as wholesalers of capacity or as reinsurers—in particular, treaty reinsurers—leaving private companies to serve as the principal retail insurers. Working together, public and private insurers can extend capacity, and provide better, more innovative products and greater responsiveness to customer needs.

Amplifying on the complexities inherent in the Argentine meltdown, James Alford points to the heightened role that bank regulators will play in shaping the demands on the political risk insurance industry. Prior to September 11 and the crisis in Argentina, he observes, political risk insurers were moving in the direction of providing "all risk" borrower default insurance that lenders fervently desired. It is not clear what may emerge, but the outcome will depend on what is learned from the experience in Argentina and how bank regulatory requirements evolve.

The experience in Argentina encompasses the interruption of currency conversion, transfer restrictions, "pesification" (with resulting mismatches between assets and liabilities), abrogation of contracts and tariff agreements, changed bankruptcy laws, and contradictory rulings and interpretations by local courts. In some cases, "pesification" has diminished the burden of liabilities; in other cases, it has destroyed borrowers' balance sheets, when assets and liabilities were converted at different rates. Many borrowers experienced overwhelming liquidity problems, leading to requests that lenders grant credit extensions, observe standstills, or reschedule payments. Lenders, investors, and insurers found themselves hyperfocused on time lines for claims determinations, settlements, and eventual payouts.

In the midst of the Argentine upheaval, Alford points out, bank regulators, led by the Federal Reserve of the United States, have begun to specify that borrowers be covered by comprehensive guarantees, explicitly covering borrower defaults and nonconvertibility. It is by no means clear, concludes Alford, that traditional political risk insurance can meet these demands, and provide sufficient risk transfer to warrant the cost of the coverage, or offer genuinely comprehensive coverage that is affordable to the buyer.

Note

1. Moran, Theodore H. (ed.) 2001. "The Multiple Pledge-of-Shares Problem." In *International Political Risk Management: Exploring New Frontiers.* Washington, DC: The World Bank.

PRI and the Rise (and Fall?) of Private Investment in Public Infrastructure

Kenneth W. Hansen
Partner in the Project Finance Group
Chadbourne & Parke LLP

The Origins of Demand for the PRI Market

Public infrastructure used to be a job for the government. The Department of Energy provided power, the Department of Telecommunications intermediated telephone calls, and the Department of Transportation managed trains, planes, and ports. The participation of the government in public infrastructure varied, of course, in different countries, between (and within) sectors and over time. The subways in New York City were built by (and as) private enterprises, but later on became municipal operations. While roads in the United States, including toll roads, were generally publicly built and maintained, railroads were typically, at least until recently, private enterprises. Airlines in the United States have always been private, though most airports are public. Until recently, power, water, natural gas, and telephone services were provided in the United States by privately owned, but publicly regulated, monopolies — the so-called public utilities. In most other parts of the world, however, these services were the business of the government, not only to regulate, but also to provide. Notwithstanding such variations in practice, well into the 1980s, it was the norm to consider the development and operation of core infrastructure to be the responsibility of the public sector.

Then came the elections of Margaret Thatcher and Ronald Reagan, and the fall of the Soviet empire—each event reflected, and contributed to a sea change in public perceptions about how to build and operate infrastructure. Deregulation and privatization spread from one sector to the next. Erstwhile public monopolies were abolished, sold, or subjected to private competition. In some cases, public assets and operations were simply turned over to private management—in other words, outsourced. In other cases, such as the introduction of independent power projects and the break-up of Bell Telephone in the United States, new models for the development, operation, and management of an industry had to be adopted. Still others reflected opportunities created by new technologies, such as the impact of mobile telephone service and the Internet in the telecommunications industry. Under a myriad of models, and in varying degrees, trust was put in the free market over public management, to meet society's infrastructure needs. There was a time lag in the arrival of the privatization movement in the emerging markets, but it quickly came to define the cutting edge of infrastructure development. The impetus for the past decade of aggressive privatization in emerging markets had two sources—one ideological and one pragmatic. The ideological driver was belief in the wisdom and efficiency of the market; the pragmatic motivation was budgetary.

The Cold War is often remembered for its conflicting visions on whether the government should favor individual liberties or collective "economic freedoms" (e.g., freedom from hunger and unemployment). The core organizational tension, however, concerned the proper role of government in managing the economy. Was it better to assure chosen outcomes through a planned and managed economy, or to leave economic outcomes to the vagaries of the market? Should private interests and actions determine collective outcomes? Could these private interests, perhaps, be guided by legislated incentives or even constrained by applicable regulations? Would these regulations put us all in a world for which no one bears overall responsibility?

Such free market outcomes, guided by Adam Smith's "invisible hand," seemed to correlate with faster economic development, cleaner environments, and safer workplaces worldwide. The economic miracle worked by the so-called "Chicago boys" pulled Chile out of economic chaos and launched it on a growth path that continues to bring prosperity today. It transcends the welfare achieved by Chile's more richly endowed neighbors, and persists despite various degrees of economic disruption and crisis in the region. No command economy could boast comparable results.

In contrast, public sector operations, even within market economies, broadly bore the stigma of "good-enough-for-government," and an attitude of such disinterest in clients that it would bankrupt any business dependent upon pleasing customers! Further, it seemed, moving along the spectrum to the more state-dominated economies and the socialist countries, as more was entrusted to the government, less was done and was done "less well."

Many emerging market governments were ready for the new party line of "power to the private sector." To exaggerate the instinct only slightly, "anything government did, the market could do better"; that is, privatizing power, telecommunications, roads (making them toll roads), airports, airlines, trains, and ports. If one really wanted to go to the cutting edge, then privatize hospitals, prisons, schools, and water systems. Outsource public operations to private providers wherever possible. One could expect more reliable, more efficient services at lower cost. When such activities were taken off the public budget, taxes could be lowered, budgetary deficits could be reduced (or eliminated), inflation could be curbed, and the currency could be strengthened. This was a heady prospect for the governors of any developing country, which had a history of deficits, inflation, the occasional currency collapse, and deficient infrastructure. Of course, turning out entrenched bureaucracies from portfolios closely guarded, even if mismanaged, for generations was not likely to be a politically simple exercise, if it was feasible at all. Emerging markets are replete with examples of ministries-of-this-and-that, which appear more as impediments to the fulfillment of their respective public missions than defenders of the public interest.

The expansion of the role of the private sector in the development and operation of public infrastructure may well have sputtered along with far less significance had ideology been its sole motivation. But ideology was at least supplemented, and often dominated, by a second impetus—budgets.

Widespread economic growth in the 1990s led many poorer countries to a vision of progress, even if it was constrained by the ability of critical infrastructure—especially, power, transportation, and telecommunications—to keep pace. But public sector funds in poorer countries are sorely limited in the best of times. Thus, the widespread economic upturns of the 1990s followed on the heels of the debt crisis of the 1980s in the Third World, and many countries were unable (or unwilling) to compound national indebtedness with the additional public debt required to finance the cost of infrastructure required for progress.

Private developers and financiers offered—and, indeed, aggressively lobbied for—a different approach. Concessions were sometimes privately negotiated, and often publicly auctioned. Opportunities were aggressively pursued by a myriad of new power and telecom development companies in prospective host countries as diverse as Brazil, Egypt, Honduras, and Vietnam. Asia was a hotbed of projects, with aggressive development programs in India, Indonesia, Pakistan, and the Philippines. South America also had major projects up for bid across the continent.

The private development of public infrastructure offered a means to tap state-of-the-art technologies, and to do so without further burdening public coffers. Indeed, auctioning concessions and selling off public assets—particularly those operating in chronic deficit—offered immediate benefits to national fiscal circumstances.

Thus, the stage was set in the early 1990s for an upsurge in worldwide demand for private sector developers and operators of erstwhile public services. It was clear, however, that, for major projects in most developing countries, the capital and technological requirements would force foreign investors to fill the demand for private sector investments.[1] A proliferation of established and new companies, particularly from Europe and the United States, focused on developing and operating infrastructure projects, left no shortage of prospective foreign private sector partners for a government seeking to privatize public operations. A principal impediment to making many of those potential matches was, however, that prospective opportunities arose in countries where the economic, legal, political, and overall business environment was not only foreign to prospective developers, but also unstable and substandard, in their view.

In particular, these prospective investors feared political risk. Investors correctly perceived that the success of their ventures would depend not only on their technical and management skills, and on developments in the relevant markets, but also on local political considerations. Concerns ranged from expropriation (by governments that could oust the private sector from these sectors as easily as they had invited it in) to political violence (consider Colombia, where a number of major projects went forward, notwithstanding narco-terrorism and civil warfare) and to currency inconvertibility (as many of these countries have histories of chronically poor fiscal and monetary management, with one weak currency replacing another). Fortunately, help was available for many investors and projects, from a few commercial insurers and from public political risk insurers, whose specific goal is to encourage

investments in developing countries by insuring against losses arising from such risks.

The Origins of Supply in the PRI Market

At the start of the 1990s, Lloyd's of London was the leading commercial provider of political risk insurance. The principal public
agencies providing such support for project developers were OPIC
of the United States, and MIGA of the World Bank Group.[2] Each got
its start, indirectly, with World War II.

OPIC

Following World War II, officials in the Truman administration,
charged with designing the Marshall Plan for rebuilding war-torn
Europe, were anxious to supplement public monies with private
investment.[3] Private investment in acquisition, repair, and restart-
ing of commercial operations, such as a bombed-out factory, would
release public funds for other purposes, such as rebuilding a
bombed-out bridge or school. In addition, to the extent such private
investments were successful, they would provide employment,
income, a market for the products of supplier businesses, a flow of
product to customers, tax revenues, and an overall return to normal
economic activity. With all due respect to the importance of emergency aid and other public programs, it was investment in, and the
operation of, self-sustaining private businesses that brought the
return of productive economic life to post-war Europe.

Unfortunately, American business was not particularly interested.
As proud as they may have been of their government's humanitar-
ian mission in restoring a good quality of life to war survivors, the
managers of leading American enterprises, as guardians of their
shareholders' capital, were justifiably skeptical of post-war business
opportunities in Europe.

First of all, Europe was seen as politically unstable, and a volatile
region prone to periodic regional warfare. The region could easily
destabilize again, long before reasonable returns on new investments
could be achieved. And the political risks to investors did not end
with warfare. The Soviets had marched halfway across Europe, and
their influence may not have stopped there. Powerful, growing Communist interests had taken root in the legislatures of all the major
countries in the region. Socialist governments in England, France,
and Italy appeared in 1948 to be at least a risk, if not an inevitable

likelihood. Communist takeovers, conjuring up images of widespread expropriation of private enterprises, were unlikely to mix well with foreign direct investment (FDI). Finally, even if the region were to avoid both warfare and Communist takeover, and if investments were to prove profitable, those profits would come in local currencies. After the war, European currencies were overvalued and subject to extensive exchange rate controls, posing a real risk that profits might prove impossible to transfer back to the United States.

In due course, the Marshall Plan was supplemented by legislation providing for U.S. government insurance to U.S. investors, against each of the risks of currency inconvertibility, expropriation, and political violence.[4]

Postwar reconstruction efforts, after achieving their objectives in Europe, evolved into development programs for less-developed countries. A leading example was the World Bank—formally known as the "International Bank for Reconstruction and Development (IBRD)." From the beginning, the IBRD looked toward a longer-term mission of Third World development, in addition to the immediate challenge of European reconstruction.[5] Similarly, the political risk insurance program of the United States government survived the Marshall Plan years and began to focus on supporting business investment in poorer countries. The rhetoric was, if American foreign economic policy was well-served by American businesses investing in job creation in Western Europe, would not American interests be similarly well-served by expanding American investments in the less-developed nations of Africa, Asia, and Latin America?

In 1961, with the passage of the Foreign Assistance Act, the various development programs sponsored by the United States government—including investment insurance against political risks—were consolidated under the umbrella of the newly established Agency for International Development (AID).[6] For the next decade, AID administered the government's issuance of PRI in the developing world.

By 1969, Senator Jacob Javits led the charge to make the political risk insurance program independent of AID.[7] His concern was that AID was too much of a government bureaucracy to administer a business-promotional program efficiently and effectively. The PRI program had developed a reputation of being bureaucratic and slow, under the aegis of AID and was primarily a resource for large corporations only. A smaller business, lacking a Washington representative to shepherd its insurance application through AID, could easily become lost in the bureaucracy. Even if the insurance coverage were to emerge from the process, it was unlikely to do so within a time frame affordable for a small business. Finally, small businesses would not be able to afford the transaction costs involved in trying to access this type of government support.

Senator Javits's brother, Benjamin A. Javits, published a book entitled *Peace by Investment*, in 1950, in which he argues the importance of private investment as a vehicle for economic development and a supplement to official aid.[8] It is interesting to speculate whether this book influenced the Marshall Plan planners when they adopted PRI as an element of their development program. In any event, it would be truly surprising if the senator had been unaware of his brother's thoughts in this regard when, 19 years after the publication of his brother's book, he himself concluded that AID was ineffective in promoting development through private sector investment, and persuaded Congress to move the PRI program to an independent agency.

Established in 1969, OPIC began operations in 1971.[9] The purpose was to create a business-oriented organization, staffed by business officers and lawyers with private sector experience who could administer the PRI program in a less bureaucratic, more efficient, and generally more effective manner, thus promoting private investment in less developed countries. Notwithstanding the new charter, the core authorizations to issue political risk insurance could be traced to the original Marshall Plan enactments, authorizing policies to cover the same triad of risks—currency inconvertibility,[10] expropriation,[11] and political violence[12]—and subject to similar limitations, such as availability being limited to U.S. investors.[13]

OPIC faced an immediate challenge to its viability—it inherited the insurance contracts previously issued by AID. By 1973, that pre-existing coverage had yielded roughly half a billion dollars in claims, based on the expropriation of U.S. investments in mining and telecommunications by the government of Dr. Salvador Allende, in Chile. The claims substantially exceeded initial reserves provided to OPIC when it was established. So as OPIC opened its doors for business it did so under the cloud of possible insolvency.[14]

The immediate crisis passed with the settlement of the claims by the successor government in Chile. The point was made, however, that, though the OPIC statute provided for its operation on a self-sustaining basis,[15] the viability of its business operations could not be taken for granted.

Notwithstanding the insolvency risk that greeted its opening, over the next 31 years of operations, OPIC has been spectacularly successful as a business. It has been profitable in every year of its operations, reaching a high of $214.6 million in fiscal 2001.[16] Its reserves against possible claims payments, which left it short-handed in the early 1970s following the Chilean claims, have since grown to exceed $3.5 billion—more than adequate to cover any seriously imaginable worst-case scenario for OPIC.[17]

MIGA

The financial success of OPIC encouraged the World Bank to offer similar support to investors in developing countries, but without being constrained by OPIC's limitation to investors from the United States. Although the idea for creating a multilateral political risk insurance agency emerged in the 1950s, no particular progress was made toward that end until World Bank President A.W. "Tom" Clausen revived the idea in his first address to the World Bank's Annual Meeting in 1981. The Convention establishing the Multilateral Investment Guarantee Agency was submitted to governments for signature on October 11, 1985.[18] Subsequent to the signature of 29 countries and the subscription of over 50 percent of its capital, MIGA opened for business in June, 1988.

Although MIGA was in no way constrained by the legislative authorizations and limitations imposed on OPIC by Congress, the agency derived great confidence in the successful precedent set by OPIC's then 17 years of successful operations. The influence of OPIC on MIGA was assured by aggressive recruitment from OPIC's ranks to staff the new agency. Leigh Hollywood, a senior OPIC insurance manager, was hired as MIGA's senior underwriter. Lorin "Laddie" Weisenfeld, OPIC's Assistant General Counsel for Insurance, was recruited to MIGA's legal department. In due course, MIGA also brought on board OPIC's senior policy analyst, Gerald West, and a number of OPIC insurance officers.

Consequently, it is not surprising that MIGA offered investors coverage substantially similar to that of OPIC, importing some of their limitations as well. For instance, OPIC's charter prohibits offering political violence coverage against losses stemming from actions taken to achieve "labor or student objectives." No such constraint is imposed by the MIGA Convention. Yet the "General Terms and Conditions" typically applicable to MIGA coverage provide that "[t]he coverage for War and Civil Disturbance ... does not extend to acts undertaken primarily to achieve labor, student, or other non-political objectives."[19]

Commercial Political Risk Insurers

A continuing presence in the political risk insurance market through the years has been that of the venerable Lloyd's of London. Other commercial insurers were also available to supplement the capacity of public agencies, but their coverage was far more limited than that of the public agency providers—with regard to the countries where it was offered and, especially, the term of the policies. The tenor for commercial coverage was likely to be up to three (and in rare circumstances, seven) years, in contrast to the 20-year term that was normal practice for OPIC, and the 15- to 20-year term for MIGA coverage.

The private market responded to the dramatic increase in demand for foreign investment in emerging market infrastructure, during the 1990s, with a relative explosion in capacity. Several new insurers opened for business.[20] Others increased their capacity, term, and the number of countries for which coverage was available. To the disappointment of the demand side of the market, however, the scope of the coverage offered by MIGA and new commercial insurers was substantially similar to the prior precedent set by OPIC and Lloyd's.

Tensions in the Contemporary Market

The expansion of demand for, and supply of, investment insurance against political risks in emerging markets in the 1990s exposed a qualitative mismatch between what investors wanted and what the market was used to providing. This was particularly true with respect to coverage for expropriation and currency risks. It is no surprise that products conceived in the wake of World War II and the Bretton Woods Conference, as part of the Marshall Plan, would not fully service market needs going into the 21st century.

Devaluation Insurance

One area of dramatic mismatch in the current PRI market concerns currency risk. The market offers—since the days of the Marshall Plan—currency inconvertibility coverage. What the demand side of the market now needs is a hedge against devaluation.[21]

The relevance of inconvertibility coverage began to diminish a year before OPIC even began its operations; in 1972, President Nixon withdrew the United States from the Bretton Woods system, ending the worldwide regime of fixed exchange rates that had prevailed since World War II. Nonetheless, inconvertibility coverage continued to be a mainstay of OPIC's annual sales, and, from time to time, OPIC had to pay inconvertibility claims.

The 1997 Asian economic crisis, however, dealt a severe blow to market acceptance of the inconvertibility insurance product. Currencies in Indonesia and Thailand collapsed in value. Contractual undertakings tied to the U.S. dollar were widely breached, interrupting project cash flows and leading to debt defaults. Although many project lenders carried conventional political risk coverage on their investments, including currency inconvertibility insurance, no currency became inconvertible. While chaos reigned in East Asian currency markets, the markets remained open. This confirmed the suspicion of lenders that the important risk to mitigate was not inconvertibility, but devaluation.

Unfortunately, there is a lack of satisfactory means for mitigating devaluation risk in emerging markets projects. Conventional sources of currency hedges—including various types of forward or currency swap contracts—are not available in the emerging markets, at least not for the terms of financing required by infrastructure projects.

The classic response, in power projects and other local-currency-generating projects, has been to assign devaluation risk to the offtaker. The Asian crisis and related Indonesian devaluation rightly undermined the market's confidence in that approach, as project after project was confronted with breaches by offtakers who feared that power price increases triggered by the maxi-devaluation would be politically infeasible to pass on. Five years later, the lawsuits, restructurings, and political risk insurance claims continue, without any value added from inconvertibility coverage.

For years, project lenders have approached political risk insurers—both public agencies and commercial insurers—seeking some form of insurance against devaluation risk. Until recently, the market presumption was that such comfort was impossible to provide and unreasonable to expect.

OPIC, however, challenged this presumption. In May 2001, OPIC issued a devaluation guaranty supporting $300 million in 15-year bonds to refinance the acquisition costs of the recently privatized AES Tiete hydroelectric generating stations in Brazil. AES, Banc America Securities,[22] and OPIC devised arrangements that enabled the AES Tiete bonds to pierce the sovereign ceiling for Brazil and to achieve an investment grade rating,[23] even as the value of the Reis slipped in the days before closing.

The devaluation coverage is not insurance in the traditional sense, but rather OPIC's guaranty of the U.S. dollar value of the project's local currency net revenues. OPIC's support is structured as a standby foreign exchange liquidity facility that the project company can draw upon if, as a consequence of devaluation, it would otherwise have been unable to make its dollar debt service payments. Through the use of various triggers, OPIC coverage distinguishes exchange rate risks from operational risks— OPIC supports the exchange rate risks and leaves the project and its lenders to use other devices to deal with the operational risks. OPIC disbursements, then, become a junior loan to the project company, whose repayment is subordinated to current payments on the bonds. The structure thus devised could be used to protect any project that generates local currency, and is otherwise commercially sound, against defaulting on its dollar-based debt because of serious local currency devaluation.[24]

The basic economic theory underlying the product is "purchasing power parity"—the proposition in international economics that exchange rates adjust to reflect the relative buying power of each currency; that is, exchange rates adjust to inflation. AES, Banc America Securities, and OPIC worked with financial and legal advisors, and with international economists at Wharton Economic Forecasting Associates, to develop the devaluation product.[25] The Wharton analysis was comforting to OPIC, because it concluded that significant deviations of currency values from rates predicted by inflation tend to be of limited duration. While headlines capture dramatic devaluations, they do not tend to report the return of exchange rates to more predictable levels — either because exchange rates subside to more familiar levels or because inflation catches up, in either case reestablishing purchasing power parity. The Wharton analysis also suggested that even dramatic devaluations are likely to pose only a temporary problem for an otherwise healthy project, unless the dollar debt is disbursed when the local currency is significantly overvalued. The consequence for the OPIC devaluation guaranty is that, although exchange rate disturbances may occasionally require drawing from OPIC's standby facility, a project that is otherwise financially sound in local currency terms should be able to repay those draws relatively easily.

As long as project revenues increase in proportion to local inflation, so the project can operate successfully in local currency terms, the OPIC foreign exchange liquidity facility ensures that the local currency net revenue, together with OPIC disbursements, are adequate to meet hard currency debt service payments when an exchange rate disturbance erodes the dollar value of those local net revenues.

The OPIC devaluation guaranty product offers an attractive alternative to offtake agreements tied to the dollar. As with Indonesia in 1997, and Argentina today, dollar-tied offtake agreements may not effectively protect a project and its investors from devaluation risk. When severe devaluations occur, offtakers face strong customer resistance to price increases triggered by international currency market events that seem far removed from local life. The risk of offtaker default becomes a high likelihood. In contrast, if prices under an offtake agreement are tied to local inflation only, then price increases will also be tied, and be proportionate, to the economic changes surrounding both the offtaker and its downstream customers. Thus, for political and economic reasons, such offtake contracts are less likely to be breached or repudiated in times of economic turmoil than are dollar-tied offtake contracts.

This pilot project for OPIC has not yet been adopted as a regular product. That next step will depend, in part, on whether there is adequate demand from appropriate projects in the marketplace. Appropriate projects would be those with strong local currency project economics, and project revenues that adjust reasonably quickly to local inflation. In addition, appropriate countries would not include those with currencies perceived to be artificially supported or otherwise overvalued, thus creating the risk of a one-time devaluation unrelated to inflation.

Whether OPIC is willing to offer this product to new projects will presumably depend on how it succeeds in its maiden voyage, not only in achieving the desired bond rating (which it did), but also in keeping an otherwise viable project afloat against currency volatility. Fifteen months post-closing, the Brazilian Reis has, as of the recent presidential election in Brazil, devalued by roughly 70 percent, but AES Tiete remains in good standing with its bondholders and OPIC.

Interestingly, while OPIC and the market await the possibility that AES Tiete will become the first of a new breed of financing structures—or remain a unique event—at least one commercial political risk insurer has decided to join the fray. In November 2001, Sovereign Risk Insurance Ltd. unveiled its "Real Exchange Rate Liquidity (REX)" product, which appears to follow the lines pioneered by OPIC. As the first anniversary of that announcement approaches, Sovereign has yet to announce any closed transactions, but it appears, nonetheless, that the idea of devaluation coverage from political risk insurers has gained ground.

Mitigating the Risk of Government Breach:
The Search for Enhanced Expropriation Cover

Expropriation cover was first conceived to address the risk that a government might seize a private business. Traditionally, such insurance specifically excluded coverage of government failure to perform affirmative undertakings, such as honoring payment promises to an investor. That is, expropriation coverage envisioned active interference by government, not an omission in keeping promises.

Such coverage failed, however, to mitigate what came to be seen as the chief political risk of public-private partnerships in the last decade: breach of contract by the government. Investors necessarily relied on a host of government undertakings to formulate their bid and make their investment. Typically, the government would promise to purchase a projects' output or guarantee payment by a state agency that had promised to purchase the project's output. It would be critical for the success of the investment that the government honor its promises.

Naturally, developers asked political risk insurers to cover the risk that the host government might fail to honor its project support obligations. Developers viewed this as a core political risk best borne by PRI providers. Insurers, however, have found it a difficult stretch to move beyond traditional expropriation cover and to stand behind host government performance risk.

As a general matter, product innovation is not easy in the political risk market—and for good reason. Political risk is not easily (or at all) subject to the statistical analysis that supports other types of insurance. While there is extensive data available regarding the incidence of auto collisions, death, house fires, and illness, the probability that a business suffers expropriation, currency inconvertibility, or political violence over the next twenty years—the maximum term of OPIC coverage—is beyond any mathematical model.

The clear alternative to statistical analysis has been to simply copy behavior that has proven successful. OPIC's two decades (as of the early 1990s) of profitable operations offers a model for prospective commercial competitors that appears feasible and tempting to copy. Further, veering from that model posed unquantifiable risks of financial disaster.

Although commercial insurers are free from the legal strictures of the MIGA charter and OPIC statute, thus enabling them to respond legally to investors' demands for novel coverages, they hesitate to take on new risks that can neither be subjected to statistical analysis nor supported by any acceptable track record. Such a track record is only available if the conventional Lloyd's, MIGA, or OPIC coverages are mimicked. Consequently, commercial insurers, even though they are motivated by commercial interests rather than any policy agenda, have proven to be as conservative as the public agencies in the risks they have been willing to underwrite. As discussed below, the principal innovations in the PRI marketplace have emanated from the public agency insurers, notwithstanding their legal and policy constraints.

Beyond this general bias toward product conservatism, there have been particular challenges in expanding traditional expropriation cover to insure against government breaches of contract. First of all, expropriation without compensation violates international law.[26] In contrast, however, international law also reserves to states the right, absent special circumstances, to breach contracts with impunity.[27] In the United States, the government waived its sovereign immunity, through legislative action,[28] to being held responsible for breaches of contract, with the establishment of the Court of Claims. But that waiver of immunity was a sovereign choice, which could be rescinded and, without which the U.S. government, like other governments that had not waived such immunity, would be free to break contractual promises.

The challenge to political risk insurers is how to provide insurance against governments breaching contracts, which the respective government has the power and the legal right to do without incurring any enforceable obligation to pay for the damages they cause to their contractual counterparties.

OPIC has offered a model to address this issue through its "contractors and exporters" coverage, which was specifically conceived to support businesses entering into contracts with governments.[29] With this coverage, OPIC would not insure against general breach of contract, but it would insure one particular clause of the contract—the arbitration clause—if the contracting government ratified the New York Convention.[30] If nonpayment or any other dispute were to arise under the contracts, the insured would need to pursue arbitration against the counter-party government in order to perfect a claim against OPIC. If the government were to refuse to participate in the arbitration, or somehow frustrate the arbitration from going forward, or if it were to lose the arbitration and then fail to pay the award against it, then, in each case, OPIC would cover the insured's loss.

As demand increased for coverage of government obligations supporting the development of infrastructure projects, OPIC resorted to a limited version of the contractors' and exporters' coverage, agreeing to simply cover a host government's failure to pay an arbitral award. Whether the government's successful frustration of arbitration in the first place would be enough to establish a claim deemed negotiable, and varies from case to case. Further, some coverages require the insured to win an arbitration as well as to have the award successfully confirmed by a nonappealable judgment of host country courts. One might reasonably ask—how much comfort could an investor take from political risk coverage that requires such cooperation from host country courts in order to perfect a claim? This is illustrative, however, of the challenge that insurers face in offering coverage against government action; that is, breach of contract—which for better or worse, the respective government may have every legal right to take, under international and local law.

MIGA has adopted a similar approach. Its breach of contract cover provides compensation for: a Loss due to the inability of the Guarantee Holder to enforce an [arbitral] Award against the Host Government, provided that . . . [inter alia] . . . the Guarantee Holder has made reasonable efforts to exhaust all remedies to enforce the Award against the Host Government for a period of 365 consecutive days from the date of the Award; and . . . . the Host Government's refusal to enforce the Award is arbitrary and/or discriminatory.[31]

Thus MIGA does not require, as a general matter, confirmation of the award by local courts (and neither, typically, does OPIC), but the unpaid award by itself is not enough. Enforcement must be pursued for at least a year, and the failure to pay must be "arbitrary" or "discriminatory." Under the MIGA coverage, if the government somehow frustrates the arbitral process from going forward, then no claim payment will be due.

Project developers have pressured insurers to provide claim payments upon proof of breach, without having to go through arbitration, particularly when the occurrence of the breach is reasonably obvious. This puts pressure on the insurance providers to decide the merits of the dispute prior to reaching arbitration.

While agency insurers have resisted taking that step, some progress has been made with commercial insurers. Several insurers offer "nonhonoring of guarantee" coverage under which, if a payment default occurs, and the supporting guaranty payment also fails to occur, proof of those facts alone (plus, perhaps a waiting period) will suffice to support a claim.[32] Aside from this, however, commercial insurers have appeared to be as conservative as agency insurers in venturing beyond the terms of traditional expropriation coverage.

This is somewhat ironic, as many developers expected (and the newly established commercial providers encouraged those expectations) that commercial insurers, freed from the legislative, charter, policy, and even political constraints facing agency insurers, be well-situated and competitively motivated to offer novel coverages, finely tuned to the business demands of contemporary infrastructure deal structures. Things have not worked out that way. Risk considerations have, to a great extent, kept commercial insurers on the same path as the agencies.

The lack of legal recourse for investors against breach of contract by governments is the reason for the norm in the PRI industry to insure only agreements to which a government has specifically waived its right to breach with impunity (i.e., without compensation), by submitting dispute resolution to binding international arbitration, and consenting to the enforcement of any resulting arbitral award against its property.

Partial Risk Guaranties

Another area that the political risk insurance industry has developed, in dealing with the risk of government breach of contracts in infrastructure investments, is negotiation of government performance guaranties by multilateral development banks—the so-called "partial risk guaranties." The World Bank led this charge.

Under its charter, the World Bank is only authorized to lend money to governments, or when the loan is backed by a sovereign guaranty.[33] As infrastructure development was delegated to private developers and lenders, the World Bank found its lending program for such projects substantially marginalized. World Bank consultants may see fiscal wisdom in developing a new power plant or road with private rather than public funds, and the benefits of world-class expertise of foreign developers and project operators, but such a project cannot benefit from World Bank lending, since it requires a government guaranty. This breaches a core tenet of the private infrastructure development approach: keeping project costs off the public balance sheet. Thus, for purely private projects (e.g., a generating plant selling power "inside-the-fence" to private businesses), there remains little for the World Bank to do besides consulting.

Most projects continue, however, to include the host government as a critical participant. It may be critical for a project's economics to have the government standing behind the terms of the concession (e.g., exclusivity). The government may also be involved in purchasing the project's output, or providing fuel for the project. The government may have guaranteed performance or payment by offtakers/suppliers whose own credit ratings are too weak to adequately support financing for an important project of the size proposed. In any of these cases, if the government breaks its promise, the project could fail and the debt and equity investments would be lost.

The term of the debt supporting many important emerging market projects exceeds the life span of their respective host governments, particularly in the former Soviet Union. It certainly exceeds the prospective terms-in-office of the specific individuals who signed the various governmental undertakings upon which the project's economics are based.

Soon after MIGA was established, the World Bank decided that although it could not lend to private projects, it could legally, and with much developmental benefit, guarantee commercial loans to a project against the specific risk that the host government might fail to perform its contractual undertakings in favor of the project. The Bank can make that guarantee legally because, as a condition of issuing it, the World Bank concludes a back-up agreement with the host country, in which the government promises to reimburse any pay-out that the World Bank has to make as a consequence of the government's breach of its promises to the project. This allows the financial recourse to a host government that is required by the World Bank's charter.

Whereas conventional expropriation coverage conceived of insured projects as being businesses independent of the government, the partial risk guaranty was invented with private-public joint ventures in mind. These partial risk guaranties—offered by the Asian Development Bank,[34] the European Bank for Reconstruction and Development,[35] the Inter-American Development Bank,[36] and the World Bank—fill a large hole in the fabric of effective project risk mitigation, which was created by the proliferation of private-public partnerships in the past decade.

While partial risk guaranties have been an exciting development in theory, their actual track record is limited. At the World Bank, this outcome has two explanations. First, partial risk guaranties have been offered as a source of project support "of last resort." Project developers have been encouraged to seek debt financing from the

IFC and investment guaranties against political risk from MIGA. Only if such support were unavailable, and only upon successful navigation of several other bureaucratic and policy barriers within the Bank, would an application for a partial risk guaranty have any prospect of receiving serious attention.

The very value of the partial risk guaranty lies in the fact that more conventional investment support programs of the World Bank Group's IFC and MIGA are not adequate to address the sovereign risks of projects that depend critically on host government undertakings. As discussed earlier, MIGA's breach of contract coverage, patterned after OPIC's, is restricted to standing behind arbitral awards. If, for instance, a host government is not willing to submit to arbitration in a foreign tribunal (and some constitutions prohibit their doing so), then MIGA coverage is likely to be of little help. Similarly, the IFC, as a lender to a project, is subject to, and possibly deterred by, the same risks of governmental breach that the partial risk guaranty program addresses. Consequently, these three branches of the World Bank Group offer private investment support that is wonderfully complementary. The World Bank's insistence on considering them substitutes rather than complements, has limited the effectiveness of the partial risk guaranty program in the past decade.

Partial risk guaranties from other multilateral development banks (MDBs) have had limited impact, primarily because of their newness —they have begun to be issued only in the past three years.

A second factor stunting the growth of host government demand for partial risk guaranties has been their accounting treatment within the issuing institution. The face amount of a partial risk guaranty has, typically, been fully counted against a country's borrowing limit. Thus if a host government accepts a $100 million partial risk guaranty, it does not receive any cash, only enhanced credibility, permitting the privately sponsored project to go forward. The host government's ability to borrow from the issuing MDB for public sector purposes (e.g., schools and roads) is, however, reduced by the entire $100 million. Consequently, partial risk guaranties have been favored in countries where MDB borrowing has been below the maximum. This has rendered the program substantially useless for the poorest countries, which generally borrow up to their maximum limits and are often unwilling to assign, in effect, a portion of their credit limit to the private sector.

Despite the barriers encountered, the future of insurance against governmental breach of contract seems reasonably bright. First, the willingness of both agency and commercial insurers to insure a government's compliance with arbitration clauses seems well established. While the demand side continues to press for more than the providers are typically willing to offer (e.g., for a claim payment upon occurrence of a breach), adequate solutions have allowed the projects to go forward, although not always with the participation of all investors. The investors left behind are generally banks that would have been willing to support the project if stronger support (e.g., more immediate claim payments) were available from PRI providers. Second, multilateral constitutions appear to understand that they can play an important role in buttressing the credibility of undertakings by their member governments. Unfortunately, while risk mitigation products have evolved, risks have also appeared to grow as a lengthening roster of host countries has taken breach of government undertaking from risk to reality.

Conclusion

Recent experience suggests that political risk insurance providers have been wise to go slow in accepting some of the political risks that project developers and lenders were inclined to hand to them.

The record of governments honoring obligations has been besmirched by a series of dramatic defaults.[37] Pakistan started the ball rolling in 1997 with its widespread repudiation of power purchase agreements and the declaration that they had been procured by bribes. The truth was that Pakistan failed to grow into its previously projected need for the power and, consequently, it could not afford to pay for it. Indonesia followed shortly after with its cancellation of various power projects in mid-construction, when they were offered the carrot of possible reinstatement if offtake arrangements were renegotiated on more favorable terms for the government.

Enron's infamous Dabhol Power Project, in India, also became victim to the trend of government "buyer's remorse." During the fall of 2000 and the spring of 2001 (within a few months of the beginning of commercial operation of "Phase I" of the project), the state-owned offtaker started to default on payments, and, in due course, both the state and the central governments breached their respective offtake guaranties. In June 2001, Phase I ceased operations, and construction of Phase II, which would have roughly tripled the capacity of the plant, was suspended, turning the largest independent power project in the emerging markets into one of its largest financial and legal messes.

Most recently, Argentina has contributed the new weapon of "pesification" to the arsenal of host government techniques for undermining the expectations of foreign investors in an emerging market. Further, the newly established electricity regulating authority in Turkey announced (roughly simultaneous with the achievement of commercial operation by the deal-of-the-year triad of Intergen-sponsored power projects) that the power purchase agreements of all independent generation projects in Turkey were going to be renegotiated.

It is no wonder that FDI into emerging markets has been reduced to a relative trickle. The Director of the World Bank's energy department has stated: "Private participation and investment has not paid off recently, and can no longer be relied on to fulfill expectations . . . in fiscal 2002, private investment in energy projects throughout the developing world fell almost 50 percent, compared to a high of $46 billion spent in 1996-1997. And private investment in energy sector projects is showing further signs of decreasing. . . ."[38]

This is a particular tragedy for countries that continue to see private development of public infrastructure as the right way forward. But it is clear that private-public partnerships, as they evolved in the 1990s, are widely being rethought by foreign investors as much as by their hosts.

It is also clear, however, that infrastructure development and operation by various ministries is not likely to return as the dominant model in many countries. The convenience of private capital and the value of private sector operating expertise are too great, and the related efficiencies are too well demonstrated, for things to go full circle. Rather, the next step will be a striving for greater sophistication in private-public partnerships. The private members will be less casual about the risks of doing business with, and depending upon performance by, host governments that are, after all, sovereign, which may well mean they can treat an investor badly with impunity. Consequently, private development of public infrastructure projects becomes more difficult—but no less necessary.

Political risk insurers watch all this with a mixture of relief (to the extent that they refused to underwrite government performance), foreboding (where they issued coverage to threatened projects that have not yet hit the headlines), and serious regret (where they bet on governments that proved to be an "obsolescing bargain).["]39

As private-public partnerships are forged in the future, allocation of political risk, especially the risk of public sector nonperformance, will be at the core of the challenge in reaching closure. Governments will feel greater pressure to enhance their credibility, either because of past lapses or because recent bad press about them disappointed investors. Governments that resisted offshore arbitration will have no choice if they want to close deals. Finance Ministry promises may need to be backed by offshore collateral accounts or letters of credit.

Notwithstanding changes in deal structures and sovereign undertakings that may develop, there continues to be a (probably expanding) role for political risk insurers in underwriting sovereign performance risk. Much of that coverage will come from public sector insurers, such as MIGA, OPIC, and the MDBs, who, through their diplomatic and business relationships with the host government and their respective bilateral[40] and multilateral agreements, are better positioned than commercial insurers to reduce government performance risks. Further, their resources for claims resolution makes them better able to bear other risks as well.

Of course, as deals become harder to close, some that would have made good development sense, will not go through. Others, particularly in the more creditworthy emerging markets, will find their way to closure, with developers and lenders simply accepting sovereign performance risk. That leaves, however, a large class of potential transactions that make both business and development sense, which only happen if a third party (a bilateral or multilateral agency, or a commercial political risk insurer) is willing to stand behind the government's promises.

Thanks to their ongoing diplomatic and financial relationships, and their respective international agreements, public agency insurers are better positioned than commercial insurers to bridge the gap between the apparent sovereign risk and the level that may be acceptable to private investors. If, with their combination of policy motivation, specific international agreements, and diplomatic and financial relationships, agency insurers are unwilling to bridge that gap in a particular transaction, it is unlikely that a commercial insurer will step in to do so.

Consequently, the future appears likely to offer a critical role to public agency insurers to take, as they have in the past, center-stage in accepting sovereign risks. Commercial insurers will continue to focus on the less risky projects and markets. They are also likely to cooperate with the public agencies as coinsurers, where they can take advantage of agency agreements in joint settlement efforts in the event of a claim.

With the public agencies on the front lines, having made pro-
grammatic strides in their ability and willingness to stand behind
governmental performance of infrastructure-related obligations, the
key question in getting projects to closure will be whether the agencies can see public sector performance (especially after Argentina,
Indonesia, Pakistan, and now perhaps Turkey), as a reasonably
insurable risk? The interests of foreign investors and of emerging
market development depends on host governments proving themselves worthy of such support.

Notes

1. This was a dramatic shift from the preceding 20 years or so, when
it was presumed that the arrival of foreign capital and influence was
likely to undermine the quality of the economic and political life in a
country of modest means. Attempts to explain why rich countries are
rich, and poor countries are not, were dominated by a literature that
accused multinational corporations of using corrupt and unfair bargaining strength as a means to sap poor countries of their natural
resources—i.e., "dependency theory."

2. Many bilateral ECAs have also been providers of political risk
insurance, but, with a few exceptions (e.g., EDC of Canada), they normally support only debt investment, whereas MIGA and OPIC com-
menced with a focus on equity investors, though their operations
have also grown to support bank loans, syndicated loans, and, in the
case of OPIC, bond offerings.

3. *See* Benjamin A. Javits, *Peace By Investment* (New York: United
Nations World Books, 1950).

4. *See* Mutual Security Act of 1954, Pub. L. No. 83-665, 68 Stat. 832 §
413(b)(4) (1954) (amending the Mutual Security Act of 1951, 65 Stat.
373 (1951)).

5. International Bank for Reconstruction and Development (World
Bank), Articles of Agreement, Art. I (1947, as amended 1989).

6. Foreign Assistance Act of 1961, Pub. L. No. 87-195 (1961) (current
version at 22 U.S.C. § 2151 (2002)).

7. *See* Foreign Assistance Act of 1969, Pub. L. 91-175 (1969) (current
version at 22 U.S.C. 2191 (2002))

8. *See* Benjamin A. Javits, *Peace By Investment*, Op. cit..

9. OPIC was formally established by the 1969 amendments to the
Foreign Assistance Act of 1961. *See* Foreign Assistance Act of 1969,
Pub. L. 91-175 (1969) (current version at 22 U.S.C. 2191 (2002))

10. Foreign Assistance Act of 1969, Pub. L. 91-175 § 234(a)(1)(A)
(1969).

11. *Id.* at § 234(a)(1)(B).

12. *Id.* at § 234(a)(1)(C).

13. *See Id.* at § 238(c) (providing U.S. citizenship or related criteria for eligibility for OPIC insurance).

14. For a review of the development and settlement of the Chilean expropriation claims, *see* Peter Gilbert, "Expropriations and the Overseas Private Investment Corporation," *Law And Policy in International Business*, vol. 9, 515-550 (1977).

15. Foreign Assistance Act of 1969, Pub. L. 91-175 § 231(a) (1969).

16. *See* www.opic.gov; *OPIC Annual Report 2001*.

17. For a perspective on OPIC's future, see Theodore H. Moran, *Reforming OPIC for the 21st Century* (Washington, DC: The Institute for International Economics, 2003).

18. *See www.MIGA.org/screens/about/convent/comment.htm.* After a series of detailed studies by the World Bank staff, a paper detailing a draft convention was circulated to the World Bank's Executive Directors in May 1984. Consultations with member governments resulted in a revised draft Convention, circulated in March 1985. A Committee of the Whole was created to discuss the draft Convention in June, and in September that year, the Executive Directors of the World Bank finalized the document and submitted the draft Convention to the Board of Governors recommending that the Board adopt a resolution opening the Convention for signature. The Board of Governors submitted the Convention to governments for signature on October 11, 1985.

19. See "General Conditions of Guarantee for Non-Shareholder Loans (Second Revision)" (MIGA, March 19, 2001).

20. In 1997, Zurich Emerging Market Solutions (headed by OPIC alumnus Daniel Riordan) and Sovereign Risk Insurance Ltd., established as a joint venture of XL Insurance Bermuda Ltd. and ACE Bermuda Insurance, Ltd. (headed by Price Lowenstein), opened for business. AIG also significantly expanded its political risk insurance staff and operations, as well as the range of countries and terms for which their coverage would be available.

21. For convenience, and consistency with market practice, the term "devaluation" is used here to cover both formal devaluation, i.e., a government's declaration of a change in the foreign exchange value of its currency, and depreciation, i.e., a free market deterioration of that value.

22. Anne Predieri and Robert Sheppard, both Managing Directors at Banc America Securities, had approached OPIC with an approach to insuring against devaluation based on the economic theory of "purchasing power parity."

23. The debt was rated Baa3 by Moody's Investors Service and BBB- by Fitch.

24. For details of the terms of the OPIC devaluation guaranty, *see* Kenneth W. Hansen, "New Product for Devaluation Risk", *Project Finance Newswire*, C&P, June 2001, at 9; *see also* Robert Sheppard, "Case Study: AES Tietê Acquisition", *Infrastructure Journal*, Feb. 2002, at 22.

25. OPIC retained Wharton Economic Forecasting Associates (subsequently merged to become "DRI-WEFA") to study the adequacy of relative inflation rates to explain exchange rate changes in a number of countries, including Brazil. The study confirmed that devaluation unrelated to current inflation does occur naturally. Some countries—including, in recent years, Argentina, Brazil, Indonesia, Mexico, Russia, Thailand, and Turkey — have experienced substantial exchange rate volatility. They also confirmed, however, that such divergences tend to be temporary.

26. *See* RESTATEMENT (THIRD) FOREIGN RELATIONS LAW OF THE UNITED STATES § 712 (1987)].

27. *See Id.* at § 712 cmt. h.

28. *See* 28 U.S.C. 1491 (2002). The U.S. Government is also immune from tort claims except to the extent specifically provided in the Federal Tort Claims Act. 28 U.S.C. §§ 1346(b), 2674 (2002).

29. *See* www.OPIC.gov.

30. *United Nations Convention on the Recognition and Enforcement of Arbitral Awards*, (New York 1958). A party to the New York Convention agrees, among other things, that arbitral awards rendered elsewhere will be recognized and enforced in its courts. *See Id.* at Art. I.(1).

31. "General Conditions of Guarantee for Non-Shareholder Loans (Second Revision)" (MIGA, March 19, 2001), sec. 10.1.

32. *See, e.g.*, www.sovereignbermuda.com.

33. *See* I.B.R.D. (World Bank), Articles of Agreement, art. I. § 4 (1947, as amended in 1989).

34. *See* www.adb.org.

35. *See* www.ebrd.org. EBRD is also willing to consider partial risk guaranties of equity, making it the only multilateral development lender willing to provide, in effect, political risk insurance to equity investors.

36. *See* www.iadb.org.

37. Government disregard for contractual obligations is not limited to emerging markets. California recently succumbed to a case of "buyer's remorse," which has undermined developers' and lenders' willingness to support further power project development on the West Coast.

38. Interview with Jamil Sagkin, reported in "Power in Latin America," Issue 92 (*Platts*, July 26, 2002), p. 1.

39. For more details about coverage of the "obsolescing bargain," refer to the first volume of the MIGA-Georgetown series. Moran, Theodore H., (ed.) 1998. *Managing International Political Risk*. Oxford: Blackwell.

40. OPIC, for instance, enters into a bilateral "investment incentive agreement" with each host country in which it makes its insurance available. The agreements provide for, among other things, binding international arbitration of any dispute that arises between OPIC and the host government, in connection with a claim.

Political Risk Insurance as Penicillin?
A Lender's Perspective

Anne H. Predieri
Banc of America Securities
and
Audrey Zuck
Willis

The political risk insurance market exploded in the late 1990s. New private insurers exceeded their creators' wildest expectations of new business growth, and claim payments were minimal. Most of the new growth came from lenders addressing portfolio risks, taking advantage of the arbitrage between market pricing and regulatory provisioning costs, and the boom in infrastructure investment in developing countries. As the Basel Committee develops a new regulatory framework with potential implications for traditional arbitrage, and the cloud of potential Argentine claims continues to loom large, lenders and insurers will be forced to re-examine the equation. In addition to skepticism about whether or not political risk insurance (PRI) does what it is supposed to do—that is, mitigate risk— lenders' perspectives are equally affected by the broader economic downturn and shifts in business strategies intended to maximize shareholder value. This has tempered the demand for traditional lenders' PRI. Nonetheless, the need for structured risk mitigation solutions cannot be eradicated. This chapter examines the symptoms that will continue to require treatment, and the role of PRI—the medicine of choice—in its evolution.

The Patient's Condition:
The Broader Context of Banks and Capital Markets

Before prescribing medicine, the patient's condition must be properly assessed. Lenders are operating in a business cycle that not only involves a general global economic downturn, but also signals the end of the "new economy." Clients are retrenching, in order to shore up their own capital structures at home and to address corporate governance issues in the wake of Enron and other corporate scandals. A recent survey, reported by the World Bank at the Energy Forum in June 2002, indicates that less than 6 percent of investors intended to expand their energy investments in developing countries, while over 52 percent were less interested in (or were retreating from) their investments in emerging markets. The threat of rating downgrades has also focused attention on the level of parent/sponsor support for various projects, forcing many investors to sell assets, rather than expand or invest in capital improvements. Lenders naturally tighten credit standards in such market conditions, which affects their willingness to book new assets and results in widespread pressure to reduce overall credit exposure to certain sectors and numerous individual companies. General economic difficulties have been compounded by the collapse of the telecommunications sector, and the profound impact on the energy sector from the collapse of Enron and other trading scandals. Finally, insurers themselves are subject to their own capitalization challenges, given declining investment returns, in some cases, increased capital costs associated with ratings pressures, and reduced credit limits, which sometimes translates into lower counter-party exposure limits by lenders.

This generally gloomy economic climate has been exacerbated by behaviors intended to maximize shareholder value. Banks allocate capital investments based on shareholder value-added calculations. Even profitable lines of business may be eliminated to reduce expenses, unless meaningful growth potential drives a comparable increase in shareholder value. The current focus on the velocity of capital is as important as the continued pressure to reduce overall balance sheet utilization. (When allocated to long-term assets, economic capital earns a much lower return than when it is "churned" with shorter-term assets to generate new fee income to enhance shareholder value.) Business models based on incremental balance sheet exposure will not survive when banks can successfully maintain market share and industry leadership with reduced exposure (reduced credit risk also reduces exposure to volatility, and reduced capital investments for a business generally correlates with a corresponding increase in shareholder returns). Business results must be recognized on a quarterly basis, and recent swings in stock values highlight the vulnerability to even shorter cycles. The net impact of these phenomena is an elimination of opportunities for strategies based on significant long-term balance sheet commitments. These balance sheet pressures, and the current credit squeeze associated with the economic and business cycles, are occurring in the wake of consolidation throughout the banking industry. Bankers often joke that, when two banks merge, "one plus one equals one half" and, subsequently, it cuts the combined credit appetite to less than that of either of the predecessor entities. These trends emphasize the importance of the capital markets as the primary source of liquidity for the future.

Equity markets have, similarly, demonstrated an unprecedented intolerance for volatility, and mark-to-market requirements have highlighted the uncertainty inherent in emerging market investments, regardless of the strength of the underlying credit fundamentals. The increased participation of capital markets traders, and the development of derivative products in emerging markets, further fuels the volatility associated with a short-term mentality. Capital markets react quickly, and current market conditions leave an increasingly limited appetite for "storied" credits associated with complex risk mitigation structures. (The credit structure may, in fact, be solid with most risks well-mitigated, but investors do not want to take the time to understand the story and/or take the risk that they don't understand something that could result in a loss.) Indeed, many investors require the full credit margin for emerging market investment grade assets, regardless of whether or not credit enhancements are utilized to mitigate many of the emerging market risks, simply because of the volatility associated with the investment. Partial risk guarantees, by definition, cover only specified risks, and these products have not protected several series of assets from significant downgrades, thereby further fueling investors' general mistrust of risk mitigants.

Tighter credit constraints are now matched by an unwillingness to accept potential ratings downgrade risk. In some cases, investors have expressed the fear of personal job risks that eliminate certain investment grade categories, regardless of the return. Argentina's precipitous decline, and continuing corporate governance scandals erupting from preferred issuers have resulted in increasing pressure for rating agencies to be more proactive in highlighting early warning signals, to avoid the embarrassment of moving from investment grade to bankruptcy virtually overnight. Waiting until after the events occur may be too late for investors to take action in response to ratings adjustments, yet precautionary ratings adjustments that foretell potential problems generate pressure on the issuer that could lead to an actual credit quality degrading, in a self-fulfilling prophecy. As a result, there is virtually no appetite for borderline investment grade transactions, where a single downgrade could have catastrophic portfolio results from either increased capital charges or required asset sales at a loss. Patients generally survive the common cold, but investors are wary of emerging market risks carrying anything less than a full financial guaranty from highly rated entities in current market conditions.

In addition to credit constraints, difficulties encountered by infrastructure projects in virtually every region of the world have significantly tarnished the views of lenders and insurers. Even official insurers are somewhat leery of covering new pioneer projects. These early projects lay the groundwork for future investments, with a broader role for private insurers and, ultimately, sustainable economic growth in new developing countries. If "insurers of last resort" retreat, the private market cannot be expected to fill that gap. Investor awareness of uncovered regulatory risks has also risen, and with it, so has a reluctance to forge ahead at politically acceptable rates of return. The array of problems has also led to heightened skepticism regarding demand projections for a variety of investments. The energy sector dominated infrastructure investments throughout the 1990s, so the collapse of this sector is a crowning blow.

In sum, this somewhat sudden retreat of equity investors inevitably reduces the demand for debt and related lenders' coverage. Ironically, where demand still exists, most notably in Brazil, insurer capacity is extremely limited or is only available at usurious prices. The vicious cycle continues as the lack of demand in the broader market impedes insurers' ability to expand their portfolios outside Latin America, in order to create new capacity for the few remaining open markets. As of early 2003, Mexico appears to be the only Latin American market open for significant levels of new lending, enjoying direct access to the capital markets, and having limited PRI requirements.

Compounding the uncertainty surrounding lenders and investors are the difficulties faced by insurers. Certainly, the events of September 11, 2001, heightened the awareness and perception of risk among lenders, insurers, investors, and shareholders. Insurance providers are subject to increased scrutiny of their financial health, given the cost of September 11. Greater ratings pressures and global equity market declines have resulted in diminishing portfolio values, and raising new capital to stabilize the situation is a costly proposition for insurance companies in the current market. The risk appetite of primary insurers has, indeed, shrunk, but not necessarily because of the risks involved in specialty product lines. In many cases, reinsurance capacity is reallocated to the improved returns now available in more standard lines of coverage. In some cases, reinsurers have tightened controls over the risks they are willing to reinsure, and in others, real financial capacity constraints have resulted in reduced lines of coverage. In this context, questions are being asked about the commitment of insurers, who recently took on specialty lines such as PRI, and whether there will be a reversal to core business lines (such as property/casualty), resulting in further reductions in market capacity. So far, however, PRI providers are holding a steady course.

Symptoms to be Treated

The current crises in emerging markets can be likened to an epidemic—certainly, fear of contagion from infected countries has prompted strong reaction from international institutions, and investors are fleeing emerging markets as if from Typhoid Mary. The crisis in Argentina, market spasms surrounding the 2002 election in Brazil, economic difficulties worldwide, governmental actions against foreign investors in a number of countries, and a general concern among investors about political stability in Latin America and other emerging markets have highlighted the risks of investing and, to a certain extent, have called into question the value of coverage provided by traditional PRI products.

With regard to Argentina, the lack of a cohesive political response to the economic crisis has prevented even the minimum reforms and restructuring necessary to prevent a severe depression resulting from default, devaluation, and banking collapse in the country. Argentina is not a short-term problem, and help is not in sight as long as the patient refuses to take any form of medicine.

In Brazil, the phenomenon of risk as a perception rather than a reality was apparent in the extreme market reaction during the campaigning leading up to the 2002 elections. Market reactions reflected more a fear of uncertainties than concern over actual economic fundamentals, as demonstrated by the failure of a $30 billion bailout package from the IMF that was provided to calm the Brazilian markets. Despite the calm that descended upon the country after President Lula's victory, the market, particularly the foreign exchange market, may continue to punish Brazil in the short- to-medium-term, as questions persist regarding the new government's actions. Ironically, this punishment may end up converting investors' fears into reality, as the resulting high interest rates and investors' demands for high yields may increase the debt burden to intolerable levels.

In Asia—especially in India and Indonesia—government actions that contravened power purchase agreements and other fundamental commercial contracts underpinning foreign investments, have resulted in concern over the sanctity of contracts, the need to properly align interests and allocate risk, as well as the difficulty of pioneering foreign investment in either highly or poorly regulated sectors. Elsewhere in Asia, the situation is very different—competition for good projects means spreads are often too low to cover the cost of credit enhancements, and PRI is not a familiar tool. In Africa, economic and commercial risks are too high to entice enough investors to these markets, especially when these risks are coupled with relatively high political risk. In Eastern Europe, the perception of traditional political risk has waned, particularly in countries slated for entry into the European Union, although the market and economic risk perception is still higher than in Western Europe.

Comparing certain Asian and Latin American situations with post-crisis Russia, which is now a growth market, having pulled its act together after a massive default, one can conclude that a positive government response to economic crisis is key to reversing these difficulties for both lenders and investors. In other words, the real cure for these very symptoms must come from within. PRI offers protection rather than a panacea, and the effectiveness of the protection is often subject to the severity of the surrounding infections.

In the face of virtually unprecedented market volatility, one would expect risk mitigation solutions to be frequently prescribed, but the specific symptoms may or may not be cured by traditional forms of PRI. It is important to remember that insurance is only intended to cover an actual loss caused by specified risks. It will never address the inherent volatility associated with these investments in the normal course of business, unless it is a full financial guaranty or a form of credit insurance.

The series of broad market crises, described in the general conditions above, has been accompanied by highly publicized court cases over insurance products that were previously considered either too arcane or too mundane to merit attention. Nonetheless, the difference between insurance products and financial guaranties has been highlighted, and the now subdued market has returned to more traditional specified performance areas, such as construction risk. Many investors are becoming increasingly wary of the potential gaps in insurance products that are designed to cover named perils—isolating specific risks rather than unconditionally guaranteeing recovery. A year ago, the prospects for alternative risk transfer ("ART") products looked promising, but new ART applications may well go the route of the new economy.

New Medicine for New Strains of the Disease and New Patients

Perhaps an appropriate analogy for political risk insurance is that it is like penicillin—PRI was an effective antidote to many political risks when it was first developed and when emerging markets were just beginning to emerge, but it is a treatment that must continue to evolve to be effective against different strains of the disease that have emerged. Certainly, PRI has been extremely effective in the past, not only in situations where it paid claims, but it also allowed investors to look past overt emerging market country risks by providing a backstop to conversion and transfer mechanisms, thereby ensuring (perhaps as a last-resort mechanism) that funds could be remitted. There are many anecdotes about the benefits of the "halo effect" of PRI backing by a multilateral, government, or private institution, in preventing host government actions that might otherwise end in expropriation of the foreign investment. The presence of PRI has allowed investors to focus on industry and country fundamentals that affect commercial strength, economic returns, and broader political factors.

The expansion of products trying to more closely address investors' needs was one of the drivers of the explosive growth in the political risk insurance market, along with the introduction of new entrants to the market and the increased appetite for longer tenors and increased amounts of coverage. Reasons for the recent reversal of that trend include significant claims, heightened perception of risk, poor performance by insurers' investment portfolios, and more cautious underwriting. The private PRI market's boom in the past few years has provided the capacity and creativity required to meet clients' needs, and despite concerns over the recent shrinkage in market capacity, it will continue to be an important and thriving complement to public providers. Private political risk insurers provide the same range of products as public providers, but can often provide a more flexible application of the product, such as global programs. Since they are not hampered by the same public policy constraints, they often have a much quicker response time, as well as the ability to put coverage in place in a short period of time.

Looking at the PRI market as a whole, it is hard to generalize about corporate providers or the London market; for example, each provider reacts according to its individual goals and constraints. On the other hand, those that have developed direct relationships with lenders have grown much more rapidly, while London continues to enjoy strong levels of demand primarily from equity investors.

Public providers, while enjoying strong credit ratings due to governmental backing, often suffer from the perception that their decisions—either to provide coverage or to determine claims—may be politicized and are, therefore, not reliable. Their public policy goals, ranging from ensuring developmental benefits, worker's rights, and environmental protection, also place an additional burden on their clients. More formal decision-making processes can make the timing of obtaining approvals to offer coverage excessively burdensome and bureaucratic.

These drawbacks are offset by a countervailing attitude in the market that public providers of PRI are more likely to pay claims, because they do not need to worry about commercial considerations such as the effect of claims payments on their credit rating or on shareholder value. Indeed, claims payment is arguably more consistent with the mission of the public provider than distributing profits, or at a minimum, the public policy goals to strengthen investment climates and the private sector in developing self-sustaining economies, offers a rationale for paying rather than avoiding payment. Further, public providers often have unique salvage options, and successful settlements with local governments can, in turn, offer opportunities to lure private investors back into the country.

Rating agencies, while carefully scrutinizing "outs" in insurance policies (in the form of exclusions of coverage or the insurer's ability to terminate coverage) also appear to be more comfortable with these "outs" in public insurance coverage, even when they are imposed for public policy reasons, rather than when they are in a private insurer's policy. This perceived willingness to pay is bolstered by the perception of a more transparent claims process upheld by OPIC's publication of its claims payment record, including its memoranda of determination of claims.

Public providers of insurance have also benefited from heightened risk perceptions: since September 11, 2001, many institutions seeking political risk insurance coverage have expressed greater

comfort when PRI is provided by a government-backed or multilateral institution. Most lending institutions, and undoubtedly a
number of other investors , track their exposure to political risk
insurers, and often establish limits for each exposure, particularly
when the PRI coverage—such as non-honoring or contract frustration coverage—results in a transfer of credit risk from borrower to
PRI provider. These limits are more likely to be constraining on
lenders' ability to take additional exposure to a private insurance
company (particularly if that company's credit standing is in question) rather than on their ability to take additional exposure to a
governmental or multilateral provider.

Recurrent publicity about disputes over claims liabilities has
heightened concerns regarding insurers' willingness—as well as
ability—to pay. While the claims in dispute are not in the political
risk insurance area, the availability of public alternatives with public policy incentives to pay has taken on increased importance.
Given the limited information available on private insurers' claims
payment records (what is available is mostly anecdotal and not all
positive), it is harder to judge their willingness to pay claims. S&P
recently revived its Financial Enhancement Rating system, which
gauges insurers' willingness to provide timely payment, and has
attempted to highlight the differences between financial guaranties
and insurance policies so that investors can better judge the strength
of their coverage. This is an indication of the increased importance
of understanding when insurers will pay—not necessarily restricted
to the political risk arena.

One positive development has been increased cooperation among
PRI providers, allowing risk sharing, greater capacity availability
for clients, and more seamless coverage. Public/private insurer
cooperation has also borne fruit, which has huge potential benefits
in terms of being able to extend tenors, increase capacity, and
expand the role of private insurance in countries or projects where
private insurers might not be willing to provide coverage, without
the backing of an official provider. However, clients will be looking
to ensure that this cooperation actually results in greater flexibility,
and not a retreat to the lowest common denominator. The growth
of the private market in and of itself offers a significant contribution
in terms of increased alternatives for flexible, timely coverage.

Whether through public or private providers, the PRI market has
been active and creative. New treatments have been developed:
arbitral award default coverage; convertibility/transfer cover for
capital markets; liquidity facilities to cover devaluation for inflation-

indexed revenue streams; and others. This creativity and activity has resulted in the presence of a relatively new, but increasingly significant, group of users: bondholders in the capital markets.

Notwithstanding the successful arbitrage with cross-border provisioning costs in the commercial bank market, political risk insurance does not remove country risk altogether. Like all antibiotics, it is designed to treat specific bacteria rather than address the general economic risks of operating in different markets. Doing business in a foreign country requires operating in potentially difficult environments, including uncertain regulatory regimes that are not covered by traditional PRI. Capital markets investors will always benchmark foreign issues against the sovereign yield, and always need to find value in exchange for lower returns theoretically justified by the risk mitigation. There is no cure for the common cold, and no business can be protected from those inherent risks, but there is limited tolerance for partial or unproven solutions in today's market.

In general, capital markets issues have only been covered for currency transfer and convertibility risks, with two exceptions: the AES Tietê transaction in Brazil, which benefits from a unique form of devaluation coverage developed by Banc of America Securities and issued by OPIC in 2001; and a transaction in Belize, for which nonhonoring coverage was issued by Zurich Emerging Markets Solutions. PRI coverage for capital markets issues is commonly referred to as "enhanced inconvertibility coverage," as it also includes coverage for expropriation of funds. Broader applications of expropriation coverage have not yet been tested in the capital markets, because the claim determination process for an expropriation claim is generally much more difficult than confirming the existence of currency controls. It often requires proof of international law violation and can be subjected to extended arbitration processes, making it extremely difficult to guarantee timely payments. We are currently working on potential new applications of expropriation coverage for issuers in the capital markets, and we envision broad demand for these products if they are successfully developed.

Not surprisingly, the success of enhanced inconvertibility coverage for capital markets issues was based on the arbitrage achieved through the ratings upgrade obtained with PRI. PRI has enabled issuers to access the U.S. capital markets at their local currency rating, rather than their foreign currency rating, often piercing the sovereign ceiling and improving the transaction rating by as much as six notches over the uncovered rating. The wider the divergence between the local and foreign currency ratings of an issuer, the more valuable the PRI becomes.

Rating agencies, therefore, play a critical role in the successful application of PRI to the capital markets. In addition to driving the price of a transaction, ratings also define the investor universe, in that investor portfolio capacity is frequently subject to ratings parameters as well as counter-party credit limits. Ratings also drive capital charges for many investors. Thus, the enormous liquidity available in the capital markets is in many ways controlled by standardized models and the views of the analysts assigned to a given transaction. There are only three relevant rating agencies (Fitch IBCA, Duff & Phelps; Moody's Investors Service; and Standard & Poors), and the lowest common denominator often applies, leaving a rather narrow filter for the ultimate risk assessment.

In addition to the underlying risk assessment related to the selection of PRI coverage requirements, PRI products involve documentation risk that must be analyzed and reflected in the overall transaction rating. Rating agencies also recently developed models to assess partial guaranties, as these risk mitigation products continue to evolve. Like many forms of PRI, partial guaranties for corporate issues do not reduce the likelihood of default, but are analyzed in the context of total recovery in a bankruptcy scenario. As a result, it is often uneconomical to provide the credit enhancement required to achieve a sufficiently high rating. For example, a guaranty covering almost 70 percent of a given issue is required to increase the rating from borderline to strong investment grade (Baa3 to Baa1, on the Moody's scale). More than 90 percent is required to move the rating into a high-grade quality rating, and a 99 percent guaranty of a below-investment grade issuer only achieves an Aa rating, even when provided by an Aaa guarantor. Obviously, an Aaa financial guaranty would be more efficient and effective.

The Current Situation: Human Trials

The current situation, and near-term outlook, can be likened to the "human trials" phase of testing medication—certainly, in terms of testing PRI for lenders. Insurance providers are reviewing the first claims (at least on a large scale) under PRI policies provided to lenders. Lenders are faced, often for the first time, with the difficult task of compiling definitive facts and marshalling compelling arguments, in order to prove the validity of compensation for their loss under the terms of the insurance policy. Many lenders may have had to dust off their PRI policy, since the insurance was often bought as a prerequisite for credit approval or to satisfy syndication requirements, not necessarily as a tool that was tailored to ensure the best risk mitigation possible, especially for inconvertibility coverage alone.

Long waiting periods under expropriation coverage also pose difficulties to investors that struggle to keep projects going until the terms of their equity insurance policies allow them to walk away, or that try to maintain commercial salvage options should claims be denied. Similarly, lenders with pending PRI claims are forced by the exigencies of their borrowers to make difficult decisions that may impact their insurer, should the insurer pay a claim and step into the lender's shoes. Logically, this situation should require consultation with the insurer—and, indeed, insurance policies require consultation and insurer approval of material decisions. On the other hand, insurers are often reluctant to provide guidance, out of the fear of inadvertently giving validity to the claim even before it is properly judged, as well as due to concern about liability, should the lender follow the insurer's advice only to be left with the consequences if the claim is denied.

Just as lenders learn from workouts, insurers learn from claims. It will be important for insurers to take to heart the lessons learned by insureds during this claims trial period, in order to maintain the relevance of their products. Current solutions to breach of contract risk generally rely on an arbitral award default. In reality, however, governments have many ways of frustrating the arbitration process. Some larger, more sophisticated governments can be very clever in depriving investors of their fundamental rights within the perceived boundaries of local law, thereby frustrating the insured's ability to obtain an arbitral award or to prove expropriation. It is not inconceivable for yet another inter-creditor issue to be introduced, if an insured lender has to resort to arbitration with its insurer in this process, thereby greatly complicating the consultation process required under the insurance policy.

Like all ongoing trials, the situation is fluid. In many countries, poor political management has contributed to the economic crises leading up to inconvertibility, or to the imposition of currency controls that have had a greater, more immediate impact on borrowers' credit positions. However, these crises create greater problems than those addressed by most traditional political risk coverages. At first blush, it was the popular opinion that Argentina was a classic inconvertibility situation, but few claims have arisen from it as of late 2002, and most claims have involved trade credit or expropriation. Also, as stated by Andres de la Cruz, partner at Cleary, Gottlieb, Steen & Hamilton, "A devaluation coupled with an inconvertibility event can quickly become a credit event if a borrower earning local currency revenues can no longer honor its foreign currency debts."[1] While the Argentine devaluation may not in and of itself be a covered event, the imposition of Central Bank controls on transfers, pesification of debt, freezing of bank accounts, and other subsequent government actions that violate numerous contracts (and perhaps even laws) have led to a number of claims being filed under PRI policies for Argentina. However, PRI policies generally have waiting periods that must elapse before claims can be filed—these waiting periods were extended—and generally up to 180 days — as insurers took on more exposure in Argentina. This has contributed to the fact that fewer claims than might have been expected have been paid early on, although a number of claims are now maturing and must be judged on their merits; that is, whether the (ever changing) circumstances in the country continues to meet the definition of a "covered event" under these policies. Perhaps, even more importantly, as time elapses and the political events breed economic difficulties, it becomes increasingly difficult to leave local currency deposits in escrow while an inconvertibility claim matures, rather than applying the cash to shore up the underlying borrower's ongoing commercial viability and enhancing overall repayment prospects.

The insurance market and its outlook have changed significantly. There is a significant lack of capacity in markets where demand has been the highest, such as Brazil, and there have been estimates that the market shrank 30 percent since September 11, 2001.[2] While overall rates have not changed significantly, political violence rates—particularly for war or terrorism—have skyrocketed. One client told us that coverage that used to cost $1.5 million was being quoted at $8 million. This situation has tested a standard requirement in loan agreements for emerging markets: that the project company must carry sufficient insurance, including for political violence. Given the often vastly increased cost, companies and lenders have had to wrestle with difficult cost-benefit analyses. Although the situation has stabilized somewhat, concern remains over cancellations or non-renewals of political violence coverage in the property/casualty market. This is less of an issue in the investment insurance market, where coverage is written for longer terms and is not cancelable, except in limited circumstances. Going forward, coverage tenors have shrunk—fewer insurers are offering longer tenors, and they now cherry-pick the projects they wish to cover. Moreover, at longer tenors, capacity limits are frequently smaller. It seems unlikely that there will be new entrants in the market any time soon, despite the hardening of the market.

Finally, the current testing of PRI coverage and the claims process have had some unanticipated side effects: the divergence of interests between PRI-covered lenders and uncovered lenders is proving to be as thorny as the pledge of shares issue that was the focus of so many debates in recent years. The conflict of interest between debt and equity is as visible between covered and uncovered lenders, but lenders face difficult voting situations and inter-creditor negotiations for every decision, not just when dealing with final claim compensation requirements. Moreover, it appears that the difficulty of linking default to a covered risk pushes the old pledge of shares issue way down on the list of priorities, as it may be only the last of many hurdles rather than the primary issue.

Political Risk Insurance: When Is It the Right Medicine?

The events covered by political risk insurance have not changed dramatically, but the perception of the relative value of traditional coverage may well be waning. PRI continues to provide meaningful relief for specific symptoms, and the preventative qualities of PRI provided by official insurers were reaffirmed in 2002, in most regions of the world. Ironically, while the market moved away from purchasing all three prongs of the traditional prescription —namely, inconvertibility, political violence, and expropriation coverages — to a reliance on enhanced inconvertibility, in most cases, political violence in small doses and expropriation in more visible cases are producing more value, in terms of potential recoveries through PRI claims, than the inconvertibility coverage that satisfies basic liquidity requirements. Nonetheless, the importance of liquidity, in an era when most lenders are captive to the "originate to distribute" model, cannot be underestimated, and the exemption from provisioning requirements is likely to continue to support strong underlying demand for enhanced inconvertibility coverage.

The challenge going forward is to determine whether these covered PRI events constitute a sufficient portion of the emerging markets risk and to justify the premium cost as a percentage of the overall risk margin. Experience seems to illustrate that uncovered risks may have a higher likelihood of occurrence and, therefore, could create a higher default risk, suggesting that the appropriate risk margin may exceed politically and/or commercially acceptable margins. Lenders and investors are increasingly focused on devaluation, as opposed to currency controls, and overall credit deterioration, as opposed to isolated political events. Interestingly enough, subsovereign risk is a much lower priority in the current market than it was expected to be when these topics were discussed at the preceding MIGA-Georgetown symposium in 2001.[3] On the other hand, regulatory risk is certainly considered a political risk by foreign investors, and may now be given higher priority than breach of contract. However, it is admittedly no small challenge to develop effective political risk insurance for regulatory risks, given the inherent legitimacy of the governmental actions involved. Finally, even the most creative users of PRI haven't yet identified a cure for the inherent volatility of emerging markets exposure that plagued several segments of the vibrant market of the 1990s.

The rapid and widespread information flow associated with the increased competition of multi-sourced investments in a truly global economy puts obvious downward pressure on profit margins. Similarly, the enormous liquidity in the financial markets, and the vast engines available to distribute debt, result in further compression of these margins for lenders, even in emerging markets. Notwithstanding the increase in perceived risks, therefore, there is less ability to increase margins to facilitate a disaggregation of risks to be covered by PRI. Additional pressure to reduce total returns and capital costs to politically acceptable levels, as a result of public scrutiny of infrastructure projects deemed to have been negotiated on a corrupt or "sweetheart" basis, highlights the dilemma—increased risk perception and required investor returns are currently incompatible with local consumers' willingness and ability to pay for the investments.

Further, premiums charged by many investors for a "storied" credit, with complex structural credit enhancements, is also increasing. Many institutional investors have simply exited the emerging markets, except for truly high yield plays. Those that remain compare the yield on an investment-grade quality, emerging markets issue to the uncovered sovereign yield, rather than to comparably rated alternatives, and charge a significant premium, regardless of credit enhancements. This market behavior offers significant potential for mono-line insurers and other true financial guaranties, many of which may require PRI for their own risk mitigation.

This paper is not intended to be a death certificate for PRI! Far from it. Rather, it intends to urge a reevaluation by users and providers of PRI, of the risks of investing in emerging markets. Careful thought must be used to determine which of these risks can be most effectively covered by traditional PRI products, what new products or evolution of traditional products need to be developed, and whether there are more effective alternatives. Securitizations, A/B loans structures, partial risk and partial credit guaranty programs offered by multilaterals, and other structures that address specific risks, should be considered as viable alternatives. Ultimately, the diagnosis must be patient-specific and the political risk insurance coverage prescribed must target the symptoms exhibited by the particular structure being contemplated. Otherwise, you might as well take two aspirins and call us in the morning!

Notes

1. *LatinFinance* April 2002, p. 16.
2. Ken Horne, Senior Vice President at Marsh Inc., quoted in *Business Insurance*, August 12, 2002.
3. See in particular Part I of *International Political Risk Management: Exploring New Frontiers*, Theodore H. Moran, volume editor, published by the World Bank in 2001.

Commentary on Political Risk Insurance in the Aftermath of the September 11 Attacks and the Argentine Crisis:

An Underwriter's View

Daniel W. Riordan
Executive Vice President and Managing Director
Zurich Emerging Markets Solutions

The political risk insurance market faced the most challenging conditions of its history in 2002. Demand for political risk insurance coverage in emerging markets was significantly reduced, as global trade and investment flows continued to diminish. The final numbers for foreign direct investment in 2002 are expected to be half of that in 2001.

With the decline in trade and investment continuing into 2003, there has been a corresponding reduction in demand for PRI from most major customers. International banks, the fastest growing PRI customer segment, have been reducing their exposures in emerging markets, especially Latin America. Private sector infrastructure investors and contractors, who contributed billions of dollars of new equity capital, equipment, and expertise to the power, telecom, and transport sectors of emerging markets, have largely focused on divestment opportunities as the attractiveness of these investments has waned. Further, capital markets investors began to shy away from emerging markets in 2002, after significant investments in this area in 2000 and 2001. No re-emergence of investor or lender interest in emerging markets is expected in 2003.

Growth in demand for political risk insurance (PRI), which had been robust over the last five years, contracted significantly in 2002. The limited areas for growth on the demand side include manufacturing and service companies. These few growth sectors have been on the rise since September 11, as previously self-insured corporate companies seek balance sheet protection and other alternatives to expensive terrorism cover.

The appetite of underwriters to offer coverage to manufacturing and service company investors is not universal. With the expansion of political risk coverage for lenders, many underwriters have grown comfortable with this coverage, and are less interested in writing traditional expropriation-type coverages.

Given the current state of world economic and political conditions, most underwriters have very limited interest in accepting higher risk markets. For example, Argentina and Brazil are very difficult to cover, due to risk and capacity concerns. Mexico is very popular with underwriters, and ample capacity can be secured for projects in this country. Surprisingly, most underwriters are willing to extend significant coverage amounts for risks in Russia, a market that was "off-limits" until only a few years ago.

There is increasing demand for specialized political risk coverages. Comprehensive (political and credit) coverage is in high demand from some banks and exporters who find political risk insurance alone no longer meets their needs. Limited capital markets opportunities have developed, based on exporters' needs and demands for an innovative way to use non-honoring sovereign guaranty coverage.

For example, Zurich Emerging Markets Solutions (ZEMS) concluded the Belize Mortgage Trust Bond Issue in March 2002, providing for securitization of mortgages issued by the Development Finance Corporation of Belize (DFC), an agency of the Government of Belize (GOB). The ten-year $44.5 million bond issue is secured by a pool of multiple assets (e.g., DFC mortgages and small business loans). Payment of principal and interest in U.S. dollars is guaranteed by the DFC, and is supported by an unconditional and irrevocable GOB guarantee mitigating devaluation risk. If the GOB fails to make all, or any portion of, the Government Guaranty payments, ZEMS will pay compensation in U.S. dollars, subject to certain limitations and exclusions, to the trustee (the insured), in an amount equal to 90 percent of the portion of the failed payment for 100 percent of the Class A Bonds. This nonhonoring of sovereign guaranty by ZEMS received an 'A3' rating by Moody's and an 'A' rating by Fitch.

Demand Side Issues in a Hard Market

There has been significant decline in PRI capacity in 2002, due to hard market conditions in the insurance industry, the dearth of reinsurance capacity, and an exodus of primary insurance carriers and reinsurers from the market. The size of the political risk market has been reduced by one-third in 2002, and is expected to shrink further in 2003. Declining capacities and higher ceding commissions for reinsurers are expected to result in the hardening of prices, reduced tenors, and restricted coverages.

How Will Buyers Cope in the Current Market?

Customers in the current market would be well advised to lock in current rates and now available tenors . They should study their coverages and read their policies, knowing what is covered and what is not. It is always advisable to resolve policy-wording issues upfront to avoid a dispute later.

Further, customers should seek collaboration of public and private insurers whenever appropriate or needed. Increased collaboration often yields greater capacity, better products, and improved responsiveness for the customer. Flexible coinsurance and facultative reinsurance arrangements are increasingly available in the market.

Is PRI Still Relevant in Today's Marketplace?

Many experts in the market suggest that Argentina is a test case. I concur. Argentina will test the PRI product and the sustainability of the market. It will also be a test of the customers, and their understanding of the product. Claims are expected and some have already been paid. These claims will most likely come in stages rather than all at once, depending on the underlying coverages.

There is no doubt that banks and investors have suffered significant losses as a result of the turmoil in Argentina. However, with a variety of political risk and credit insurance products in the market, time will tell whether these losses translate into valid claims. I suspect we will see more credit insurance policies triggered than political risk policies due to the unfolding of events, but it is still too early to tell. In the event that losses in Argentina do not produce valid claims, there will be significant questions raised about the value of political risk policies, including pressure on underwriters to develop new coverages or to provide increasing levels of comprehensive coverage.

Some lenders may consider comprehensive coverage or non-honoring of sovereign guaranty coverage, in response to an inability to claim against political risk covers for the unique events in Argentina. This will not eliminate the need or demand for currency inconvertibility and transfer risk ("CI") coverage; rather, it will be recognized that CI cover alone cannot hedge all potential sovereign risks. For similar reasons, equity investors may judge expropriation cover to be inadequate, opting for broader confiscation, expropriation, and nationalization ("CEN") coverage instead, which includes arbitration award default provisions.

Is there a "Public Policy Incentive to Pay" Claims, as suggested by the Lender's Perspective Paper?

Public agencies, such as OPIC, have historically considered claims on their merits (i.e., the validity of claims), and do not base their determination on public policy or political considerations. Let us hope this is the case, considering taxpayer funds are involved!

The previous chapter "PRI as Penicillin: A Lender's Perspective" suggests that public agencies have a "public policy incentive to pay claims," and perhaps the private insurance market has an opposite interest. This line of argument is seriously flawed, as it is missing the key word "valid." I believe any public agency claims director would take similar issue with this argument, as they have historically, and to the contrary, based their determination of a claim on professional and thorough evaluations of "valid" claims and not on political considerations. Private insurers also have highly professional claim directors who work hard to provide high quality service to customers, basing their determinations on the validity of claims, not on political factors.

Do Rating Agencies Favor Public Insurers Over Private Insurers for Capital Markets Transactions?

Representations in the Lender's Perspective paper indicating that rating agencies are more comfortable with capital market transactions enhanced by public agency PRI coverage are also unfounded: S&P, Moody's, and Fitch have each rated privately insured capital markets transactions, and are comfortable with PRI-enhanced capital markets transactions involving private PRI insurers. In fact, there have been more rated emerging market bond issues insured by private insurers than those insured by public insurers (including 10 rated bond issues insured by Zurich alone, between 1999 and 2002).

The Future of Public and Private Market PRI Insurers

Public agencies will continue to retract from the political risk insurance business as the private market grows to fulfill the needs of investors and lenders. Public agencies will continue to provide the necessary additional capacity for large projects, and serve segments that are not served by the private market: namely, small business and high-risk markets.

Political risk insurance is a profitable business for private insurers, but only for those willing to invest in the expertise required for this highly specialized business. As a profitable business, the private insurance market will continue to grow, albeit at a gradual pace and with dependency on available sources of reinsurance.

Future collaboration between private and public insurers will be focused on treaty reinsurance. Public agencies will serve their public policy roles by serving as wholesalers of capacity or reinsurers, enabling the private market to act as the primary retail provider of products and services to the market. The result will be an innovative and responsive marketplace.

Commentary on Political Risk Insurance in the Aftermath of the September 11 Attacks and the Argentine Crisis:

A Lender's Perspective

James D. Alford
Vice President
Citibank

From a lenders' perspective, I agree with the analogy of Ann Predieri and Audrey Zuck: like penicillin, political risk insurance in its traditional form is limited in its ability to "combat" the broader range of risks being experienced today, and its popularity as the "drug of choice" is waning.

Clearly, lenders and investors are looking for more robust or comprehensive coverage to mitigate sovereign actions experienced in Russia and Argentina. As Predieri and Zuck point out, insurers have made significant strides in the past several years to expand and strengthen their product offerings. Prior to the events of September 11 and the Argentine melt-down, they were moving further towards providing "all risk" borrower default insurance, which would provide customers the robust coverage they have been seeking. However, on the way to the hospital, the new wonder drug was hijacked by September 11, Argentina, and similar catastrophes. Now, we are left to discover whether it is the particular product that has been destroyed—or the formula itself. At the same time, we must determine if the supply of old penicillin administered to infected patients is sufficient to nurse them back to health.

At Citibank, I believe the future path of politcal risk insurance (PRI) as a risk mitigant depends on two main drivers: the lessons learned in Argentina and bank regulatory requirements.

Looking at Argentina first, there are a number of complex, sometimes contravening, issues and circumstances at work.

Sovereign actions include "pesification," which has resulted in targeted mismatches of assets and liabilities, changed bankruptcy laws, interrupted currency conversions and transfer restrictions, abrogated contracts and tariff agreements, and contradictory rulings and interpretations by local courts.

In certain circumstances, borrowers' nonpayments and defaults have been protected under law changes, allowing them to realize a windfall where liabilities have been pesified. In other cases, pesification has resulted in an expropriation of borrowers' balance sheets, where assets and liabilities were converted at different rates. There have been numerous loan defaults—some driven by market conditions, others by government decree—and most lenders have been inundated with requests for credit extensions, standstills, and reschedulings.

At the same time, events have caused tremendous commercial and individual local liquidity problems, like those experienced in Russia in 1998–99.

The range of insureds and the types of transactions affected are extensive: banks, bondholders, construction projects, equity, real estate, trade, utilities, and working capital.

A broad range of insurers have also been affected: agencies, ECAs, multilaterals, and private insurers. The entire gamut of perils has been experienced: borrower nonpayment ("comprehensive"), breach of contract, convertibility and transfer, expropriation, nonrepossession of collateral, political violence, and so forth.

Collectability and timeliness are important. Lenders and investors are keenly focused on time lines for claims determinations, settlements, and payouts. On the lender's side, bank regulators are equally focused on these matters.

For insurers dealing with an already challenging underwriting environment, how claims and exposures play out will have a significant impact on what can be offered to the insureds going forward, and on what level of reinsurance support will be available to syndicate their underwritings.

Turning to the regulatory dimension, bank regulators have a different view on country risk reporting, which is tied, in large part, to the Argentine situation.

Reporting guidelines are specified in the FFIEC 009 Instructions document: insurance policies that cover specific assets, and that guarantee payment if the borrower defaults or if inconvertibility occurs for any reason, should be treated as guarantees.

Previously, the two phrases in the above sentence were viewed as "either/or" prerequisites for mitigating country risk exposures. The latest guidance from the Federal Reserve, however, is that insurance must be comprehensive; that is, it must cover borrower defaults, including inconvertibility.

Predieri and Zuck have concluded that users and providers of PRI need to reassess the risks of operating in emerging markets, and that the treatment must be patient-specific. However, in reality, the convergent paths of users and providers over the past several years, has been derailed by the events of 2001, and they are now being pulled in opposing directions. Can traditional PRI provide sufficient risk transfer to warrant its cost? Can insurers offer meaningful amounts of "comprehensive" coverage? If so, at what cost? The answers are not clear, but are critical in resolving the question of whether PRI can continue to reliably facilitate investment in the emerging markets.

PART THREE

Shall the Twain Meet?
Finding Common Ground or
Uncommon Solutions

Overview

Theodore H. Moran, Editor

Part Three brings together Felton "Mac" Johnston, President, FMJ International Risk; Charles Berry, Chairman, Berry, Palmer & Lyle Limited; and Witold Henisz and Bennet Zelner, Assistant Professors at Wharton and Georgetown University respectively. Additional commentary is provided by David Bailey, Vice President, Sovereign Risk Insurance Ltd. and Edith Quintrell, Manager, Insurance, at the Overseas Private Investment Corporation, who provide perspectives on how the political risk insurance industry might evolve to meet the needs of insurers and reinsurers, on the one hand, and investors and lenders, on the other.

Even in the face of a substantial volume of possible claims, accompanied by retrenchment by political risk insurers and their reinsurers, Mac Johnston provides an optimistic perspective on the political risk marketplace. His reading of the history of the industry supports the notion that investors, lenders, and insurers have always had to learn as they go, accumulating new experience—and sometimes developing new products—to help them cope with constantly surprising future events.

Addressing the question of whether investors have adequate knowledge about the insurance they are paying for, and of whether insurers know what risks their policies cover, John-

125

ston points out that even the most intelligent buyers have diverse judgments about the value and usefulness of what they purchase, and even the most experienced sellers of insurance have to make complex projections that extend beyond the words in the policies they sell.

It is implausible to suppose, argues Johnston, that when the industry started writing coverage for infrastructure projects, investors and insurers fully appreciated the dimensions of the performance obligations being assumed by sovereigns, on a case-by-case basis and in the aggregate. Nor is it reasonable to imagine that the industry had adequately thought through the dilemma that host officials would face in dealing with foreign currency-indexed tariffs and take-or-pay purchase contracts during an exchange crisis. It is unlikely that participants on all sides in the political risk industry could have imagined that the IMF and the U.S. Treasury would pressure host country governments to abandon their solemn commitments to private infrastructure investors, in an effort to restabilize their economies.

The conclusion to be drawn from this failure to foresee such contingencies , argues Johnston, "is not that none of this business should have been written, but rather that we learn as we go, and we keep trying to do things better. That is the nature of the business."

Despite a common supposition that public sector bureaucrats might be stodgy and unimaginative, Johnston points out that in this learning process, MIGA and OPIC have matched the private market in inventiveness, pioneering long-term lender's coverage, capital markets coverage, and a devaluation product. At the same time, public agencies have been able to play a deterrent role that private insurers cannot duplicate. They have been able to act as a channel to explain the fairness of an investor's case. They have been able to provide political cover to officials looking for the resolution of a problem. They have been able to help guarantee a settlement. These functions serve the needs of host country authorities, as well as investors and lenders.

But there is a danger that public agencies may stretch the preferred status they confer upon lenders and investors too thinly, asserts Johnston, returning to a theme that he and others have highlighted in preceding MIGA–Georgetown volumes.[1] The umbrella of preference created by MIGA and other public agencies may discourage investing and lending by parties who do not share in it. And too many claimants on preferred status may mean that no party enjoys preference when a crisis hits.

In the end, one can be optimistic about the political risk insurance market, even in the midst of uncertainty and retrenchment, concludes Johnston. "Claims represent bad news for insurers and insured alike, but they help us to understand the risks and the policies that address them, and to make improvements."

In the area of confiscation policies, however, argues Charles Berry, the creativity of the industry in designing new coverages has mixed and muddled three separate, distinct traditions, involving expropriation, breach of contract, and political force majeure. This has caused a lack of clarity about what risks are, and are not, being transferred.

Expropriation concerns the regulatory, not the commercial, acts of government, Berry points out. The expropriation tradition springs from a government's decision to nationalize an investment without prompt, adequate, and effective compensation.

Breach of contract, in contrast, usually concerns the commercial acts of government. The breach of contract tradition originates in the trade and export credit insurance markets, where it is assumed that a breach occurs when it is impossible to unravel its cause.

Political force majeure deals with regulatory acts of government that are of general application, are not discriminatory, and are usually taken to regulate the economy (hence, they may fall within the category of regulatory acts that are not expropriatory). The political force majeure tradition derives from the London marine political risk insurance market, where coverage related to legitimate acts of government without any expropriatory tests. A typical example is a U.K. export embargo, which the proper authorities decree under existing law, without insurers having recourse to the government.

Scrutiny of these three distinct traditions, Berry points out, illustrates what is wrong in the wordings of PRI contracts. He demonstrates in some detail how these are separate coverages, with separate principles. To underwrite these risks correctly, and price the insurance correctly, requires keeping them separate. Trying to patch these three traditions together, by requiring a violation of international law, simply muddles things, argues Berry.

The MidAmerican case in Indonesia illustrates the problem of mixing these three coverage traditions.[2] The actions of the Government of Indonesia, in derailing the arbitration process, triggered a test of the expropriation coverage in the political risk insurance policy. Had the government not engaged in such misbehavior, it would have been a direct breach of contract case, under circumstances in which the Indonesian government was substantially overcommitted and unable to meet every single commercial obligation in full and on time. At the end of the day, the MidAmerican case was considered under the rubric of expropriation, even though, in reality, it was not.

Berry's step-by-step analysis of the differences between breach of contract, political force majeure, and expropriation covers—and his argument that the first two risks need to be seen as different from expropriation risk, not as a type of expropriation risk—provides valuable direction to insureds and insurers trying to ask the right questions when assessing what they wish to buy and sell, respectively.

Political risk management requires active strategies by international investors that extend beyond the structuring of financial and insurance protections, argue Witold Henisz and Bennet Zelner. In designing such strategies, investors can use several methods to increase their bargaining power regarding host authorities. One method is to employ technology that only company executives can utilize effectively. Another method is to mobilize home government authorities and industry associations to lobby on their behalf, or threaten to report poor treatment to rating agencies, multilateral banks, and private lenders. Investors may also collaborate with host country players who have political, economic, or other institutional clout.

Investors increase their chances of good treatment if they frame their objective in terms of goals that have broad appeal in the host country—such as a "level playing field" or "no government handouts"—rather than simply asking for a higher profit margin.

Henisz and Zelner point out the possibility of negative feedback effects from strategies to bolster an investor's position in the host market, however. A powerful local partner may become a liability when the political climate changes. Aggressive lobbying by foreign corporations can be viewed as interference. Even operational successes of foreign investors can carry potential political risk liabilities. Rational cost-cutting measures can lead to power failures that incite local resentment against foreign owners. Efficiency gains can lead to levels of profitability that appear to host country citizens as "profiteering."

In the early days of the political risk insurance industry, points out David Bailey, coverage was designed to protect the investor against proactive hostile interference—in the extreme, expropriation—by host governments. Insurers argued that contract wording was "broad" rather than "vague," and since not all covered events could be anticipated, it was considered reasonable not to spell out precisely what would trigger a claim.

As governments began to play a more direct role as suppliers or off-takers to large infrastructure projects, however, there was a need for greater clarity in identifying the specific host country commitments that were covered, or excluded, in insurance coverage. This was the origin of "breach of contract" protection. The issue of who bore the devaluation risk when revenues were paid in local currency, while capital costs were denominated in hard currency, increased in importance. Finally, terrorism emerged as a more clearly visible threat.

As a result, on the client "wish list," Bailey suggests, demand for protection against expropriation has evolved into demand for protection against nonpayment; demand for protection against nontransfer and inconvertibility has evolved into demand for protection against devaluation; and demand for protection against political violence has evolved into demand for protection against terrorism.

Arbitration Award Default cover has gone part way to protect against losses due to breach in host government commitments. The exchange risk products developed by OPIC and Sovereign, described earlier, have helped with devaluation exposure. Terrorism coverage is moving forward with specific exclusions, such as "biological and chemical" carve-outs similar to existing nuclear exemptions.

Coverage for institutional lenders has been stimulated by proposals for regulatory changes under Basel II, asserts Bailey, and by the growing awareness of officers and directors that failure to pay adequate attention to risk mitigation carries grave consequences.

The result will be "increased transparency," as all parties— investors, lenders, and insurance companies—identify and agree, from the start, who is responsible for bearing what risk. While this may result in project delay, as policy language is formalized, it will be increasingly demanded by shareholders and reinsurers.

The final issue pertains to releasing claims information. The PRI industry has, traditionally, not been very open to publicizing claims details. This approach, asserts Bailey, is not in the best interest of the industry's future and, as Chairman of the Berne Union Investment Insurance Industry, Bailey urges the release of aggregate claims information by all Berne Union members.

In contrast to Charles Berry, Edie Quintrell argues that "sometimes simpler, somewhat vague language may be better." It is impossible to predict exactly how, and in what form, political risks may emerge. If political risk insurers try to become too precise in drafting policy wording, the coverage may not fit the specific circumstances, when the need for protection arises. In the case of creeping expropriation coverage, for example, an effort to define too strictly when the waiting period begins and ends, and when the outcome qualifies as total expropriation, may produce a product that is less useful than the one currently available.

It is also important to recognize the limitations under which some insurers operate. OPIC's statutory authority allows coverage of expropriation, inconvertibility, and political violence. Breach of contract must be covered, therefore, under the rubric of expropriation, and must relate to political rather than commercial risk. Quintrell acknowledges that it is an increasingly blurry area, when governmental entities are involved as buyers or sellers of a given insured project. Private insurers have more freedom to provide hybrid coverages that blend political and commercial considerations. Despite the constraints within which OPIC operates, however, Quintrell concludes, the pressure from clients has continually pushed OPIC to innovate, and to ensure that its coverage remains responsive to evolving needs.

Notes

1. Shanks, Robert B. 1998. "Lessons in the Management of Political Risk: Infrastructure Projects." *In* Theodore H. Moran, (ed.), *Managing International Political Risk.* Oxford: Blackwell. Johnston, Felton (Mac). "Preferred Creditor Status: Husbanding a Valuable Asset." 2001. *In* Theodore H. Moran, (ed.), *International Political Risk Management: Exploring New Frontiers.* Washington, D.C.: World Bank.

2. For details, see Martin, Julie. 2001. "OPIC Modified Expropriation Coverage Case Study: MidAmerica's Projects in Indonesia—Dieng and Patuha." *In* Theodore H. Moran, (ed.), *International Political Risk Management: Exploring New Frontiers.* Washington, D.C.: World Bank.

Finding Common Ground or Uncommon Solutions: An Independent Consultant's Perspective

Felton (Mac) Johnston
President
FMJ International Risk Services, LLC

In 1996, I wrote an article about the prospects of political risk insurance that struck a lot of people as too negative. This was in the days when there was great euphoria about the opening of developing countries to "economic reform," and when public and private PRI activity was burgeoning. I took a cautionary view, asking "Who would dare predict a quiet opening to the twenty-first century? And who would predict that the current enthusiasm of global markets for private-sector investment will be universally permanent, or that infrastructure investors can count on the rules and commitments of governments remaining immutable for decades to come?"

I think I am condemned to live my life as a contrarian, because now, despite the substantial volume of claims and incipient claims chickens coming home to roost, and retrenchment by political risk insurers and their reinsurers, I am optimistic about the future of this marketplace! Things may get a little worse before they get better, but I think PRI will resume being a vibrant and innovative business that plays a vital commercial and policy role.

I will return to my optimism about the marketplace later, but first I want to answer a few of the larger questions addressed in this volume:

1. Do investors know what they are paying for?

There are several ways to answer this question.

Some investors know more than others. (Those with imperfect knowledge are a boon to brokers, lawyers, and consultants associated with this industry.)

Some investors care more than others. If the only reason to want coverage is to have the ability to score additional exposure as a domestic risk, how much do you really need to know? This isn't like buying a loaf of bread. It is a complex set of products. And no one knows for sure what events will occur, and exactly how the policies will respond to those events.

2. Let's put the question a little differently. Do investors know what they need, and does having this knowledge help them to make wise decisions?

Most investors are intelligent buyers—but intelligent buyers have different perspectives, and can reach different judgments about the value and meaning of what is available to them. Sometimes investors make the wrong judgment about what they need and the implications of buying a product.

Every underwriter knows a story about an investor who, in hindsight, didn't buy the right coverage or who bought too much/ not enough, or made some other error in judgment. Looking back, the mistakes people make regarding political risk insurance can seem pretty dumb. That's what makes hindsight so much fun, if you are judging someone else's decisions! But making good judgments about coverage—what to buy and what to negotiate—can be difficult. The complexities of the product are hard to grasp, and the future is hard to fathom. This difficulty, and the desire to avoid tough decisions, is probably why some companies buy insurance as a matter of policy, and without too much effort, adjusting what they buy to perceived risks. Given how much we cannot know, it is hard to blame those who take this route.

What isn't always clear, however, is how buying insurance affects investment decisions. It is typical for the cost of insurance to be factored into hurdle rate calculations, and for the hurdle rate to reflect the risk of cross-border investing, without also factoring in the risk-reducing benefit of the coverage. If risk-reduction does figure in the calculations, my impression is that not too much attention is paid to the details of the coverage. Again, these are not easy things to think through.

3.   Do insurers know what they are covering?

Yes, I think they do. In the sense that they are familiar with their
own products, and assume that the buyer is forthright about why
he needs the coverage. Of course, some underwriters are more careful and thorough than others, and their judgment can be undermined by haste or eagerness to book business.

But there is another, broader dimension to knowing what you are
doing, beyond knowing what the words say, and appraising what
the investor is doing and understanding the particular risk environment. For example, when we underwriters started writing coverage for infrastructure projects, were we thinking hard about the
history of private infrastructure projects in developing countries?
Did we really appreciate how much the sovereigns were taking on
(case-by-case and in the aggregate), in terms of their performance
obligations? Did we fully appreciate the dilemma presented to
authorities by an exchange crisis: do you impose exchange controls
and, thus, keep indexed tariffs low, or do you let the currency plum-
met and then have to either enrage the public by raising tariffs or
make good on your guarantee? And did we imagine that, in such a
crisis, the IMF and the U.S. Treasury would suggest a sovereign
should abandon its performance obligations?

Maybe other underwriters knew or anticipated all of this, but I
did not.

I am not saying that none of this business should have been written, but rather that we learn as we go, and we keep trying to do
things better. That is the nature of our business.

There is another sense in which you could say that political risk
underwriters do not know what they are doing. The PRI market is
an almost purely anecdotal market—there is no organized statistical data about the marketplace, or about claims/losses. We do not
"know" much about the PRI marketplace, in a way that most other
insurance products are understood and for which data is available.
It partly reflects a general private market tendency to discourage
acknowledgment that policies exist, an understandable reluctance
to share information with competitors and maybe even with customers, a lack of standardization, and the fact that PRI is not regulated like other insurance markets. This problem is not likely to be
fixed any time soon. Even if confidentiality problems can be dealt
with, the data will not be comparable to the statistics available for
more conventional perils. Still, an independent information clear-
inghouse could be a good thing for insurers and insureds alike.

Next, I want to address the subject of the relationship between public and private sector insurers.

What the public market uniquely offers—whether in the form of deterrence or preferred creditor status—cannot be replicated by the private market, although it can be shared. This "sharing" is a key element in the relationship between the two sectors.

But public agency insurers, or at least some of them, also perform services that help the private sector and the overall development process. These services deserve more attention.

The first is innovation and product development. Far from the conventional image of a plodding bureaucracy, unimaginatively cranking out shopworn products that compare unfavorably with those offered by the inventive private market, some public agencies have been major innovators. Long-term lenders coverage, capital markets coverage, and a devaluation product emerged first from the public sector. It isn't that private insurers lack good ideas, or that public agencies don't have plenty to learn from the private market, but it is the public agencies, in general, that are prepared to invest substantial resources to develop a product whose commercial success may not be assured. If the products work, and if there is demand, private insurers will quickly replicate them.

The other benefit of having public agency insurance is its deterrent role. Some public agencies can bring to bear resources and bona fides, to resolve or deter investment disputes, that private insurers lack. Both MIGA and OPIC have played this role very successfully. Sometimes the solution comes in the form of guaranteeing a settlement. In other cases it involves convincing the host government of the fairness of the investor's case, and the importance of respecting investors' rights. It can also include giving a little political cover to officials looking for a way out of the problem.

As we search for the right formula to preserve the benefits of public agencies, without throttling the opportunities and development of the private market, we need to exercise a little restraint, and avoid killing the goose that lays the golden eggs.

For public agencies to maintain their essential usefulness and relevance, it is not sufficient to be useful to and relevant for private sector insurers. There is no one right way to do these things, but in trying to avoid undermining the private sector, public agencies must remember that their main priority is to serve investors' needs and that if the mechanisms for not undermining private sector insurers are unacceptable to investors, the public sector agency raison d'etre ceases to exist. The fact is, without strong support from

buyers, the public agency insurer will not be around to share benefits with the private insurer, or to benefit investors and developing
countries.

Another kind of restraint should be exercised. Public agency
insurers need to be careful about how thinly they stretch their collective preferred status. Too much preference discourages investing
and lending by the people who do not share in it. And too many
preferred creditors will, at some point, mean there may not be
enough preference to go around. This, of course, will undermine the
whole concept. The need to limit preferred status is not just a political risk insurance matter either, but it certainly affects insurers.

What are my reasons for optimism?

As I said at the outset, I am an optimist about the market. We
have come a long way over the years, and retrenchment is not the
same as turning back the clock.

Here is what I consider the good news for political risk insurance.
There is a lot more capacity today than ten years ago, even if capacity today is less than it was one year ago. Retrenchment is not collapse; it is part of the market cycle. And, although political risk
coverage is not a mainstream insurance product, it is not utterly off-
beat any longer. It has earned legitimacy and has been accepted by
all the major players.

There is a lot more competition. There are more players, in more
places, from the public and private sectors. Private markets offer
products whose terms are competitive with public agency policies.
And competition is good for the buyer.

At the same time, there is more cooperation between public and
private insurers, to everyone's benefit.

There is a growing body of experience—including claims experience—and a growing body of experienced underwriters. Claims
represent bad news for insurers and insureds alike, but they help us
to understand the risks and policies that address them, and to make
improvements. As to the talent pool, I took an informal survey of
the major private sector sources, and except at Lloyd's, the number
of investment insurance underwriters has at least doubled over the
last five years or so. Most of them have at least a couple of years of
experience in the field, and a considerable number of private market underwriters have previously worked in public agencies doing
this kind of underwriting. Cross-fertilization is a good thing. It contributes to mutual understanding and facilitates cooperation.

Finally, there is innovation. We have new products, such as capital markets coverage, and a willingness by insurers to adapt cov-

erage to special circumstances. Another aspect of innovation is the willingness to rethink old issues: the pledge of shares issue is getting priced away.

Demand—and the political risk that drives it—is not going away. It may witness a temporary decline for a while, but it will experience resurgence sooner or later.

All of this is not to say there are no problems or challenges for the business. Managing the current cycle of claims and learning from them, addressing the problem of subsovereign risk, sorting out the overlap between sovereign risk and credit risk, gaining a better understanding of political violence risks and how they should be addressed, and many other problems confront us. But the foundation has been well laid, and the prospects for the future are good.

Shall the Twain Meet? Finding Common Ground or Uncommon Solutions: A Broker's Perspective

Charles Berry
Chairman
Berry Palmer & Lyle Global

In investment insurance, "common ground" can be an elusive commodity. There is a familiar theme in the PRI market, namely, that the cover insurers and reinsurers want to sell is not quite the cover investors want to buy, and the cover policyholders want to buy is not really what the insurance market wants to sell.

A central part of a broker's role is to help find this common ground, to achieve "a meeting of the minds." And while our role is to represent the interests of the policyholders, our work is not entirely a zero sum. We believe that clear and simple policy language, based on a shared and common understanding of the principles underpinning the coverages provided, will benefit both sides—the insurer and the policyholder.

However, when it comes to reviewing the policy wording produced by private and public investment insurers, the oft-used school report expression comes to mind: "Could do better!"

My perspective is not simply that of a broker seeking broader coverage on behalf of clients (though I would be disingenuous not to admit that is where my instinct lies). Rather, my focus is on clarity: clarity of language, and of thought concerning the underlying principles and conventions that have underpinned the successful underwriting of political risk insurance for many years.

Traditionally, investment insurers focused on three risks: currency inconvertibility, expropriation, and political violence. Client pressure has forced insurers to address other areas of risk, specifically breach of contract and political force majeure. My concern here is less about currency inconvertibility and political violence, though I will comment briefly on these later. Rather, I would like to focus on breach of contract, expropriation, and political force majeure. These three are distinct and separate, and should not be addressed under the umbrella of Expropriation; all three have a long and successful, but different, tradition in the insurance industry. Investment insurance policy language, in attempting to incorporate breach of contract and political force majeure perils, has not always succeeded in providing the clarity of thought and wording that is needed.

We find ourselves amidst difficult times. Argentina and Iraq hang over our business like specters at the feast. Capital providers, including reinsurers, are asking primary insurers searching questions about the adequacy of the returns they receive for the risks they run. At the same time, the corporations that pay the premiums are asking questions about the value of the investment insurance policies they purchase. The fact that our industry feels pressure from both sides of the market is a reflection of the uncertainty that exists in the minds of decisionmakers as to exactly what risks are, or are not, being covered by the investment insurance policies.

This puts clarity of thought, and of wording, right at the top of the agenda for the investment insurance industry today. Unless there is a meeting of the minds as to which risks are, and which risks are not, transferred by investment insurance policies, capital providers can take no comfort that risks are being properly priced and risk portfolios are being properly managed, and policyholders have no confidence that they are receiving value for the premiums they pay. For these reasons, I make no apologies for reverting to the underlying principles that have long guided different sectors of the PRI market, and I make no apologies for pointing out the lack of clarity in wordings where I see it.

It is a truism in the insurance industry that you learn far more about a class of business through handling claims than by placing policies. My general opinion on investment insurance wordings is forged in the crucible of claims experience. Berry, Palmer, & Lyle has had a number of interesting investment insurance claims over the years, ranging from Latin America to the Middle East, and from Africa to the CIS. However, the two largest claims that we have settled arose from the Indonesian crisis of 1997–98. These claims have greatly influenced my current views.

The first of these claims, involving MidAmerican's Indonesian power projects, is well known. The claim is described in detail in

Julie Martin's paper in the preceding MIGA–Georgetown volume on *International Political Risk Management.*[1] The loss was shared between OPIC and a group of private insurers. We placed the private market portion, which followed the OPIC wording, for $72.5 million. The claim was paid in full, and promptly, once MidAmerican obtained the necessary trigger judgments against the Indonesian government.

However, despite the fact that the policy was delivered in full and on time, I am not satisfied with the OPIC policy wording that was used. The claim involved a breach of contract. Breach of contract was addressed in the wording, but consisted of "a modified form of expropriation coverage." Happily for MidAmerican, the Indonesian government did enough to enable the company to meet the additional tests necessary to satisfy insurers that the breach was "expropriatory." However, despite the satisfactory outcome, the case convinced me that it is not desirable to write breach of contract cover by modifying expropriation language, nor is it desirable to make separate breach of contract language subject to "expropriatory" tests.

The second claim remains a private matter. The quantum of the settlement eventually achieved was similar in magnitude to the private market's portion of the MidAmerican claim. While the settlement figure was close to the full policy limit, the policyholders (and brokers) were disappointed not to receive full settlement; in addition, settlement was only achieved following lengthy and protracted negotiations with underwriters about the basis of the claim.

The claim should have been a straightforward matter: in a nutshell, the policyholder's project and related agreements had been cancelled by a decree of the Indonesian government. This host government action was not prompted by any action, or inaction, of the investor or any of their partners, rather, it appeared to be prompted by the IMF. The effect of the decree was clear: the investors were left with a half-built project, and, metaphorically speaking, with a large amount of money poured into a very black hole.

But was the decree that cancelled the project "expropriatory?" Was it selective? Was it discriminatory? Was it a breach of international law? Or was it a bona fide, nondiscriminatory action taken by the government in its ordinary course of regulating economic activity? (Not all these tests applied to the actual policy.)

These are the sort of questions that delight the investment insurance professionals (and enrich their advisors). But we also need a reality check. If a government decree cancels a specific project and does not clearly trigger a cause of loss under an investment insurance policy, policyholders will discredit the value of the coverage.

This is neither the place to go into the details of the language of that specific policy, nor to reiterate all the lessons we learned from this experience. My message here is that many of the standard market wordings available from investment insurers provide insurers and their legal advisors with better grounds for legal argument than the actual, modified wording used in this particular case.

While some wording could have cast aspersions onto the notion that the decree was expropriatory, there is no doubt that the decree was political force majeure. There is certainly a difference between the two. While all expropriations may fall under the heading of political force majeure, certain host government acts of political force majeure are definitely not be categorized under Expropriation. Sometimes Political Force Majeure cover may be a cleaner, better alternative. Clearly, investment insurance policyholders who have their project unilaterally terminated by the host government in this manner, ought to have found a way of being given a product that provides them with certainty that a covered "peril" has occurred.

Our general claims experience, in Indonesia and elsewhere, convinces me that breach of contract, expropriation, and political force majeure are separate types of host government action that ought to be treated differently. All three may be relevant to investors and lenders when contemplating investment insurance on a specific project. In addition, all three covers have been written in the insurance market for many years, albeit out of separate traditions and with differing underlying principles. It is time to highlight these different traditions and their key principles. It is this framework that guides my reflections on current investment insurance wordings.

The Expropriation Tradition

I regard this tradition as being centered on the Eastern seaboard of the United States. OPIC, and its predecessor agency in the 1960s, certainly made a substantial contribution to the development of the principles underpinning many investment insurance policies, particularly the principles of underwriting expropriation risks. OPIC's influence extends through its many alumni, and its thinking can be seen in the policy language of MIGA and key North American private sector insurers. London contributed to the expropriation tradition largely by imitation. The key principles of the Expropriation tradition are, inter alia:

No commercial actions: A distinction is drawn between the commercial and regulatory actions of host governments. This principle has been explicit in OPIC's expropriation wording, in the form of an exclusion called "Government Action" or, most recently, "Government Relationship to the Project." The principle is echoed, implicitly or explicitly, in most other Expropriation policies.

Regulatory action must be "expropriatory": While Expropriation policies cover the actions of a foreign government, taken in its regulatory or governmental capacity, not all regulatory or governmental actions are "expropriatory." This principle is incorporated in Expropriation policies by language addressing one or more of the following:

- precise definition of the effect that the governmental action must have;
- application of a test that the action must be in breach of international law;
- use of qualifying words such as "expropriatory," "selective," "discriminatory," etc.;
- exclusion of any governmental actions that are bona fide and nondiscriminatory, and are taken in the normal course of government business, such as raising revenues, regulating economic activity, ensuring public safety, etc. (I refer to this as the Bona Fide Actions Exclusion.)

Recourse to the host government: closely related to the concept that covered governmental action has to be "expropriatory," is the underlying principle that the loss should give rise to a potential course of action in law against the host government, which should provide insurers with an eventual recovery.

Given these principles, it is abundantly clear that breach of contract and political force majeure fall outside the expropriation tradition: the former fundamentally challenges the first principle, as Breach of Contract cover is centrally concerned with the commercial actions of government. Political force majeure deals essentially with government actions that, in all probability, *are* bona fide, nondiscriminatory, do *not* breach international law, and do *not* give policyholders and insurers any legal recourse (in international or any other law) against the respective government.

Worded thus, it is not surprising that talk of breach of contract and political force majeure induce feelings of nausea and vertigo among those who have been brought up in the strict confines of the

Eastern Seaboard expropriation tradition. Happily, these feelings can be calmed by turning to other, well-established traditions in other sectors of the insurance market that have come together in the past 20 years in the Contract Frustration market: a Contract Frustration policy basically blends government Breach of Contract and Political Force Majeure covers. But the traditions predate the Contract Frustration market, and it is worth revisiting them.

Breach of Contract

Breach of Contract cover has a pedigree in the insurance industry that is much longer than that of investment insurance. The basic technology and principles of this cover have long been established in the trade credit insurance and surety markets. The Contract Frustration market developed in the 1970s and 1980s by transferring the technology of ECGD and other government ECAs to private sector insurers, and by government entities focusing on breach of contract. Important underlying principles adopted by insurers, or learned by bitter experience, include the following:

The scope of cover is defined by the underlying contract rather than the insurance policy itself. In other words, the nature and extent of the coverage provided, when granting Breach of Contract cover, depend on the obligations imposed on the counterparty/government by the underlying insured contract.

These obligations may be regulatory; for example, an investor may have a "contract" with the host government that provides for certain regulatory concessions, such as tax holidays or tax rates. To the extent that the contract limits itself to such issues, a Breach of Contract cover may not go far beyond the cover provided by an Expropriation policy.

Nevertheless, most contracts that are the subject of a Breach of Contract cover involve obligations entered into by the host government in their commercial, rather than their governmental or regulatory, capacity. Hence, a conflict with one of the basic tenets of Expropriation insurance arises.

In seeking to cross this threshold, some try to downplay the significance and distinction between a government's commercial and regulatory actions. I prefer to emphasize the distinction. Based on my experience, appreciating the different risks associated with the government acting as regulator and its separate role as a buyer, seller, etc., is the most important distinction in the political risk business.

Underwriting the "commercial" acts of government takes insurers into the area of government "insolvency" risk, or government "credit" risk. While there is (as yet) no internationally agreed procedure for governments to become insolvent, in the technical sense, governments certainly become insolvent in the colloquial sense of the word. They find themselves in a position where they are unable to meet *all* their commercial obligations in full and on time. In practice, a government is just as capable of overcommitting itself as an individual or a corporation.

Here, the word "all" is all-important. I have frequently heard the argument that where a government has enough money to meet a specific obligation (which they invariably do), their failure to do so is "political." It is certainly true that when it overcommits, a government can use its own discretion to decide which creditors to pay and which not to pay. However, any insolvent corporation or individual is still able to meet "some" of its obligations: insolvency arises when they cannot meet all their commitments in full and on time. It seems reasonable to apply the same test to a government. The risk that a government cannot avoid causing losses, because they are overcommitted, should not be present in an expropriation policy—the risk of a government overcommitting itself is at the heart of most Breach of Contract policies.

Cover geared to the breach, not the underlying cause of the breach: Coverages in the credit insurance, surety and the Contract Frustration market, all focus on the *fact* of the breach, not on the underlying *cause* of it.

Breach of Contract specialists recognize that it is impossible, in practice, to disentangle the web of causation that leads an entity, including a government, to breaching a contractual commitment. While there may be, in principle, different underlying pressures that cause a government to default on a contractual obligation, trying to dissect them into "commercial" causes and "political" causes is impossible in practice.

The MidAmerican case illustrates this difficulty. It so happened that the Indonesian government took certain actions to thwart the enforcement of the arbitration award, which thus triggered the necessary "expropriatory" hurdles in the policy wording. Luckily for MidAmerican, the government of Indonesian did this. Furthermore, had MidAmerican been able to appeal to a super-sovereign court, capable of enforcing arbitration awards against the Indonesian government, that court would have had no alternative but to instigate what would have been the equivalent of Chapter 11 proceedings.

The fact remains that, at that moment, the Indonesian government was hopelessly overcommitted. Specifically in the power industry, it had significantly overcommitted to buy electricity, under power purchase agreements, U.S. dollars or a hard currency equivalent. In general, Indonesia had over-borrowed and was incapable of meeting all its commercial obligations in full and on time; it was already in discussions with its government ECA creditors through the Paris Club. In reality, MidAmerican's inability to enforce its international arbitration award was due to a combination of political and commercial reasons.

Breach of Contract cover is written around key conditions. Due to the nature of the risk underwritten, and specifically to ensure that in a claim situation, insurers are subrogated to recourse against the defaulting party (particularly useful when the party in default is a government):

For the protection of insurers, these key provisions should include:

- a condition or warranty that the underlying contract is signed and in force;
- a condition forbidding the policyholder to change the contract materially without the insurer's agreement;
- an exclusion relating to disputes between the parties to the insured contract;
- an exclusion of losses arising from the failure of the policyholder to perform the insured contract.

Political Force Majeure Tradition

The political force majeure tradition in the political risk insurance industry is the contribution of the London market. Political force majeure risk is a cover that is steeped in the tradition of the London market in general, and in Lloyd's in particular. Much of this cover is based on war risk and expropriation risk associated with tangible assets, such as aircraft and vessels. However, for many years there has been a market for various political contingency risks. Indeed, the Political Force Majeure market had its origins in the so-called "contingency" market in London. One of the early manifestations of political contingency, or Political Force Majeure cover, was in the event cancellation market, particularly major sporting and other events such as the Olympic Games and the World Cup.

The most common manifestations of the Political Force Majeure market today are the "pre-delivery" political contingency risks, underwritten on a daily basis under Contract Frustration policies and trade disruption policies; examples of government-related political force majeure, covered on a daily basis, include contract termination covers, export and import embargo covers, and license cancellation covers.

Political force majeure also embraces war risk, which cause cancellation and abandonment. Indeed, the Forced Abandonment cover seen in many investment insurance policies is a prime example of a Political Force Majeure policy. However, I would like to focus on political force majeure in the form of government action.

The key principles (or conventions) that guide the political force majeure tradition include:

- *A wider grant of cover than in Expropriation policies*: While Political Force Majeure cover deals with governments acting in their regulatory, not commercial, capacity, the coverages are not subject to an "expropriatory" test. Event cancellation, license cancellation, and embargo covers, for example, do not require that the government's regulatory action be in breach of international law, or be nondiscriminatory, etc.

- *No recourse to the government*: This is a related point. If you take the example of the U.K. export embargo, the U.K. government has a right to withdraw an export license or to impose export restrictions at any time. It does not have to enact any legislation; enabling legislation has already been enacted, and what is required is "the operation of a law, order, decree or regulation" by the relevant minister. Neither the U.K. exporter, nor its insurers, have any right of recourse to the U.K. government. Insurers take no comfort in the idea that these types of losses, if they occur, are recoverable from that government, though there may be salvage in the embargoed goods. Rather, they rely on the fact that these types of losses are rare, and that the premiums charged are adequate to compensate insurers for losses of this nature, when they occur.

- *The political force majeure event must cause termination*: Given the apparent broadness of the peril being insured, a key protection for insurers underwriting Political Force Majeure covers has usually been that the consequences of the event must be catastrophic to the insured contract, event, or project. This is a reasonable principle. Extra expense cover, arising from political force majeure events, is not usually provided.

My framework for reading investment insurance policies is based on the above-mentioned three traditions. I see different traditions emerging from different sectors of the insurance industry, based on different key underwriting principles.

Most investment insurers have normally focused on the Expropriation tradition. However, the nature of investment has changed in the last decade or more, particularly with regard to infrastructure investment. The need for Breach of Contract coverage has been widely recognized in the context of many investments. In addition, for many investments today, the needs of investors and lenders are closer to the tradition of political force majeure than those of Expropriation. Investment insurers have clearly been under pressure to adapt, and to a greater or lesser extent, have done so. However, generally speaking, in incorporating such covers, investment insurers could provide greater clarity by respecting the established principles governing the breach of contract and political force majeure traditions.

There are a number of generic practices that I consider undesirable. I have already admitted to having the brokers' bias of wanting to see a broader form of coverage. However, while admitting that bias, I maintain my argument that the practices I highlight may reflect a lack of clarity of thought about the type of cover intended to be granted, and definitely produce unclear wordings. As I have said, clarity and a meeting of the minds is in the interest of both parties in the investment insurance policy, namely, capital providers and policyholders.

The practices that I consider undesirable, in the context of Breach of Contract covers, are:

- *Writing Breach of Contract Cover as Part of an Expropriation Cause of Loss*: This is undesirable because, at the root, Breach of Contract cover flies in the face of one of the fundamental principles of Expropriation cover. Adding coverage by making an exception to an exclusion is not the best route to clarity. I should add, however, that I am technically ineligible to cast the first stone at this particular practice, though I am comforted by the fact that the same is true for most professionals in our industry.

  Clearly, from the policyholder's point of view, the danger is that not all the details of an Expropriation policy are adequately amended. There is equal danger for insurers: we have seen wordings that weave Breach of Contract cover very effectively into what appears, at first sight, to be an expropriation wording, thus producing a veritable wolf in sheep's clothing.

■ *Writing Breach of Contract Cover With "Expropriatory" Tests*: Breach of Contract covers that impose "expropriatory" tests, relating to the original breach and/or to the nonhonoring of a subsequent arbitration award arising from the breach, are not proper Breach of Contract covers. In a marketplace that can, and does, provide Breach of Contract cover without such tests, it would be fairer for these types of perils to be labeled and described as modified forms of Expropriation coverage, as OPIC did in the MidAmerican case.

■ *Breach of Contract Cover with Inappropriate Exclusions*: Exclusions that I consider inappropriate include:
  – An exclusion of "commercial" acts of government. In this context, an exclusion does not make sense, and ought to be seen as contrary to the intent of a normal Breach of Contract cover.
  – "Bona fide actions" exclusions, which again make no sense in the context of a Breach of Contract cover.
  – Currency fluctuation exclusions. This would be inappropriate, as would any other exclusion that attempted to unravel the underlying web of causation behind a breach. Having said that, many policies covering breach of contract are required to carry currency fluctuation exclusions. Nevertheless, a strong convention in many parts of the market dictates the purpose of the exclusion as being that insurers are not allowed to write policies that indemnify for exchange rate or currency fluctuation losses. Consequently, the intent of these exclusions is not to limit Breach of Contract coverage, where one of the underlying causes of a government's breach could be currency fluctuations or devaluations.

■ *Breach of Contract Cover Without the Normal Conditions*: These conditions include the normal protections built in for the benefit of the insurer, requiring that the underlying contract is effective and prevents the policyholder from making amendments to the insured contract without the agreement of the insurer. In addition, exclusions relating to disputes, and exclusions of failure of the policyholder to perform contracted duties, are necessary and reasonable conditions, if Breach of Contract cover is to be granted on a sound basis. It does not benefit either the insurer or the policyholder if these types of provisions are not clearly stated where Breach of Contract cover is given.

I would add, however, that disputes, exclusions, and exclusions relating to the failure of the investor to perform contractual obligations, are not necessary or desirable, if the policyholder has to demonstrate breach by establishing an arbitration award against the host government.

The subject of disputes raises another issue. Is it acceptable that Breach of Contract cover be limited, by requiring the policyholder to obtain an arbitration award against the host government? This limited form of breach of contract has sometimes been called "Disputes Coverage." Clearly, this is a hurdle the policyholder must clear, and it is likely to delay the claim settlement, possibly by several years.

Despite the obvious disadvantages, I regard this form of coverage as acceptable. It provides clarity; it enables issues concerning performance and disputes (issues that a host government will very likely raise, spuriously or otherwise, and that will, therefore, complicate any breach of contract claim) to be resolved in a proper manner; and it may, in practice, be the only basis on which Breach of Contract cover is available at all.

However, when evaluating Breach of Contract cover geared to obtaining an arbitration award, care needs to be taken to ensure that the arbitration clause in the underlying insured contract provides for international arbitration that cannot be thwarted by the host government. A "Disputes" cover dependent on local arbitration does not mitigate this political risk. Likewise, provisions that require judgments against the host government to be recognized by a local forum (in the host country) may, again, incorporate the very political risk that insurers intend to mitigate.

Turning to political force majeure, it is fairly common for private market policies to contain supplementary covers that broadly fit into the category of political force majeure, and it is worth commenting on them, as follows:

- *Forced Abandonment*: Though the wordings vary in quality, this cover is a good example of a Political Force Majeure cover being incorporated in an investment insurance program. Similar coverage is often provided by public sector insurers as part of their War and Political Violence cover.
- *Forced Divestiture*: To a large extent, this is a good example of a Political Force Majeure cover. However, some wordings (including the Berry Palmer & Lyle template) require the policyholder's own government action to be taken selectively.

This provides a good example of how language from the Expropriation tradition can infect a Political Force Majeure cover. The "selective" criteria should not apply to forced divestiture: if it refers to the selection of the foreign country against whom sanctions or other action is being taken, it goes without saying; if it refers to an action against the policy-holder, one would expect the sanctions to be directed at all investors operating in the foreign country. Indeed, one would be somewhat suspicious if the policyholder's own government selected the policyholder for special treatment.

- *Selective Discrimination*: It strikes me, in the context of most investment insurance policies, this adds little or nothing to the coverage already provided in the expropriation cause of loss. All that can be said is that, as it is usually thrown in without additional premium, it is fairly accurately priced from a value for money point of view! The title of this cause of loss disqualifies it from consideration as a political force majeure peril.

Other political force majeure perils involving actions of the host government may be added to investment insurance policies from time to time. Additional causes of loss may cover import or export license cancellation, import or export embargo, the cancellation of operating licenses, government action terminating projects and/or contracts, and so forth.

A minor issue relating to some of the license cancellation wordings is the requirement that coverage may only apply where the host government "…has no right to cancel the license in accordance with its terms and conditions." There is some ambiguity here. In instances where license has been granted subject to a particular condition, and the policyholder has breached that condition, clearly such a cancellation should not be covered, as it would have been triggered by the policyholder's own breach.

However, there is an implication in the language that echoes "expropriatory" language, and a suggestion that the host government needs to operate *ultra vires*, or in breach of international law, or in some arbitrary or discriminatory manner. This is wrong. Returning to the example of a U.K. export license, the government is perfectly entitled to cancel or revoke such licenses; coverage does not work as a Political Force Majeure cover, unless it is provided where the host government *does* have a right to cancel the license. The need for these additional coverages specifically arises because the host government could take certain specific actions that might prove fatal to the project or investment, but may at the same time be "nondiscriminatory measures, of general application of a kind governments normally take in the public interest for the purpose of ensuring public safety, raising revenues, regulating economic activities, etc."

This brings me to my principal complaint about adding more Political Force Majeure covers to investment insurance: often they are done without removing the Bona Fide Actions Exclusion. This is inappropriate. The purpose of Political Force Majeure cover is to provide coverage against host government actions that may not be "expropriatory." If covers that purport to provide additional coverage, beyond expropriation, have to pass expropriatory tests, the additional coverage becomes illusory. An expropriatory action of the host government that prevents operation of the investment or project should already be covered under the Expropriation cause of loss.

A Political Force Majeure cover needs to have clarity as to the peril; but it also needs to have a clear definition of the loss event, which will normally be the termination of a project/ contract/ abandonment of an investment. This is an area that requires care and thought, not least as there are issues of moral hazard associated with decisions to abandon an investment or terminate a project.

Nevertheless, the area in which Political Force Majeure cover (and Breach of Contract cover) is likely to be most relevant is for projects and investments that are defined in a series of contractual agreements. These agreements may deal with the subjects of breach of contract and (political) force majeure explicitly; indeed, they are as likely (or more likely) to address these issues as they are to deal with Expropriation, indicating where the real risks in these projects are. Tying the Political Force Majeure cover to formal project termination may best define the trigger loss event in a manner consistent with the general principle to be covered; a political force majeure event should have a catastrophic effect on the project or investment, and not simply cause extra expense and delay.

Furthermore, project agreements may reveal that the host government has agreed to compensate the investor for political force majeure events. This can provide recourse to the host government in contract, where none might otherwise exist in law. Generally, dove-tailing Breach of Contract and Political Force Majeure coverages, with underlying contract conditions relating to the project or investment, is an essential part of providing clarity and a meeting of the minds.

I will now briefly address Currency Inconvertibility and War cover. Generally, it is not the best time to debate the detail of Currency Inconvertibility cover; the situation in Argentina remains confused, and the detail of different policies varies. However, we

already know from Indonesia and elsewhere, that Currency Inconvertibility may be a political risk cover, but it is not a country risk
cover. Where a country crisis prompts a devaluation (the market-
oriented response to a shortage, rather than the traditional Socialist
devaluation), losses tend to manifest themselves as commercial
defaults. I like to think policyholders understand this.

Finally, a comment on the physical damage aspect of Political
Violence cover: This involves issues of indemnity. Investment insurers have tended to gear cover to Net Investment; in contrast, the
property insurance approach to War and Political Violence cover
focuses on property values. The first approach works well if the consequence of damage is abandonment. However, the property insurance approach may be far more effective when, following damage,
the investor is willing and able to rebuild or replace. This practical-
ity of rebuilding or replacing will be revealed once the circumstances and extent of the loss is established. In our view, purchasers
of Political Violence cover need to consider how well the policy will
respond in each circumstance.

Clarity of thought and wording has been my theme; "could do
better" is my assessment. If insurers, who read my analysis claim
the wording issues I have highlighted do not apply to their policies,
and only to their competitors' offerings, noone would be more
delighted than me.

My own view, however, is that most policies, as they stand today,
require at least some review. Breach of Contract and Political Force
Majeure covers are relevant, but they need to be seen as different
from the expropriation risk, not a type of expropriation risk. Drawing clear distinctions between the three can only help insurers ask
the right questions when assessing the risks they are presented with,
and charge the right price when they find such risks acceptable. This
can only be healthy for the market.

I have spent much of my time in the political risk insurance market worrying about the supply of PRI capacity, particularly from private insurers. However, despite current difficulties, I remain
confident. Investment insurance is a young class of insurance in the
private and public sectors. However today there is a talented group
of specialist underwriters and brokers who are committed to the
class. They have been developing experience and expertise that will
ensure the class continues to attract capital. There will be problems
of capacity, particularly at this stage of the insurance cycle. However, I am convinced that the political risk and investment insurance
business is very much closer to its beginning than it is to its end.

Therefore, with the passage of time, I have begun to worry less about the supply side of our business: today I increasingly worry about the demand side. Do policyholders believe they get value for their money from investment insurance?

Those of us who have made our careers in the PRI market would be fooling ourselves if we did not think this is an issue today. We need to convince policyholders that investment insurance provides value for money. My view is, often, insurers provide good value to policyholders, but this value is not consistent and it is not transparent. Value for money remains an issue, and at the heart of the issue is clarity of thought (and of wording) about the risks that are/are not transferred.

I hope that insurers reading this paper find my comments fair and, possibly, useful. However, having been somewhat critical of insurers, perhaps I could close by being just slightly critical of some policyholders. My criticism, though, is transparently self-serving: I believe policyholders could make better use of the services available to them from specialist brokers in this class.

The time to assess value for money is when you buy the policy, not when you have to make a claim. And though many clients in the market have dedicated professionals involved in this class, with great knowledge of the business, almost by definition, individual companies cannot have the breadth and depth of experience of specialist brokers. Specialist brokers are good at judging value for money; we have a framework for evaluating policy language, we know the industry, we are in touch with the market, we know about pricing, and we have claims experience. Nevertheless, we certainly come across policyholders who have not taken advice, or have not been properly advised, and who have consequently received very poor value for their money. This is not good for them; and it is not good for our market.

By definition, you cannot ask your insurers whether they are delivering the best value for your money. So, before you buy your next policy, why not ask us? It goes without saying that a broker must deliver value for money; and the fact is, we do.

Note

1. Martin, Julie A. 2001. "OPIC Modified Expropriation Coverage Case Study: MidAmerica's Projects in Indonesia—Dieng and Patuha." *In* Theodore H. Moran, (ed.), *International Political Risk Management: Exploring New Frontiers*. Washington, DC: The World Bank.

Political Risk Management:
A Strategic Perspective

Witold J. Henisz
The Wharton School
University of Pennsylvania

Bennet A. Zelner[1]
McDonough School of Business
Georgetown University

Although insurers often treat political risk as a country-specific phenomenon, substantial variation in the probability and magnitude of
loss exists at the firm level. Individual firms confront different
sources of policy uncertainty and political influence, depending on
their familiarity with the local environment, nationality, network of
global stakeholders, partner status, size, and technological leadership. Sophisticated managers address political risk by employing
tailored risk mitigation strategies to reflect specific factors affecting
a firm's risk profile. Insurers may, therefore, determine the proper
scope and price more accurately and efficiently, by assessing the fit-
ness of a given political risk mitigation strategy.

This paper provides a simple framework that can be used to make
such an assessment. The framework revolves around a firm's bilateral "bargain"—its explicit or implicit agreement about what portion of its returns will be appropriated—with a host country
government. Over time, the government is likely to face economic,
electoral, or financial incentives to increase the fraction of the firm's
returns that get redistributed among buyers, competitors, suppliers,
or the broader polity. We develop our framework by, first, identifying the factors that imbue a foreign firm with "bargaining power,"
which it may exploit to protect its initial bargain. Next, we consider
how a firm's industry position affects the optimal form of the arguments its managers make, in attempting to influence the policy-
making process. Finally, we discuss the dynamic integrity of a firm's

political risk mitigation strategy; that is, the extent to which the strategy balances short-term profitability with resistance to future political backlash that could result from the appearance of privilege or inequity. The choices that Management makes in these three areas affect the probability and likely magnitude of a firm's loss from adverse government behavior.

In our analysis, we draw from extensive field interviews in the cellular service and electricity generation industries of 13 emerging markets in Central Europe, East Asia, and South America, to support our arguments.[2] Managers of all the firms we visited stressed the importance of their government and public relations functions in reducing the probability and severity of attempts by public officials—acting in the interest of competitors, consumers, potential entrants, suppliers, or other interested parties—to squeeze profits out of the firm. Such attempts, typically, took the form of policy decisions that altered the terms of existing contracts, structure of the market, or the firm's latitude to set prices or make new service offerings. Key determinants of success, which many interviewees pointed out, include active monitoring of political and regulatory areas, as well as active participation in policy debates.

Noninfrastructure industries may face less policy uncertainty, or fewer policy initiatives, that affect them directly. Nonetheless, managers who recognize that political risk is ubiquitous, and learn to manage it effectively over time, have an opportunity to outperform their counterparts in a wide array of industrial and country environments. In the words of one manager, "governance is as important as value." Indeed, surveys of multinational managers across industries repeatedly underscore the impact of the policy environment on international investment decisions and outcomes.[3] For example, a survey of 3,951 firms in 74 countries found that corruption and judicial unpredictability were the second and third most serious obstacles to doing business, following only taxation.[4] A similar survey of the largest global multinational corporations found that "unconventional" risks, such as corruption, crony capitalism, and political risk, cost firms $24 billion in lost revenue in 1998 alone, leading 84 percent of subsidiaries in emerging markets to fall short of their financial target and, ultimately, to an 8 to 10 percent diminution in total corporate returns.[5] Another recent report, concerning the economic significance of governance (broadly defined), found that investors contemplating entry into countries with "opaque" governance (e.g., China, the Czech Republic, Indonesia, Romania, Russia, South Korea, and Turkey) faced the equivalent of a 33 to 46 percent increase in corporate income taxes, relative to the cost of entering a country with stronger governance (e.g., Chile or the United States).[6] Similarly, an analysis of portfolio debt flows found that bondholders in countries with opaque governance demanded premiums of 9 to 13 percent.

While these aggregate statistics are compelling, they mask the underlying firm- and project-level heterogeneity acknowledged by industry participants. Consider, for example, the following comments:[7]

> "…effective political risk analysis is not just a question of evaluating country risk. Instead, risk assessments must identify the implications of economic, political, and social conditions for each project…. The key to analyzing the political risks facing a project is to identify the winners and losers, and assess their relative abilities to help or hinder a project, whether directly or by influencing a host government."[8]

> "I prefer to focus on what my assured can bring to a risk. My reasoning is, if you back the right assured, you can usually keep problems from occurring in the first place— and if they do happen, you have an excellent chance of mitigating your loss.[9]

> "There is no such thing as abstract political risk, in my opinion. Political risk very much depends on who you are and what you are doing in a country.[10]

> "Zurich's view is that the insured is the most crucial part of risk assessment, because it is the experience and capabilities of the insured that will ultimately have the largest impact on risk in the long term."[11]

These practitioners highlight an insured's familiarity with the local environment, network of global stakeholders, nationality, partner status, size, technological leadership, as relevant criteria for political risk analysis. Our framework provides insight into why these criteria matter, and augments this initial list with new considerations.

Creating Bargaining Power

Ultimately, any attempt to influence a policy decision requires managers to participate in the political debate. Their success depends as much on their bargaining power relative to the host government as it does on the actual arguments they make (which we consider below). Investor bargaining power is often argued to be at its maximum in the negotiation phase, when the investor has the capital and technology that the government needs to create jobs, output, promote additional foreign direct investment, and technology transfer. It tends to decline after the investor has sunk its capital. Some of the factors that can affect the rate of decline lie outside Management's immediate control. For example, government officials are typically thought to be more sensitive to the demands of a large firm, providing substantial local employment and income, than they are to those of a smaller firm offering fewer benefits to their constituents. Global size may also convey the benefits of reputation to investors, or provide room for added flexibility in response to adverse policies that similarly increase policymakers' sensitivity to investor needs.

Yet, managers may still improve their firm's bargaining position by making choices that *are* within their control, in order to increase the host country's dependence on the local subsidiary. A common means of doing this is to deploy nonreplicable technology (embodied in the production process or in an intermediate product) owned by the parent firm. One oil company with drilling operations in Russia, for example, deployed advanced technology that only its specially trained engineers could operate through a freeze and thaw cycle of permafrost.[12] The oil company's leverage was high, because the Russians would have been unable to maintain production if the company and its employees left the country. The incentives for government officials to squeeze the company through adverse policy changes were, therefore, much lower than they would have been had the company used generic technology that the Russians would be able to operate even in its absence.

Even where the range of technological choices that managers can make to increase their bargaining leverage is limited, they may find opportunities to create leverage through external relationships. One such channel is the foreign company's home country government. Interviewees in Poland (speaking of the 1989–92 period) and Taiwan described their governments' susceptibility—especially given their role in U.S. foreign policy—to lobbying efforts undertaken by the U.S. government on behalf of American firms. Observers in Central Europe highlighted the recent lobbying prowess of the French and German governments on behalf of France Telecom and Deutsche Telekom, respectively, in light of the host governments' desire for EU accession, at the earliest possible date.

Foreign investors may also exploit direct ties with home country political officials, to create external leverage relative to a host country government. One former regulator told us that when he "assessed a $4 million penalty on the companies from [country x] and [country y], they claimed force majeure, and put their embassies to work to lobby our government." Another prominent example involves Texas-based Enron Corporation's investments in Argentina. A former regulatory official in Argentina (now a Congressman) claims to have received a phone call in early 1989 from George W. Bush, the son of then President-elect George H.W. Bush, which delivered "a subtle, vague message that [helping Enron] could help us with our relationship with the United States."[13]

Finally, even in the absence of a specific source of external leverage, the more nebulous threat of an angry public, combined with good old-fashioned brinksmanship, can be quite effective. One interviewee recounted a perilous 90 minutes in his project's history: "[Our pricing dispute] came down to a final phone call with the Ministry, where we threatened not to put our plant into operation, resulting in lawsuits from the contractor and offtaker, which would result in a counter-suit by us against the government. We promised them that this would be a very public and very dirty affair, and asked them, 'What are you going to do?' Less than two hours later, we agreed on a price."

Managers often create external leverage through nongovernmental organizations (NGOs) as well. For example, one manager described his threat to alert the financial rating agencies of worsening relations between his company and the government, as an important source of external leverage. Others emphasized the leverage they were able to attain through their ties with international banking syndicates, government-sponsored political risk underwriters (e.g., COFACE, ECGD, the Export-Import Bank, MITI, OPIC, etc.), and multilateral lending agencies (e.g., the ADB and the IFC). Investors in wireless telecommunications, for example, have relied on the WTO to reduce formal local ownership requirements and liberalize the sector. For publicly traded firms, shareholders—especially foreign and institutional ones—can provide external leverage as well, according to an investor in Chile. So, too, can ties with industry associations, which can participate in lobbying and public education, like the Association of Foreign Generators did on behalf of investors in the Philippine electricity sector.

Efforts to build bargaining power are especially important when a new market includes politically powerful incumbents who possess strong ties to government institutions or officials. Because a foreign entrant can do little in the short run to sever such ties, managers need to analyze the nonmarket environment as carefully as the market environment, in order to develop realistic performance expectations. Alternately, managers may want to undertake a detailed analysis of the nonmarket structure in order to evaluate potential local partners, whose political ties could then benefit the foreign entrant.

The Czech electricity market provides an example. Many private entrants allege that the government accords special treatment to the partially privatized former monopolist, the Confederacion de Empresarios de Zaragoza (CEZ). They claim that the regulatory formula used to determine the fees to be paid to CEZ, for access to the national transmission system, are "cooked up to help CEZ," which has massive debt through its subsidiary. Even the Ministry of Finance has attacked the lack of transparency in the design of the new formula.[14] United Energy has filed a lawsuit claiming that the fee was calculated by a consultant hired under closed tender, rather than by open competition. Nonetheless, the formula remains in place for the time being, demonstrating just how powerful an incumbent's ties to the government can be. As is often the case, CEZ's ties date back to the preprivatization period—that is, prior to entry by any of the private firms—suggesting that an analysis of the nonmarket environment might have identified the possibility of privileged regulatory treatment. Moreover, the unfortunate experience of the investors who did enter, has led many international operators to stay away from the Czech market altogether—unless they can enter by buying into a privatized CEZ.

In the wireless telecommunications industry, a similar situation exists with fixed-line carriers, mainly those that retain some degree of state ownership, and enjoy preferential political treatment as a result. One interviewee explained, "All the rules are right. The problem is the execution. The outcome, the execution, they always favor [the fixed-line carrier]." Another lamented that it is "hard to fight a player and a referee that are on the same team," and a third averred that the fixed-line incumbent "takes advantage of its relationship with the (government). They postpone deadlines and cooperate reluctantly...they lobby to reduce the budget of the [regulator], which reduces its ability to hire professional experts to inspect and monitor them." For these reasons, in many cases, foreign entrants have allied themselves with fixed-line incumbents through equity investments, partnerships, and the like. Examples include the recent partnership between France Telecom and Telekomunikacja Polska (TPSA) in Poland, the acquisition and partnership strategies of firms such as Bell Canada, MCI, Telecom Italia and Telefonica in Brazil, and France Telecom and Telecom Italia's joint ownership of Telecom Argentina.

Sometimes, existing political ties require a deeper political analysis than an evaluation of the incumbent(s) alone. In the Polish cellular sector, for example, a political coalition has dictated the structure of the market, to the disadvantage of the state-owned fixed-line operator and its foreign partner, France Telecom. In 1996, the Polish Peasant Party (PSL) controlled the Minister of Telecommunications and, consequently, also held the reins of the state-owned firm, TPSA. TPSA chose not to participate in a GSM license tender that year (much to the consternation of its American joint venture partner, Ameritech), paving the way for the government to award new licenses to two new private consortia. TPSA's decision appears puzzling, without recognition of the strong ties among the PSL, its coalition partner, the Left Democratic Alliance (SLD), and the two new consortia that received the license. According to one interviewee, "These consortia were created for political reasons, by people without experience in the market." Another concurred, "The Polish partners had no operational experience in telecommunications, but did help with lobbying." The Financial Times summarized the relationships: "One license would be awarded to Elektrim [the former state-owned trading enterprise that had a monopoly on foreign trade in electricity and telecommunications products in the Communist era], which has political links with the SLD, the senior governing coalition partner, while the other license would be awarded to Ciech [the former state-owned trading enterprise that had a monopoly on foreign trade in oil and chemical products in the Communist era] with strong links to the PSL."[15]

Similar examples abound elsewhere. In Thailand, the Prime Minister has proposed legislation restricting foreign investment, but provided an advantage to the telecommunications firm AIS by "grandfathering" in its shareholders. Our interviewees in Taiwan ascribed the success or failure of private wireless telecommunications entrants, relative to the incumbent Chunghwa Telecom, to their ties to the DPP and KMT parties.

Entrants seeking to create leverage vis-à-vis foreign governments have several options. In addition to making clever choices about technology, they can utilize various external channels to increase their bargaining power, and they can also choose to ally themselves with incumbents who already possess such power. Assessing the nonmarket environment of a potential host country is a necessity in any case, in order to make realistic projections about the future.

Framing the Arguments

We now shift focus from the structure of "bargaining" with a host country government to its content. Simple demands for more profits are seldom successful. Instead, such demands must tap into some policy goal, such as "fair competition" or a "level playing field," that resonates with a broad class of constituents and, thereby, increases popular support for an initiative. Moreover, the precise form of such arguments depends on the position of the firm in the industry, as well as the extent to which the firm is in a defensive or an offensive position.

Foreign entrants, taking the offensive on their own, often argue for the long-term benefits of free competition—with the stipulation that a system of asymmetric regulation, favoring entrants over incumbent(s), is initially necessary to create a level playing field. Consider some of the specific arguments made by entrants in the wireless telecommunications sector, which were virtually identical in the countries we visited:

> "Of course we have pushed for asymmetry. Our concept is for a level playing field. If one firm starts with a huge lead, you are not going to get competition by treating everyone equally. Unless you tilt the market, so that the dominant firm cannot abuse its market power, you will never have true competition."

> "It's like giving a 70 mile head start in a 100 mile race, and asking who will win."

> "However hard we try to improve the situation, the structure of the market itself makes it hard to catch up with the frontrunners… What we want is not outright favors but a market environment where frontrunners and latecomers are allowed to stage fair competition."

When on the defensive, rather than the offensive, foreign entrants tend to focus more on the inefficiency of the incumbent rather than

its power in the market. In Hungary, for example, fixed-line operators, caught off-guard by the substitution of mobile telephony for
traditional service, sought redress from the government through the
imposition of a universal service fee and a reregulation of fixed-to-
mobile tariffs to compensate them for the higher costs of serving
rural and relatively poor regions. The ensuing public relations bat-
tle saw entrants highlighting the mistakes made by incumbents, in
an attempt to avoid these cost burdens: "The only one way that they
can survive is from subsidies. They go to the government to
demand something from the mobile sector. The government is
afraid that if they don't give them what they ask for, they will go
bankrupt, and 30,000 to 40,000 customers will have no local service.
It would have been much better to let them go bankrupt, then we
would not be in this blackmailing situation today."

Another interviewee concurred, "They saw no way to survive the
takeover of mobile telephony, other than to lobby the government
to change the interconnection regime…Fixed-line services are still
perceived as the way to reach the masses. Mobile is somehow ugly:
compact, expensive, high profile, a symbol of status, and trendy."

A cellular operator in another country summarized the concerns
of new entrants regarding such appeals: "The bottom line is that
[they] want some of our money. Everything that they say translates
as 'we want some of your money.'"

The nature of the arguments changes when an entrant allies
itself with an incumbent. The offensive posture, then, takes the
form of an argument for unfettered competition: "After 2006, we
need to have equal terms. We can't try to make up for the past. At
the time, the bidding was open. Those who won the bids have a
right to win."

> "The danger of asymmetric regulation is that it will be
> applied in a manner that discriminates against the large
> operators, without regard to whether they arrived at their
> position through a special deal or through efficient busi-
> ness practices."

> "I question whether these new entrants are even that effi-
> cient. They have such a heavy reliance on government."

> "The late entrant applications were not conditional on
> asymmetry. They didn't even mention it. Now they give
> all these reasons." "The problem is that [they] priced their

service below cost and ran into serious financial problems…Now, they are asking for asymmetric regulation."

"Most of the disputes come from the third operator. They
ask for better treatment…arguing that they are poor."

Another interviewee explained the reason for the operator's weak
position, as follows: "Their license stipulated certain fixed prices.
They claimed, at those prices, they couldn't make a profit and asked
for better terms, but they knew the fixed prices when they bid."

When on the defensive, the incumbent and its foreign partner
focus on the incumbent's inefficiency. In this case, however, it was
done by citing the burden of additional costs incurred to serve a
public need. They note that incumbent firms with current or past
state ownership typically face great difficulties in reacting quickly
to changing market conditions, due to government bureaucracy,
government regulations, and a lack of influence with other relevant
branches of government. A spokesman for Chunghwa Telecom in
Taiwan presented this perspective in an interview with *Communication International*: "It is difficult for Chunghwa to improve its
mobile networks, as equipment procurement is still under MOTC
control. [Private] operators can buy what they want and expand at
any time, but we cannot, as we have to go through a tender procedure," said a spokesman for Chunghwa.[16] Furthermore, Chunghwa
officials claim that they are forced by the government to make 80
percent of their investments in extending local loops, which brings
in only 30 percent of revenue due to implicit and explicit subsidies.
Chunghwa also claims that the government pressures them to offer
interconnection to new cellular operators at a discount, to avoid any
cases of market failure.[17]

Officials at state-owned companies in other countries lamented:
"My first impression when I started working for [dominant firm]
was that I needed to respond to the market, but I couldn't because
it's always perceived as predatory. I have had many frustrating
experiences. As a result, we are perceived as being slow. It's not
true." Also, "of course the private sector wants to keep their money,
but what are we to do if we have no payments and few subscribers?
It takes time to develop competition… We have been a state-owned
enterprise for a long time. We have never conducted our business
like a business." Another public sector official proposed an interesting solution: "A level playing field requires the government to
make sure that everyone has the same costs."

Feedback Effects

A third consideration, which is particularly important for managers devising political risk strategies, is the strategy's dynamic integrity, specifically the possibility of a "feedback effect". The broader literature on political risk management advises the adoption of *ex ante* safeguards, for example, taking on a local partner with privileged access to the government, or shortening the period during which capital returns are at risk, by structuring a deal to front-load the cash flows.

However, a local partner becomes a liability if it uses its privileged access at the expense of the foreign investor (Henisz, and Williamson, 1999). Similarly, the front-loading of returns may invite excessive scrutiny of a project. The use of foreign partners may create a perception that a project is not "local" enough. Government commitments are not necessarily credible. Foreign lobbying is often perceived as meddling. International arbitration can be lengthy, and works only when accepted by all sides. Political risk insurance or other financial hedging instruments are available for limited terms, and rarely reach beyond the replacement value of assets to encompass expected cash flows. Investors must, therefore, assess each potential safeguard with respect to the original hazard it is intended to mitigate, and the new risks and costs that it introduces.

One prominent example of such a trade-off is the use of local partners by investors in Indonesia and Malaysia. Because the formal institutional supports for private infrastructure investment in these countries were so weak, investors were forced (often literally) to rely on relationships and family ties as contractual supports: "Malaysia is a difficult place to understand. The electricity sector is closely interwoven with the political process. You can only try to get the tightest kind of contractual arrangements, then you have to work on relationships." Another interviewee reiterated: "You have to use the culture... a certain amount of patronage is necessary in any government project... there's a price for everything." Yet another, "Here, outlawyering is a waste of money. Ultimately, it doesn't protect you anyway. The key component is finding the right local partner."

In Indonesia, the political and regulatory officials "found" partners for the investors. One interviewee told us that "an Indonesian partner was suggested to us. There was no way to avoid that." The experience appears to have been repeated in virtually every Independent Power Project (IPP) contract there. Cikarang Listrando, the first major private power project in Indonesia and, later, the first to sell power back to the national grid, was owned by President Suharto's cousin. President Suharto's son had a 10 percent stake in the next major project to be signed through his business concern, the Humpuss Group. The infamous Paiton project passed from President Suharto's second son, Bambang, to the brother of President Suharto's son-in-law. Bambang later resurfaced as a director for the company that took over East Asia Power in 1997. The three-phase Tanjung Jati plant included, among its many investors, Suharto's second daughter (phase A); eldest daughter (phase C); and a close associate of the Minister of Planning, who was brought into the venture by an adviser to the Minister of Mines Energy (phase B). Suharto's eldest daughter also controlled a 20 percent stake in another project, although this stake was subsequently reduced to five percent. Cal Energy shared ownership of its Dieng project with the Association of Retired Officers Businesspeople (Himpurna); and of its Patuha project with the son of the Minister of Mines and Energy. In addition, Suharto's oldest son was reputed to be a partner of CalEnergy, although the firm vigorously denied this link. Finally, presidential confidante Mohammed Bob Hasan owned 10 percent of another prominent independent power project (IPP). In all, 26 IPP projects were approved or, in the words on one interviewee, "shoved down the throats of PLN [the incumbent SOE], as all the kids and cronies elbowed in and demanded their own power purchase agreements (PPAs)."

Following the 1997 crisis, partnering practices proved to be of some help to private investors in Malaysia. One interviewee mapped out the surviving IPPs, in the following fashion: "One furthers the interests of the BumiPatra, and was supported by the ex-deputy Prime Minister who is now in jail, one furthers the interests of Mahatir, another supports Mahatir's good friend who had difficulty in his other businesses, the remaining two are large diversified Bumipatra multinationals that are shrewd political operators..." Despite widespread doubts regarding its economic viability, the largest IPP in Malaysia (the Bakun hydroelectric project) continues to resurrect itself, due in no small part to the friendship between its chairman Ting Pek Khiing and the Prime Minister.[18]

In Indonesia, however, the partnering practices ultimately backfired and magnified investors' exposure to the crisis. In May 1998, President Suharto's longtime confidante, B.J. Habibe, replaced him and initiated a systematic campaign against the corruption, cronyism, and nepotism ("KKN" in local parlance) that characterized the Suharto regime. The Indonesian state audit agency subsequently reported that it had "found indications of corruption, collusion, and nepotism on all 27 [private power] contracts" and, thus, believes that it has legal standing to terminate these agreements. Thus, the rational calculation to play by Suharto's rules, and partner with the president's family and friends, created tremendous liabilities for private investors in the anti-KKN campaign that followed the end of his regime.

Another strategy that may backfire is an otherwise rational pruning of maintenance and other overhead costs. For example, support for the privatization program in Brazil waned substantially after a blackout in Sao Paulo, during the Christmas holiday in 1997. Record heat and a poor preprivatization maintenance history were certainly contributory factors, but the press and the public focused largely on the 40 percent reduction in personnel (some of whom had to be rehired to teach existing workers how to repair jury-rigged transformers), as well as the utility's record profits and weak regulatory supervision.[19] Another example comes from Hungary, where the state-owned electricity utility MVM launched a campaign criticizing the supply security and performance of new market entrants. In Buenos Aires, customers who had been without power for almost a week of high temperatures, following a fire at a power station operated by the Chilean firm Edesur, marched in the streets nightly, banging pots and pans and setting tires and automobiles on fire.[20] An engineer, interviewed by the news media, claimed that the delay in reinstating power was caused by the layoff by Edesur of thousands of skilled Argentine workers like himself.[21]

Ironically, even in the absence of such flashpoints, profitable entry strategies may themselves create a backlash against the status quo policy regime. Consider the experience of the Chilean generators, in the Argentine example. Researchers document a striking decrease in the average variable costs of one privatized generating company (CHILGENER, later GENER) due largely to increased efficiency in the amount of electricity generated per unit of coal input.[22] Further, there were even sharper declines in total cost, due to an increase in the capacity utilization of CHILGENER's plants from approximately 50 percent in 1985 to 83.4 percent in 1989. Energy line losses fell from 20.9 percent in 1986 to 8.6 percent in 1996, or almost 60 percent.[23] Labor productivity increased from 376 clients per worker in 1987 to 703 in 1997.[24] The ratio of GWh to employees at ENDESA increased from 2.23 in 1989 to 7.62 in 1996.[25]

Despite the dramatic efficiency gains described above, the Chilean system was not without its detractors or its problems. From the onset, critics argued that wealth had essentially been transferred from the state and/or consumers to the shareholders and managers of the newly privatized enterprises. As evidence, they point to the thousand-fold appreciation of electric companies' shares between 1984 and 1994;[26] rates of return of 30 percent in 1995; return on assets as high as 20 percent;[27] and the vast gap between the 11.4 percent reduction in tariffs, compared to the 37.4 percent fall in the price of generation, combined with the reduction in line losses reported above.[28]

The perception of profiteering dominated the experience of the efficiency gains, during a conflict originating in the 100-year drought of 1998. During that crisis, the Chilean government overturned an existing law that explicitly obviated the generator's responsibility for climatic conditions, outside the wholesale pricing model that included data on hydrological conditions, over the past century. Direct political intervention by Congress undermined the ability of generators to adapt to the shortage, and mandated that they pay compensation for any shortfall, including those caused by force majeure events, such as 100-year droughts.[29] The magnitude of these fines is substantial, as the government, also responding to popular pressure, raised the upper cap from approximately $25,000 to $6.4 million, with 25 percent payable upfront, prior to any appeal.[30]

In the words of one interviewee, "Popular pressure led to massive liabilities. Now, we have the same clients and the same price, but more risk." Another interviewee said, "The government didn't want to assume the political costs in explaining the need for sacrifice. Instead, they said we are responsible. They changed the law retroactively, and instituted a monetary penalty for a condition that the law explicitly stated we were not obliged to fulfill."

Conclusion

Farsighted investors never assume that a contract is a guarantee. Rather, in the words of one interviewee, political risk "has to be actively managed. You can minimize it, but never fully eliminate it, even under the best regulatory design. You have to dance with the shadows. You have to go beyond what you see on the surface. A lot of it is relationships, not picking the right people, but rather articulating your views and cultivating ties with people who share your goals."

In the words of Dr. Ferenc Tompa, head of Regulatory Affairs for the Hungarian operator Westel: "As regulatory authorities the world over have a growing appetite for regulating everything that moves in the mobile industry, operators need to move ever faster not only to innovate, but also in the regulatory domain, to stay ahead of the regulatory learning curve."[31]

Insurers must recognize that learning, articulating, cultivating, and dancing cannot be achieved through financial engineering alone. Political risk identification and management capabilities differ across firms and industries within a given country. A firm's characteristics, direct and indirect ties, and experiences shape its ability to influence government. Its position in the industry shapes the types of appeals most likely to generate favorable outcomes. Each financial or strategic move made to counter the government generates a counter-move by the government, or third parties, which must be taken into account. Successful management of political risk, on an ongoing basis, requires the cooperation of country experts, risk analysts, and senior management. Such insight into the firm-specific nature of political risk management is an essential dimension of competition, in the turbulent and uncertain policy environment that increasingly surrounds the multinational enterprise. An insurer's ability to appreciate these strategic aspects of political risk management will directly influence the accuracy of their pricing and cover limits and, ultimately, their profitability and survival.

Notes

1. Both authors contributed equally. Author order alternates on joint work. We thank the GE Fund and The Reginald H. Jones Center for Management Policy, Strategy, and Organization, for their generous financial support.

2. The countries are: Argentina, Brazil, Chile, The Czech Republic, Hungary, Indonesia, Malaysia, The Philippines, Poland, Singapore, South Korea, Taiwan, and Thailand.

3. Kobrin, S., Basek, J., Blank, S., and La Palombara, J. 1980. "The Assessment and Evaluation of Noneconomic Environments by American Firms: A preliminary report." *Journal of International Business Studies*, 11(1): 32-47. Root, F. R. 1968. "Attitudes of American Executives Towards Foreign Governments and Investment Opportunities." *Economics and Business Bulletin*, 20(January): 14-23.

4. Pfeffermann, G., and Kisunko, G. 1999. Perceived Obstacles to Doing Business: Worldwide Survey Results. *IFC Discussion Paper 37*.

5. Merchant International Group. 1999. *The Intelligence Gap*. London.

6. Wei, S.-J., and Hall, T. W. 2001. Investigating the Costs of Opacity: Deterred Foreign Direct Investment. *PriceWaterhouseCoopers Report*.

7. Drawn from Moran, T. (ed.). 1998. *Managing International Political Risk*. Oxford: Blackwell Publishers; Moran, T. (ed.). 2001. *International Political Risk Management: Exploring New Frontiers*. Washington, DC: World Bank Group.

8. Sandy Markwick, in *Managing International Political Risk, op. cit.*, p. 55.

9. David James in *International Political Risk Management: Exploring New Frontiers, op. cit.*, p 172.

10. Charles Berry in *International Political Risk Management: Exploring New Frontiers, op. cit.*, p 181.

11. Daniel Riordan, in *International Political Risk Management: Exploring New Frontiers, op. cit.*, p 189.

12. Spar, D. 1995. White Nights and Polar Lights: Investing in the Russian Oil Industry. *HBS Case*, 9-795-022.

13. Corn, D. 2002. Enron and the Bushes. *The Nation*, February 4: 5.

14. Johnstone, C. 2001. United Energy Threatening New Energy Regulator with Legal Action, *Prague Business Journal*.

15. *Financial Times Business Reports Business File*. 1995. Politics Influence GSM Tender. 12/1/95: 6.

16. David Hayes, *Communication International*, 10/01/97 p. 75.

17. *Ibid.*

18. Financial Times Business Limited. 1997. Matathir's Bakun Lifeline Scares Forex Market. *FT Energy Newsletters - Power in Asia*, December 1.

19. Moffett, M. 1998. Sour Juice: In Brazil, A Utility Dims Public Enthusiasm for Privatizations. *Wall Street Journal*, April 27: A1.

20. Zadunaisky, D. 1999. Anger Grows Over Lingering Power Blackout in Buenos Aires. *Associated Press Newswires*, February 20.

21 Valente, M. 1999. Consumers-Argentina: Tempers Over Outage Reach Boiling Point. *Inte Press Service*, February 19.

22. Galal, A., Jones, L., Tandon, P., and Vogelsang, I. 1994. *Welfare Consequences of Selling Public Enterprises*. New York: Oxford University Press (for the World Bank).

23. Estache, A., and Rodrigues-Pardina, M. 1998. Light and Lightning at the End of the Public Tunnel: Reform of the Electricity Sector in the Southern Cone. *Economic Development Institute, The World Bank* and Rudnick, H. 1998. *The Electric Market Restructuring in South America: Successes and Failures on Market Design*. Paper presented at the Plenary Session, Harvard Electricity Policy Group, January 29-30., San Diego, California.

24. Fischer, R., and Serra, P. 2000. Regulating the Electricity Sector in Latin America. *Economia*, 1(1): 155-198.

25. Rudnick. 1998. The Electric Market Restructuring in South America: Successes and Failures on Market Design. Processed.

26. Jadresic, A. 1997. Regulating Private Involvement in Infrastructure. Processed.

27. Britan, E., and Serra, P. 1998. Regulation of Privatized Utilities: The Chilean Experience. *World Development*, 26(6): 945-962.

28. Fischer, and Serra. 2000. Regulating the Electricity Sector in Latin America. Processed.

29. Basanes, C. F., Savvedra, E., and Soto, R. 1999. Post-Privatization Renegotiation and Disputes in Chile. *Interamerican Development Bank Working Paper*, Infrastructure and Financial Market Series (IFM)(116).

30. *Global Power Report*. 1999. Chile's New Electricity Law Alarms Generators; May Kill New Hydro Units. July 9: 1.

31. Evidence of the potential for learning about political hazards in the infrastructure sector comes from Holburn, G. 2002. "Political Risk, Political Capabilities and International Investment Strategy: Evidence from the power generation industry." Processed. He finds patterns of entry in the independent power production industry over time that suggest, firms that have previously operated under rate-of-return regulation are better equipped to manage the rate review process, while firms with experience in wholesale market competition are better able to manipulate prices under complex market rules. Similarly, firms with experience in countries with a specific institutional profile (e.g., centralized political decisionmaking or a strong independent regulator) enjoy a comparative advantage in other countries with similar institutional structures.

Commentary on Finding Common Ground or Uncommon Solutions:

A Private Provider's View

David Bailey
Vice President
Sovereign Risk Insurance Ltd.

My perspective draws upon personal experience, and reflects the different hats I have worn and currently wear. I was formerly the Chief Underwriter for Political Risk Insurance at Canada's EDC, where I spent 23 years, before moving to Sovereign Risk Insurance in April 2002. I can be considered part of the public-to-private sector "transfer of resources."

I am also the Chairman of the Investment Insurance Committee of the Berne Union, which includes private and public sector political risk insurers worldwide. It is clear from our Berne Union meeting in Prague, in mid-October 2002, that the issues addressed in this volume reflect what private and public actors are faced with globally, not just in North America.

Like other insurers, Sovereign too has witnessed fewer submissions, many of which are of a size or quality that do not meet the requirements. So, overall, we have seen a marked decline in demand.

PRI pricing is likely to remain stable in the near term. This reflects two factors: first, there are only a few good projects circulating. Therefore, these are likely to be completed at a reasonable price. Second, PRI was not as severely underpriced as other classes of insurance business and, therefore, did not need dramatic rate increases to come to an acceptable risk/reward ratio.

Looking to the future, in order to understand where the industry is headed, it is important and useful to briefly look at PRI in three stages: the history, the evolution of risks and the PRI product, and, finally, the contemporary operating environment.

In the Beginning…

At the genesis of the PRI (or investment insurance) market, policies were designed to protect against losses associated with exclusively private projects. The sponsors (or equity investors) were private, the banks were private, the foreign enterprise was obviously private, and the suppliers and offtakers were all, typically, private entities. Expropriation risk, as perceived by the client and insurer, was that of overt nationalization. Expropriation coverage protected against the government interfering in a project. The covered event had to be a proactive act, rather than a failure to act or perform. Simply put, as long as the government stayed out of the way, things were fine.

Transfer and Inconvertibility risk coverage was similarly straightforward. If there was a foreign exchange shortage, a local currency equivalent of the required dollars, at an official rate of exchange, would be deposited into a pipeline. Eventually, the local currency was converted when foreign exchange became available, and the dollars came out the other end of the pipeline. It was relatively easy to concisely outline a scope of coverage for this risk.

Similarly, political violence risks, and scope of coverage, were generally understood and clearly outlined.

In general, it can be argued that the insurance policies developed to cover the three specific political risks, as they existed at the time, did so relatively well.

The Evolution…

Over time, the operating environment changed. The risks became more complex, and client sophistication and demand for insurer responsiveness increased.

The real risk of Expropriation was no longer viewed as overt nationalization, but the risk of government action or inaction having the effect of confiscation. "Creeping Expropriation" coverage was thus developed, and it satisfied client needs until there was an increasingly persistent cry for more specificity and certainty in the coverage.

I remember, early in my career, trying to make potential clients understand and believe that the insurance wording wasn't "vague," it was "broad." One of the biggest challenges in explaining Expropriation cover was to outline the circumstances under which the policy would respond. Our best available answer to the "what if" question was, typically, "That depends...." This response was obviously not very satisfactory—not only to the person hearing it, but also to the person saying it. It was an approach that had its merits—broad language acknowledged that all insurable events could not be anticipated, but unanticipated events that met the test of expropriation were insurable.

The increased desire of investors for clarity in coverage was derived from a change in government participation in projects, from a passive to an active role. Government involvement became such that the commitments they provided, particularly as suppliers or off-takers to large infrastructure projects, were absolutely crucial to the success of the projects. It became relatively easy to identify the specific government commitments that were integral to the project, and to predetermine which were to be insured and which were to be excluded from coverage. "Breach of Contract" protection came of age. Conceptually, Breach of Contract cover was a good thing. Unfortunately, there were as many different interpretations of the scope of the coverage as there were people using the term. There was considerable confusion as to "who" in the market was providing "what," under Breach of Contract. It was unclear, for the longest time, how many long-term, pure breach of contract risks were being underwritten in the market.

There has also been an evolution in Transfer risk coverage. Many countries now have floating foreign exchange rates. Therefore, as opposed to making an irrevocable deposit, foreign exchange purchasers are required to go to the bank regularly, or even everyday, to see if there is any hard currency available.

There are challenges in coming up with Transfer and Inconvertibility policy risk language to reflect that, even under a floating rate system, the insured has the obligation to take all the required local administrative steps, while maintaining principles of "reasonableness" and "fairness" to the insured.

While there have been significant developments in the perception of risks (and the related coverage) for expropriation and currency transfer, political violence risk and coverage has remained relatively unchanged. As we have heard from others, political violence risk had not, until recently, been the cause of much discussion or policy negotiation. The coverage was, usually, either not taken or was included in the insurance package for a nominal increase in premium.

The Present...

The contemporary operating environment presents a rather unique set of circumstances and challenges for the PRI market.

Client demands have intensified and become more focused on specific risks. On the current client wish list, the demand for Expropriation cover has been transformed into demand for Non-payment cover; the demand for Transfer and Inconvertibility has become demand for Devaluation cover; and the demand for Political Violence cover has become demand for Terrorism cover.

The market has been relatively responsive in terms of product enhancement and development, up to 2002.

Development and refinement of Arbitration Award Default cover has provided long-term protection against losses due to breach of government commitments, particularly prevalent in infrastructure projects. While not fully meeting clients' desires, this cover has addressed some of the restrictions and uncertainty, including eliminating the need to distinguish whether government default was taken for political or commercial reasons. In addition, many political risk insurers provided nonhonoring or nonpayment cover for sovereign guarantors and borrowers.

Specific financial products had been developed by OPIC and Sovereign, as described earlier, to partially address devaluation risk, although for a number of reasons these products have not been made widely available or used.

Political risk insurers have been less eager to take on the increased demand for terrorism coverage, caused by the dearth of capacity formerly available in the property and casualty markets. Certain insurers write terrorism coverage on a stand-alone basis. However, PRI providers are more likely to either exclude terrorism from Political Violence cover entirely, or include it with specific carve-outs. As an example, it is likely that the PRI market will have "biological and chemical" exclusions in its policies, similar to the existing nuclear exclusions.

I now turn to the question: "Do clients know what they are purchasing and do insurers know what they are selling?" The answer is that, although the majority on both sides would say they think they know, they will likely only *really* know some time in the near future—because of the claims (more specifically, the Argentine claims) which are currently in the market. It is an unfortunate truth that, in some cases, a claim represents the first time that the scope of coverage under a policy is truly scrutinized. Whereas there have been a few Argentine PRI claims paid to date, many more of these claims are in the later stages of the assessment period. A few of the larger, more complex claims are either close to, or have progressed to, arbitration or litigation. The unique combination of circumstances and government response in Argentina was not predicted, and was largely unpredictable at the time the policies were underwritten. It is expected that claims adjustors and independent adjudicators will have a difficult time judging whether any compensation, resulting from the occurrence of these events, is payable under the policies. Further, it is expected that the outcome will probably come down to the specifics of the project, the coverage, and the policy language.

As buyers and sellers have both become increasingly knowledgeable about the actual scope of coverage under PRI, the drivers and motivations have also undergone significant transformation. For example, institutional lenders' business had been a rapid growth area in the PRI market. In many cases, lenders' primary motivation for purchasing PRI had been to reduce the amount of capital that needed to be allocated against the underlying loan. Maximizing the cost/benefit ratio was achieved by reducing the cost of the PRI premium. Therefore, the objective was often to try and minimize the coverage purchased (and therefore its cost), while still retaining the benefit of capital allocation relief.

Factors, such as proposed regulatory changes under Basel II, may require banks to revisit this strategy, and will certainly make the actual scope of PRI coverage a much more important factor in banks' purchase decision.

It is not only the direct providers and purchasers that influence change in PRI demand and motivations. Many banks' directors and shareholders are actively involved in restructuring and refocusing the banks and their priorities. Direct lending to emerging markets is being significantly curtailed. Those emerging market projects that do make it to the credit committee are subject to additional scrutiny on all aspects, including the extent of risk mitigation provided by PRI. Many of the traditional, large equity investors have, similarly, cut back on their international activities, taking a "wait and see" approach. At the same time, directors and officers of companies with existing (or proposed) equity investments are now increasingly aware of the existence of PRI and the potential consequences and liabilities associated with failing to take the appropriate risk mitigation steps. PRI providers are also operating under increased attention from their reinsurers and/or shareholders, most of whom have experienced losses due to September 11, Enron, and other catastrophes, and all of whom are aware that there are claims in the PRI market.

What will be the outcome of these recent events? The short answer is: "increased transparency." Insurers will be subject to additional disclosure, to their reinsurers and shareholders, regarding their activities. Banks and equity clients will have to be more open to directors, shareholders, and regulators regarding the level of risks they accept. PRI will be treated less like a generic commodity, and more as a risk transfer tool that can be modified to meet specific circumstances. Insurable political risks are, in the simplest sense, one slice in a "pie" of risks. It is essential for all risk-takers, including equity investors, banks, and PRI providers, to identify upfront which risks make up the pie and, then, commonly agree on which risks are to be accepted by which party. When—and only when—this meeting of the minds is achieved, should the policy language be formalized and checked to ensure that it accurately reflects the agreed risk allocations. The need for this agreement may well cause some project negotiation delays, but it will certainly minimize surprises and acrimony if, and when, a loss occurs.

One additional aspect of the need for transparency is in respect to claims information. The PRI market has not traditionally been very open about releasing claims details. This approach is not in the best interest of the industry, particularly now, when the PRI product is under intense scrutiny. Although valid PRI claims are being paid, and will be paid in the future, this message does not always reach those who need to know. As the Chairman of the Berne Union Investment Insurance Committee, I strongly encourage and support the release of aggregated claims information from our members.

I remain confident in the future of political risk insurance. The product has undergone considerable enhancement and development, in response to fluid and aggressive demands from clients. While political risk insurance will continually be required to "push the envelope," financially strong and creative providers will continue to meet the challenge.

Commentary on Finding Common Ground or Uncommon Solutions:

A Public Provider's View

Edith P. Quintrell
Manager, Insurance
Overseas Private Investment Corporation

Do investors know what they are paying for, and do insurers know what they are covering?

I contend that most investors know what they are getting from their insurance policies. At OPIC, we see every kind of purchaser of political risk insurance—from large, sophisticated firms that hire major law firms to scrutinize every word of an insurance policy, to small investors who buy insurance from OPIC for the intangible value of having the U.S. government back their project. The latter are less concerned with the fine print and trust that OPIC, as a part of the U.S. government, will help them out of difficult situations and pay claims, if it comes to that. In both cases, I believe that the buyers of PRI know what they are getting, although they can only appreciate the value of the coverage at the time, with little knowledge of what might happen to their investment in the future. None of us can anticipate how, and in what form, political risk events will occur.

Insurers place political risk in clear, distinct categories (expropriation, inconvertibility, and political violence). But events are likely to happen outside these categories or, most importantly, in a way that blurs the distinction. What we think is covered by an insurance policy at one point in time might not look the same, or be so clear, after a few years. It is impossible to imagine all the possible ways that an overseas investment can be affected by political risk, and there can be no certainty that the insurance purchased today, at the time will cover every event of political risk in the future. As Mac Johnston points out, when we insurers began to cover infrastructure projects, we could not have imagined all the pressures that a sovereign might face in connection with these projects. We did not think enough about the possibility that these projects could be cancelled by decree, or that project agreements could be completely repudiated by a sovereign.

If we try too hard, however, to anticipate risks and draft wordings accordingly, we might end up in a worse situation—for example, if something else were to happen, our policies may not be flexible enough to respond to the situation at hand. I am not suggesting that we stop tailoring our coverage to specific investment structures, or that underwriters should look the other way, but I caution against trying to cover *all* bases upfront and ending up with a product that is overworked and difficult to apply to changing circumstances and conditions. Sometimes, simpler, somewhat vague language may be better.

One example is how OPIC covers "Creeping Expropriation"; that is, a series of actions taken by the host government that, in aggregate, have the effect of a total expropriation. OPIC's standard Expropriation wording, which Charles Berry correctly points out is the foundation of many wordings in today's market, is easier to apply to traditional expropriation, such as outright nationalization or confiscation. Creeping expropriation is more common nowadays, and much more complicated. For example, in the case of creeping expropriation, it must be determined *when* has the expropriation occurred. When does the waiting period begin and end? When does creeping expropriation become total expropriation? Although our policies may be vague with respect to creeping expropriation, if we try to be more specific in the wording, we could end up with language that no one understands and that does not address the situation we are trying to protect against.

Public and Private Insurer Relationship

The public market has taken the lead in product innovation and development, a legitimate role for public insurers. OPIC has certainly led in this area, benefiting both investors and private insurers. OPIC has also adopted a more flexible approach to working with the private market, including a willingness to coinsure and provide reinsurance to the private market, particularly when capacity is not available, or insufficient, for projects that are highly developmental or important to the interests of the United States. In our view, these changes, including OPIC's recent focus on additionality, can only benefit investors because, ultimately, we provide a better product to our clients, and more choice in the marketplace. OPIC and other public insurers are extremely valuable in mitigating market fluctuations and providing stability to the market, because public insurers are not subject to the cycles of the insurance market and their capacity is unaffected by developments in the reinsurance market.

Breach of Contract Issues

Charles Berry's discussion of some of the issues surrounding breach of contract and expropriation is excellent and thought-provoking. The MidAmerican Indonesian claim, paid by OPIC in 2001, is an example of close cooperation between public and private insurers resulting in quick settlement for all parties involved. This claim is also a clear example of how OPIC's coverage works in difficult situations. Although OPIC's advocacy was not successful in deterring the claim, the Corporation paid its largest Expropriation claim in record time, despite the complexity of the case.

Whether breach of contract should be offered separately from expropriation depends partly on the particular constraints under which each insurer operates. In OPIC's case, breach of contract must be defined as expropriation, given that its statutory authority for insurance is limited to expropriation (as well as inconvertibility and political violence). This means that any Breach of Contract coverage offered by OPIC as an insurance product is intended to cover only political risks. Admittedly, this is an increasingly difficult distinction to make when dealing with governmental entities or parastatals. Private insurers, on the other hand, are more flexible and can offer hybrid coverages that include commercial and political risks. They can provide many of the coverages described by Charles Berry as Political Force Majeure. Whether they want to do that is, of course, another question.

The Role of Brokers and Investors

In the end, it is the brokers and investors who force change in the PRI market. You will not get everything you ask for, but you should try. Our clients have pushed us to innovate, and to improve and make our coverage more relevant and responsive to current conditions. Many of the risks that Charles Berry describes as political force majeure can be negotiated and included as part of a PRI package. I think it is important for investors and brokers to understand the institutions they are dealing with, and in particular, the constraints under which they operate. This makes the negotiations more effective, and makes it easier to come to closure on important issues.

State of the Market

We are witnessing a hardening of the market. This will continue as long as Argentina remains unstable, and as long as we experience the aftermath of September 11, the impact of the U.S. war on terrorism, and the effects of the war with Iraq. There is still plenty of capacity available, but we are starting to see tenors shortening and insurers becoming more selective and conservative. Although I indicated earlier that investors and brokers must force change, and negotiate for better wordings, this market makes it difficult to do that. We will see insurers becoming more conservative and more reluctant to take on new risks, or to broaden their coverages. This is where public insurers, such as OPIC, can fill the gaps by providing additional capacity, longer tenors, and an appetite for risks that the private market might not be willing to underwrite.

Appendix I

Biographies of Authors

JAMES D. ALFORD

James ("Jim") Alford is a Vice President of Citibank, and Senior Risk Manager in Citigroup's Corporate Insurance & Risk Management Division. He is responsible for all business-specific and transaction-oriented insurance programs, including political and credit risk. Jim joined Citibank as a Vice President in 1986, and has held varying roles of responsibility for Citigroup's worldwide insurance programs during his 16-year tenure with the bank. Prior to joining Citibank, he was Director of Risk Management for Moore McCormack Resources, Inc., and Assistant Treasurer for their shipping group. Jim started his career as an auditor and financial consultant with Price Waterhouse in New York. He holds a B.A. in economics from SUNY College at Plattsburgh, an M.B.A. from Duke University, and earned his C.P.A. designation in 1976.

DAVID BAILEY

David Bailey is Vice President at Sovereign Risk Insurance Ltd. in Bermuda; he recently joined Sovereign from his previous role as Chief Underwriter, Political Risk Insurance at EDC in Canada. Mr. Bailey has over 18 years of experience in the PRI industry. He has led and directed the structuring and underwriting of PRI solutions for a number of high profile projects across industry sectors—in addition to product development and portfolio management responsibilities. As Chairman of the Investment Insurance Committee of the Berne Union—a worldwide association of credit and investment insurers—he is among those at the forefront of the issues facing the PRI industry today.

CHARLES BERRY

Charles Berry has worked as a London-based specialist insurance broker since 1974. He trained at Hogg Robinson, where he was involved in the early development of the political risk insurance market at Lloyd's. He became a founding director of Berry Palmer & Lyle Limited (BPL) in 1983, where he served as Managing Director before becoming Chairman in 1996. Charles Berry was educated at Oxford and Harvard, and is a Fellow of the Chartered Insurance Institute.

VIVIAN BROWN

Vivian Brown has worked on industrial and trade issues since joining the Civil Service in 1970. Most of his career has been spent in the Department of Trade and Industry (DTI). He has had two periods of secondment outside: as Head of the Commercial Department in the British Embassy in Jeddah from 1975 to 1979, and as Head of the Science and Technology Assessment Office in the Cabinet Office from 1986 to 1989. He was a non-Executive Director of the Rank Organisation's Industrial Division from 1980 to 1986.

Since returning to DTI in 1989, Mr Brown headed the Department's Competition Policy: Investigations, Deregulation, and Small Firms and Business Links Divisions. He became Chief Executive of Export Credits Guarantee Department (ECGD) following an open competition in November, 1997. He was elected President of the Berne Union in September 2001.

He has a BA and BPhil from Oxford University in Oriental Studies, specializing in Arabic.

BRIAN DUPERREAULT

Brian Duperreault joined ACE in October, 1994, with a mandate to establish the company as a premier global insurance organization.

Following a clearly articulated strategy of growth by acquisition and diversification, Mr. Duperreault has overseen the emergence of the ACE Group of Companies as one of a handful of global property casualty insurers and reinsurers. Acquisitions completed during his tenure include that of ACE Tempest Reinsurance Company Limited and Lloyd's managing agencies

Methuen and Ockham (1996); Westchester Specialty Group, CAT Limited and Tarquin plc (all in 1998), and CIGNA P&C and Capital Re Corporation in 1999.

Through such transactions, Mr. Duperreault has led the transformation of ACE from a catastrophic insurer writing a few lines of business to the global P&C enterprise with unparalleled geographic and product diversity that it is today.

Prior to joining ACE, Mr. Duperreault was the Executive Vice President of Foreign General Insurance of American International Group, Inc. (AIG), and concurrently, Chairman and Chief Executive Officer of American International Underwriters (AIU). He joined AIG in 1973 and gained international experience through a variety of senior management positions in both the United States and Japan.

Mr. Duperreault, a Bermudian, holds a Bachelor of Science degree in Mathematics from Saint Joseph's University in Philadelphia, Pennsylvania and is a member of The American Academy of Actuaries. He continues to be affiliated with Saint Joseph's University as a member of the Board of Trustees. In addition, Mr. Duperreault is a member of The School of Risk Management, Insurance and Actuarial Science (SRM) of the Peter J. Tobin College of Business, of St. John's University's Board of Trustees, and Director of the Bermudian-based Bank of Butterfield.

KENNETH W. HANSEN

Ken Hansen, former General Counsel of the Export-Import Bank of the United States, is a partner in Chadbourne & Parke's Washington office. Prior to joining the Export-Import Bank, Mr. Hansen was with the Washington office of Baker & Botts. Prior to that, he spent nine years with the Overseas Private Investment Corporation, (OPIC) where, among other positions, he was Associate General Counsel for Investment, OPIC's chief counsel for the investment funds program and for legal aspects of investment policy generally.

Mr. Hansen represents project developers, lenders—including bilateral and multilateral agencies as well as commercial lenders—and political risk insurers in structuring and implementing international project financings, privatizations, regional venture capital funds, work-outs and settlement of investment disputes, including political risk insurance claims. His sectoral experience includes power, oil and gas, pulp and paper, industrial, commercial, agricultural, tourism, and banking projects.

Mr. Hansen is a 1974 graduate of Harvard College and a 1983 graduate of the University of Pennsylvania Law School. He also holds
masters degrees in international relations from Yale University and
in public administration from Harvard's John F. Kennedy School of
Government. Mr. Hansen is admitted to the Massachusetts bar.

Mr. Hansen currently teaches "International Project Finance" at
the Georgetown University Law Center and "International Investment Law" at the Johns Hopkins University School of Advanced
International Studies. He has also taught law, economics, and
finance at a number of institutions, including Wellesley College,
Harvard University, Bryn Mawr College, and Haverford College,
and various courses in international law and finance at the Fletcher
School of Law and Diplomacy at Tufts University, George Washington University National Law Center, Boston University Law
School, and Georgetown University Law Center.

WITOLD J. HENISZ

Witold J. Henisz is an Assistant Professor of Management at the
Wharton School. He received his Ph.D. in Business and Public Policy from the Haas School of Business at University of California,
Berkeley and previously received a M.A. in International Relations
from the Johns Hopkins School of Advanced International Studies.
His research examines the impact of political hazards on international investment strategy, with a focus on the magnitude of the
technology employed in, and the market entry mode chosen for, foreign direct investments. He considers how these strategic choices
as well as other non-market lobbying or influence strategies affect
the probability that the government will seek to redistribute
investor returns to the broader polity, and the success of individual
firms in withstanding such pressure. He currently focuses on such
politically salient and capital-intensive sectors as telecommunica-
tion services, electric power generation, and semiconductor fabri-
cation. His research has been published in such scholarly journals
as *Academy of Management Journal*, *Administrative Science Quarterly*,
Business and Politics, *Economics and Politics*, *Industrial and Corporate
Change*, *Journal of Economics & Management Strategy*, and *Journal of
Law, Economics and Organization*. He has served as a consultant for
the World Bank and The Inter-American Development Bank and
previously worked for The International Monetary Fund. He is currently a principal in the political risk management consultancy
PRIMA LLC.

MOTOMICHI IKAWA

Motomichi Ikawa, a Japanese national, joined MIGA as Executive Vice President in January 1999.

Mr. Ikawa has had a distinguished career in the field of finance, economics, and private investment, including positions at the OECD in Paris and as the Director of the Budget, Personnel, and Management Systems Department at the Asian Development Bank. He has also served with the Japanese government as Assistant Vice Minister for Finance for International Affairs and Director of the Development Policy Division (1992–1993), and as Director of the Coordination Division of the International Finance Bureau (1993–1994). Between 1994 and 1996, Mr. Ikawa was Managing Director of the Coordination Department of the Overseas Economic Cooperation Fund (OECF). During this time he published *The Role of the OECF Toward 2010: The Medium-Term Prospects for OECF Operations.*

His most recent position, prior to joining the World Bank Group, was Senior Deputy Director-General of the International Finance Bureau of the Ministry of Finance in Japan, where he served as the G7's Deputy's Deputy and Financial Sous-Sherpa and was responsible for multilateral and bilateral development finance.

Mr. Ikawa attained his B.A. in economics from the University of Tokyo and was a Ph.D. candidate at the University of California at Berkeley.

DAVID JAMES

David James is the senior underwriter for Political Risks at Ascot Underwriting. Ascot was formed on November 1, 2001 as a new Lloyd's Managing Agency. The Agency is led by Martin Reith, a leading Lloyd's Underwriter, who underwrote the first MIGA "CUP" in 1996.

The Ascot vision is to create the premier underwriting agency in Lloyd's. American International Group Inc. (AIG) provides the underwriting capital for Ascot's Syndicate 1414.

David has underwritten the Political Risks account since commencing his underwriting experience with XL Brockbank in 1995. Prior to this, he practiced as a solicitor with Clifford Chance London, specializing in political risk insurance claims and policy drafting, banking, and asset finance.

David has worked extensively with MIGA since the start of the "CUP" program. With the changing focus of investors, he is currently underwriting a large political violence program in North America and Europe.

FELTON (MAC) JOHNSTON

Mac Johnston is a consultant specializing in political risk insurance and guaranties. His consulting practice primarily involves advising private and public sector political risk insurers regarding underwriting, management, pricing, product development, and staff training. He also advises investors and governments regarding the assessment and management of risks associated with private investment in emerging markets.

He was for many years Vice President for Insurance at the Overseas Private Investment Corporation, (OPIC), and his career includes experience in international banking, project finance, and military intelligence. Mac Johnston is a graduate of Harvard Business School, The Fletcher School of Law and Diplomacy, and Colgate University.

JULIE A. MARTIN

Julie Martin is a Senior Vice President of Marsh Inc. and a member of the Political Risk group. She is responsible for development and management of the political risk business in the mid-Atlantic and southeast and is based in Washington, D.C.

Julie joined Marsh after 20 years of experience in the political risk business at the Overseas Private Investment Corporation, (OPIC), the U.S. Government agency charged with promoting U.S. investment in emerging markets. Serving in a variety of positions, including as Chief Underwriter and Vice President, she worked with a wide range of clients in most emerging markets and established relationships with private and public counterparts. She was elected Chairman of the Technical Panel of the Berne Union (the international organization of the export credit agencies and investment insurers). Julie was responsible for many of the initiatives by OPIC in the political risk area, including developing the programs for institutional lenders and the capital markets.

Julie has worked extensively on designing political risk programs for manufacturing, mining, power, financial services, and other companies in most emerging markets.

She has spoken at numerous seminars and conferences on political risk and OPIC programs. Julie has an MBA in Finance from

George Washington University, a Masters of Science in Foreign Service from Georgetown University and a Bachelor's degree in International Relations from Texas Tech University.

KEITH MARTIN

Mr. Martin is the Advisor to MIGA's Executive Vice President, a position he has held since July 2002, advising on all policy and operational matters. He was previously the Senior Policy Officer at MIGA, having joined the agency in March 2000. From 1998 to 2000, Mr. Martin worked in the Insurance Department of OPIC both as an underwriter and advisor to the vice president for Insurance. Before that, he worked for two years at a consulting firm on issues related to the Central Asian nations of the former Soviet Union, primarily on development and conflict prevention issues. In 2003, Mr. Martin also taught a course at Georgetown University, with Gerald West, on political risk analysis and management.

Mr. Martin has an undergraduate degree from the School of Foreign Service, Georgetown University, and a master's degree from McGill University in Montreal; he is pursuing his Ph.D. (ABD) in political science at McGill. He has authored articles on political risk management, politics of states in economic transition, political Islam, and on Central Asian affairs.

THEODORE H. MORAN

Theodore H. Moran holds the Marcus Wallenberg Chair at the School of Foreign Service, Georgetown University, where he teaches and conducts research at the intersection of international economics, business, foreign affairs, and public policy. Dr. Moran is founder and serves as Director of the Landegger Program in International Business Diplomacy, which provides courses on international business-government relations and negotiations to some 600 undergraduate and graduate students each year. He also serves on the Executive Council of the McDonough School of Business at Georgetown. His most recent books include *Beyond Sweatshops: Foreign Direct Investment, Globalization, and Developing Countries* (Brookings, 2002); *Foreign Investment and Development* (Institute for International Economics, 1998); *Managing International Political Risk: New Tools, Strategies, and Techniques* (Blackwell, under the auspices of the World Bank Group, 1998). In 1993–94, Dr. Moran served as Senior Advisor for Economics on the Policy Planning Staff of the Department of

State, where he had responsibility for trade, finance, technology, energy, and environmental issues. He returned to Georgetown after the NAFTA and Uruguay Round negotiations.

Dr. Moran is consultant to the United Nations, to diverse governments in Asia and Latin America, and to the international business and financial communities. In 2002 Dr. Moran was named Chairman of the Committee on Monitoring International Labor Standards of the National Academy of Sciences. Professor Moran received his PhD from Harvard in 1971.

ANNE H. PREDIERI

Ms. Predieri joined Banc of America Securities LLC in September 1994 to establish an International Structured Finance office in Washington, D.C. She is currently responsible for arranging political risk insurance and government agency financing for Banc of America Securities' global corporate and investment banking transactions. Ms. Predieri brings ten years experience with the Overseas Private Investment Corporation (OPIC). At OPIC, she worked in all areas of Project Finance activities, managed the Investment Missions program, and served as Deputy Treasurer with broad corporate financial management responsibilities, including the corporation's worldwide loan workout portfolio, Finance and Insurance portfolio management and loan/contract administration, strategic planning and credit review functions. Ms. Predieri has worked with officers at all levels of the multilateral development banks and agencies in Washington, D.C. on structuring international finance transactions and arranging risk mitigation. She also has extensive contacts in the private political risk insurance market and works well with European agencies. Ms. Predieri has a B.A. with honors from Williams College and an M.A. with distinction in International Economics from The Johns Hopkins University School of Advanced International Studies.

EDITH P. QUINTRELL

Ms. Quintrell is the Manager of Technical Operations in the Insurance Department at the Overseas Private Investment Corporation (OPIC). OPIC, an independent agency of the United States Government, provides political risk insurance, financing, and investor services to U.S. firms investing overseas. Ms. Quintrell is responsible for new product development, underwriting policies and procedures, relationships with the private insurance market, pricing and product enhancements. She serves as Vice Chairman of the Berne Union Investment Insurance Committee. She has been with OPIC since 1991.

Prior to joining OPIC, Ms. Quintrell worked at the Pan American Development Foundation, a nongovernmental organization in Washington, D.C., as the Assistant Director for Public Relations. She holds a B.A. in Political Science and Latin American Studies from Princeton University and an M.A. in International Affairs from the Johns Hopkins School of Advanced International Studies. Ms. Quintrell was a Fulbright Scholar at the Universidad de los Andes in Bogota, Colombia from 1985–86.

DANIEL W. RIORDAN

Daniel W. Riordan joined Zurich in June 1997, to establish and manage Zurich Emerging Markets Solutions, a global political risk insurance group in Washington, D.C. Zurich Emerging Markets Solutions delivers world class political risk solutions to leading international investors and financial institutions who operate in emerging markets.

Zurich Emerging Markets Solutions has rapidly established itself as a leading underwriter in the political risk insurance market. The political risk group's success is based on its staff of experienced professionals, flexible and creative solutions, and responsive service to its customers.

Mr. Riordan was Vice President for Insurance of the Overseas Private Investment Corporation (OPIC), June 1994 to May 1997. He managed OPIC's political risk insurance operations generating $200 million in premiums for investment coverage in 75 countries. Mr. Riordan also served as OPIC's senior inter-agency policy advisor, and as a member of OPIC's senior management committee, which considers large financing and insurance proposals. He served in several other management positions at OPIC, including underwriter, marketing director, chief information officer, and deputy vice president. Mr. Riordan began his career at OPIC in 1982 as an unpaid intern while pursuing his graduate education.

Mr. Riordan is a graduate of the State University of New York College at Oswego and holds a Master of Arts in International Development from the School of International Service at The American University.

JOHN J. SALINGER

John J. Salinger is President of AIG Global Trade & Political Risk Insurance Co., a wholly owned subsidiary of American International Group. AIG Global is the leading private sector underwriter of political risk, domestic and export credit insurance in the world.

Mr. Salinger is a Director of several AIG joint ventures, including Uzbekinvest International Insurance Co., Ltd. (a London based political risk insurer that is a partnership with the Government of Uzbekistan) and the Latin American Investment Guarantee Co. (a Bermuda based political risk insurer that is owned by AIG and the Andean Development Fund). He has served on the Advisory Committees of U.S. Eximbank and U.S. OPIC.

He joined AIG in 1985 after twelve years with The Chase Manhattan Bank where he had international assignments in New York, London, Hong Kong, and Nigeria. At Chase he was the U.S. Trade Finance Division Executive.

Mr. Salinger was educated at Brown University, and holds a Masters in International Relations from the University of Pennsylvania. He served as a Peace Corps volunteer in Morocco and Senegal.

GERALD T. WEST

Gerald West is Director of the Policy and Environment Unit at MIGA. Prior to joining MIGA in 1991, he served in a variety of positions at the Overseas Private Investment Corporation, including 10 years as Vice President for Development.

Mr. West received his Ph.D. in international politics from the Wharton School of the University of Pennsylvania. For nine years, he was affiliated with the Foreign Policy Research Institute in Philadelphia and the Wharton School, where he conducted research on a wide range of international political and economic topics.

From 1983-1995 and again in 2003, Mr. West served as an Adjunct Professor of International Business Diplomacy at Georgetown University, where he taught a graduate level course on International Political Risk Assessment and Management. Over the last 25 years, he has lectured at many universities and has consulted and published widely on corporate political risk assessment and management.

BENNET A. ZELNER

Bennet A. Zelner is an Assistant Professor of Strategy and Policy at Georgetown University's McDonough School of Business. He received his Ph.D. from the Haas School of Business at the University of California at Berkeley, where he studied in the Business and Public Policy Group, and also received his M.S. in Economics from the University of California at Berkeley. He studies topics at the intersection of business and government, especially how differences in country- and state-level political and regulatory characteristics affect firms' investment levels and the strategies that firms employ to manage political risk. Prod. Zelner's current research focuses mainly on infrastructure industries such as electricity and telecommunications. He has published in scholarly journals such as the *Academy of Management Review*, the *Journal of Economics and Management Strategy*, and *Industrial and Corporate Change*. He has served as a consultant for the World Bank and is currently a principal in the political risk management consultancy PRIMA LLC.

AUDREY ZUCK

Ms. Zuck is an Executive Director of Willis' Structured Financial Solutions team based in London, focusing on production, marketing, and placement of political and comprehensive risk insurance, primarily for North American clients. Ms. Zuck joined Willis in 2003 from Bank of America's Agency Finance & Insurance Group, where she was responsible for structuring and implementing cross-border risk mitigants for emerging market transactions, using specialty risk insurance, multilateral financing and export credit agency solutions.

Prior to Bank of America, Ms. Zuck served from 1994–2000 at Overseas Private Investment Corporation as a Manager in Investment Insurance overseeing Europe and the former Soviet Union. In this capacity Ms. Zuck was responsible for business production, underwriting, and management of a political risk insurance portfolio of over US$2 billion. Ms. Zuck was Poland Desk Officer with the U.S. Department of Commerce from 1991–94 and previously served as Program Coordinator at The John Hopkins University Foreign Policy Institute.

Ms. Zuck received a B.S. in French and German languages (cum laude) from Georgetown University and an M.A. in International Relations from the Johns Hopkins University School of Advanced International Studies. She speaks French and Hungarian.

Political Risk Investment Insurance: The International Market and MIGA

Gerald T. West, Director
Policy and the Environment
Multilateral Investment Guarantee Agency
World Bank Group

I. Introduction

The Multilateral Investment Guarantee Agency (MIGA), a member of the World Bank Group, was created in 1988 to facilitate the flow of foreign direct investment (FDI) into its developing member countries by offering noncommercial (political) risk guarantees to investors and by providing technical assistance to host country agencies. This paper is designed to provide an overview of MIGA's recent activities and to address some issues of public-private partnerships in the international investment insurance marketplace. To put these subjects in a wider perspective, some general observations about recent global economic and political trends will be offered together with a brief description of FDI trends.

An earlier version of this paper was presented to the Conference "Political Risk 2003: Assessing Exposure and Implementing Protection Strategies" sponsored by the Royal Institute of International Affairs, London, UK, June 23, 2003. I would like to acknowledge the assistance of Maiko Miyake, Mark Berryman, and Kristofer Hamel in preparing this paper, and the several anonymous reviewers who critiqued it. This article reflects the views of the author, not those of MIGA or the World Bank Group.

II. The Global Milieu for Investment Insurers

A. International Economic and Political Environment

There are a few encouraging signs that the global economic slow-down of the last several years has bottomed out. Nevertheless, concerns over the pace and sustainability of the recovery remain significant due to a number of factors, including volatility in oil prices and the uncertainty over the future of Iraq, Nigeria, and Venezuela. The recovery is expected to be strongest in the United States, which had a short and moderate recession, although the recovery has not been as strong as expected. Europe's growth pattern has been broadly similar to that of the United States, but much weaker. Japan continues to struggle out of its recession; however, without fundamental reforms, its prospects for sustained growth are weak.

Latin America has had a severe recession, driven mainly by Argentina, which has experienced one of the most severe contractions in recent decades. So far the contagion from the crisis in Argentina has been limited, reflecting the fact that the crisis was well anticipated. Asia has been the best performer over the last year, aside from the United States; Korea has surpassed expected rates of growth. While oil prices will heavily impact growth in the Middle East, the spectre of war which hangs over the region will have an even greater impact. The economic slowdown has also affected African countries, primarily through lower commodity prices and falling external demand. However, the growth of some countries has been sustained due to improved macroeconomic policies, debt relief, and the resources released under the Heavily Indebted Poor Countries Initiative. The political turmoil in several West African countries, may affect the political and economic stability of the whole region if not quickly resolved.

The global economic slowdown of 2002–03 resulted in less interest in overseas investment in general; furthermore, collapsing equity values meant that companies had limited resources available for investment projects. Foreign direct investment into developing countries significantly declined in 2001 and 2002 after a decade of steady growth (see Figure A.1). According to the United Nations Committee on Trade And Development (UNCTAD), global inward FDI fell by 51 percent to $735 billion, and outflows by 55 percent to $621 billion. It is estimated that global investment flows (both outflows and inflows) in 2002 fell by another 30 percent, and the FDI flow for 2003 is projected to remain at the same level.

FIGURE A.1 FDI IN DEVELOPING COUNTRIES
BILLIONS OF U.S. DOLLARS

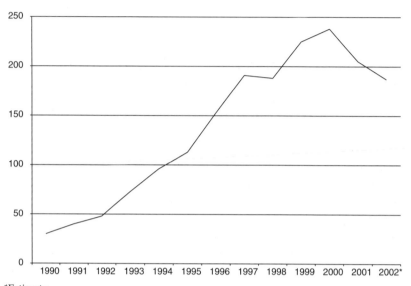

*Estimate
Source: UNCTAD

Compared to the FDI trends in developed countries over the decade, fluctuation of FDI flows to developing countries have been less dramatic. In 2001, FDI into developing countries declined by 14 percent; it is expected that another 20 percent decline will be reported for 2002, and a similar low level will occur in 2003. Behind the recent decline of inward investment there are many factors. In many developing countries, privatization activities have come under increased scrutiny, and efforts to improve the investment climate have slowed. Not only have many emerging market governments paused to reassess the costs and benefits of private investment, but also there is a heightened perception of risk in virtually every sector and region. Faced with crises in the Middle East, political and economic turmoil in parts of South America, and continued terrorist threats in every region, there seems to be no realistic prospect for sustained investor attention to emerging markets on the immediate horizon.

In terms of the sources of investment, it is notable that European investors across the board recorded a huge drop in outward investment in 2001 (data are not yet available for 2002 and 2003). Particularly significant is the case of the United Kingdom, the largest investor in the world in 2000, dropping its investment flows from US$254 million to US$39 million in 2001. Among developing countries, outward investment from Hong Kong recorded a major decrease. This implies an overall decline in investment in the region, as Hong Kong is heavily used as a hub for investment from other countries in the region.

In sum, weak net FDI flows reflect the sluggish global recovery, lingering concerns over profitability of emerging market investments, limited privatization opportunities, and concerns about the noncommercial risks associated with equity investment.

Apart from equity investments, non-bank private lending remains almost 70 percent less than the yearly average during the 1990s, and new commercial bank lending to emerging markets is expected to be completely offset by repayments. Where it exists at all, lender interest in emerging markets is constrained by country limits, and Basel II capital accord requirements may further contribute to commercial banks' reluctance to lend to developing countries in the future. International commercial banks are taking an increasingly active role in local currency lending rather than external financing to address refinancing requirements. Many banks have withdrawn from long-term lending to emerging markets altogether.

B. Investment Insurance Market

During the 1990s, demand for political risk insurance (PRI) burgeoned. Investment insurance for political risks provided by the Berne Union Investment Committee members grew from just over US$3 billion in 1990 to US$17 billion in 2001 (Figure A.2). The rise reflects the significant increase in FDI over the same period as well as the widening membership of the Berne Union (which now includes a number of private insurers). In fact, the growth of private insurers was one of the main characteristics of the market during this period, averaging 20 to 40 percent growth per year. By 1999, private insurers supplied 50 to 60 percent of PRI investment insurance capacity.[1] Qualitatively, in the 1990s there were notable improvements by private insurers, who extended their tenors, improved their coverages, and raised their country limits.

Recently, given the current external environment, the boom cycle has been reversed, and the PRI industry entered a "hard" market phase. The hardening of the general insurance market was coupled with radical reductions in reinsurance capacity; the 2003 reinsurance renewals proved to be the most difficult ever for many insur-

FIGURE A.2 TRENDS OF INVESTMENT INSURANCE ISSUED
BILLIONS OF U.S. DOLLARS

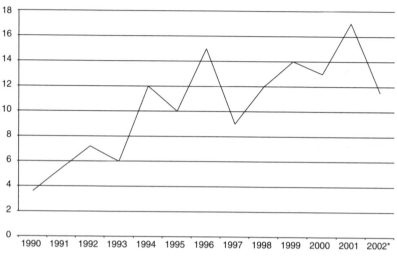

Source: Berne Union.

ers. Legislative and regulatory requirements to maintain liquidity
following September 11 losses have also forced insurers to rebuild
their balance sheets, including liquidating investments at depressed
prices, further impeding increases in capacity. Finally, insurers'
investment portfolio returns have continued to decline dramatically,
dwarfing even the magnitude of their insurance losses.

Due to the substantial decline in global FDI flows, the ratio of
insurance coverage to FDI (investment insurance/FDI to developing countries issued by Berne Union members) actually increased
slightly in 2001 and maintained more or less the same level in 2002
(Figure A.3). Over the last five years, the coverage ratio hovered
around 6 percent, at a much lower level than in the early 1990s.

Recently, there have been severe impacts on the tenors (generally
down to five to seven years or less), capacity (30–50 percent reductions for most carriers), and pricing (10–20 percent increases) of the
private political risk insurers. Moreover, investor perceptions of risk
have changed; for some investors broad economic risk factors are
now of greater concern than standard PRI risks. The result is that
investors are trying to manage political risks in different ways
(including self-insurance) or are looking to avoid political risks altogether. Demand for investment insurance is, therefore, likely to be
affected by market conditions as much as the supply of coverage.

FIGURE A.3 INVESTMENT INSURANCE COVERAGE
FDI/INVESTMENT INSURANCE

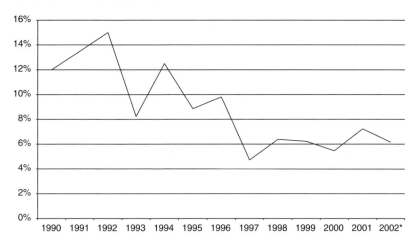

Source: Berne Union and UNCTAD.

Current market uncertainty and the existence of numerous potential claims have led investors to carefully scrutinize the perceived risks
and the true value of their investment insurance coverage. Clarity of
contract wording, specifying exactly what risks are and are not being
transferred, is now a high priority for all parties. Many investors have
concluded that currently uncovered regulatory risks are actually a
greater concern than traditional expropriation risks. Similarly, devaluation or currency depreciation is often a greater concern than transfer
and convertibility risks in a world of floating exchange rates. Investors
are keenly focused on realizing value for their insurance premiums.

The number of countries in which PRI is available reduced considerably in 2002–03. Virtually all underwriters had little or no
capacity in Brazil and were limiting coverage in the Dominican
Republic, Turkey, and Mexico. Some investors were having difficulty obtaining coverage in China and Russia. In early 2003, no one
was aware of anyone offering significant amounts of coverage in
Argentina, in which most PRI insurers already had large exposures.[2]
In terms of sectors, infrastructure, especially power—once favored
by political risk insurers—has fallen into some disfavor as a result
of the number of investment disputes and potential claims in this
industry. At the same time, a slowdown in the global economy has
reduced the demand for energy in many countries; this has caused
many prospective projects to be delayed.

III. Recent MIGA Performance

The challenging external environment in FY02 and FY03 prevented MIGA from matching its record volume of coverage issued in FY01 ($2.1 billion). In FY02, MIGA issued US$1.4 billion in total coverage for 58 contracts in support of 33 new projects and 5 expansion projects of previously supported deals. Collectively, these guarantees facilitated an estimated US$4.7 billion in foreign direct investment into member developing countries. In FY03, MIGA issued US$1.4 billion of total coverage for 59 contracts in support of 36 new projects and three expansions of previously supported deals. The guarantees facilitated an estimated US$3.3 billion in FDI, bringing the cumulative amount of FDI facilitated since the agency's inception to US$49.1 billion and the cumulative number of contracts issued to 656.

MIGA started fiscal year 2003 with a healthy pipeline of projects and achieved good results for the first half of the year, but increased geopolitical uncertainties and anxieties generated by the military intervention in Iraq resulted in lower than expected business for the whole year. This was further exacerbated by the outbreak of SARS in Asia, which had a major impact on economic activity and caused delays in finalizing projects. Increased threats and attacks by terrorists groups also caused delays. In addition, MIGA's guarantee business continued to be impacted by the low levels of activity in the global economy and the loss of investor confidence in Latin America, particularly due to the continued uncertainty in Argentina, Uruguay, and República Bolivariana de Venezuela.

As a development institution, MIGA is committed to supporting projects that will yield economic and social benefits for host developing countries. From this perspective, MIGA has built a strong record in supporting projects that are developmentally effective. In FY02 and FY03, MIGA supported many projects in the world's poorest (IDA) countries, for which private PRI coverage is particularly difficult to obtain. In FY02, MIGA provided coverage for the first time investments in four African countries — Benin, Mauritania, Nigeria, and Senegal. Moreover, in FY03, coverage was extended for the first time for projects in Burundi, Serbia and Montenegro, and Syria. MIGA also extended its efforts to support projects in post-conflict regions, helping small- and medium-sized enterprises (SMEs) and assisting investors from developing countries. (See the annex to this paper on page 206, entitled "Representative MIGA-supported Investments," for a few examples of projects.)

In terms of host country exposure, the largest share of MIGA's outstanding portfolio is in Brazil — with other significant exposures in Argentina and Peru. This position makes Latin America — with 43 percent of MIGA's outstanding portfolio — the region with the largest overall exposure (Figure A.4). Nevertheless, in fiscal year 2003, other regions of the world rose in prominence within the portfolio. The Europe and Central Asia region moved from representing 23 percent to 26 percent. The agency's portfolio in Africa also increased slightly. Despite the fact that Africa has less than 5 percent of the FDI stock of developing countries, MIGA's African portfolio is 19 percent of its total.

In terms of investor country distribution, the United States is home to the largest share of MIGA-supported investors, followed by Austria, the United Kingdom, the Netherlands, and Canada (see Figure A.5). As mandated by its Convention, MIGA tries to support investment flows from developing countries. Over the past decade, MIGA's guarantee program has been involved in 39 "south-south" projects—investments from one developing country to another—providing approximately US$1 billion in total coverage. Beyond the amounts insured by MIGA, these projects have collectively accounted for an estimated US$6 billion in additional FDI. Of the 39 "south-south" projects that the agency has supported, investors have hailed from 17 different developing countries, and have directed their investments into 19 different host countries. A number of developing countries are surfacing

FIGURE A.4 REGIONAL BREAKDOWNS OF MIGA GUARANTEES (JUNE 30, 2003)

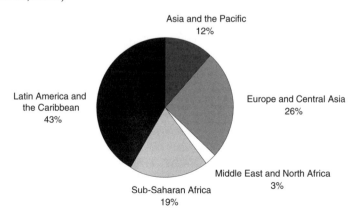

Note: Percentages add up to more than 100 percent because of multi-country agreements.

FIGURE A.5 INVESTOR COUNTRY BREAKDOWNS OF MIGA GUARANTEES (JUNE 30, 2003)

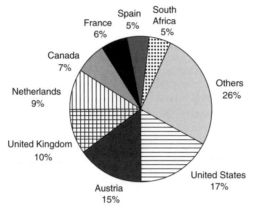

as a significant source of investment, such as South Africa, Mauritius, Turkey, Egypt, Israel, Tunisia, and Singapore.

The sectoral breakdown of MIGA's outstanding portfolio is depicted in Figure A.6. In fiscal year 2003, the infrastructure sector grew to 41 percent of total gross exposure—up 5 percent from the previous year. Since undertaking more business in the infrastructure sector is one of MIGA's strategic priorities, this development reflects the agency's dedication to focus on and achieve its mandated set of priorities. At the same time, the financial sector's share fell from 35 percent in FY02 to 29 percent in FY03, reflecting cancellations in the Latin America and Caribbean region as well as the low level of new investor activity in the sector.

MIGA has maintained an outstanding claims record over its entire history; ownership by more than 160 member countries has contributed significantly to this record. The agency has successfully and quietly resolved more than a dozen investment disputes over the years. It is difficult to discuss these successful resolutions of disputes because of political sensitivities and business confidentiality concerns. However, it can be said that they were not concentrated in any one country or region, but were disproportionately concentrated in infrastructure projects.

In 2002, MIGA helped resolve a two-and-a-half-year-old dispute between the El Paso Corporation and subsovereign entities in the People's Republic of China. The investments were insured in the mid-1990s against the failure of local authorities to adhere to terms of agreements under which power was to be purchased from the

FIGURE A.6 SECTORAL BREAKDOWNS OF MIGA GUARANTEES
(JUNE 30, 2003)

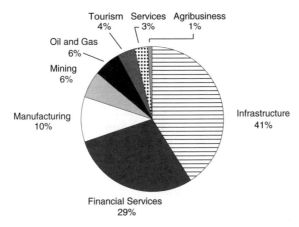

projects. The localities sought to adjust power purchase prices paid to energy producers in the wake of the economic downturn of 1997 in ways that risked violating the agreements previously entered into with El Paso. MIGA brokered a settlement that took into account the interests of both sides in May 2002, and a claim was averted.

IV. Public - Private Collaboration in a Changing Market Place

Out of the growth period of the 1990s, it became clear that public and private insurers could play complementary roles. While private insurers face fewer policy constraints and are able to respond quickly to the market, public agencies can provide coverage for investments in high risk situations, capitalizing on their ability to provide "deterrence" from unwanted government intervention as well as influencing a host government's willingness to resolve claims. Public insurers also provide stability to the entire PRI market by playing a countercyclical role when market conditions become difficult. Since public insurers tend to have a longer-term perspective and more resources to devote to developing products that may not appear to be immediately commercially viable, they have also demonstrated an ability to develop market innovations.

By working together, private and public partnerships allow more risk sharing, provide greater capacity for clients, and supply more coverage by leveraging more private capacity. Partnerships have induced extended tenors, increased capacity, and stretched the private market to specific countries where private insurers would not otherwise enter. In the event of a claim, the partnerships have allowed private insurers to benefit from public insurers' "political" influence on the host governments.

A. MIGA's Partnerships

Over the years, MIGA has expanded its public-private partnerships through a number of arrangements: treaty reinsurance,[3] facultative reinsurance,[4] the Cooperative Underwriting Program (CUP),[5] and coinsurance. All of these arrangements have resulted in increasing insurance capacity for individual projects required by investors, and ultimately to mobilize larger FDI into developing countries. To date, US$2 billion of coverage has been mobilized through facultative reinsurance and treaty reinsurance, and US$550 million of coverage under the CUP. MIGA also may take the role of a reinsurer where the agency will provide reinsurance in so far as the underlying transaction meets the requirements of MIGA's mandate. MIGA has signed 20 MOUs with various insurance partners in the public and private sectors, from both developing and industrialized countries. MIGA has taken a lead in forging collaborative relationships through the training it provides to representatives of investment insurance agencies. MIGA uses training to help promote knowledge sharing and capacity building. The programs include sessions on country risk analysis, contract drafting, and sector-specific underwriting.

MIGA's practices have not gone unnoticed. The Overseas Private Investment Corporation (OPIC) has become more flexible in cooperating with private insurers; it recently reinsured a private insurer, which it would not have previously undertaken. OPIC has also shown a willingness to share its recoveries on a pro-rata basis without fees or charges. The Export Development Corporation (EDC) of Canada has taken a lead role among public agencies in syndicating risk to the private sector, and a number of other public agencies are beginning to obtain treaty reinsurance for the private sector.

In FY02, MIGA's Board of Directors increased its reinsurance limits, from 40 percent to 50 percent of its aggregate gross exposure. The increase will give MIGA greater freedom to utilize reinsurance to better leverage its own capacity. MIGA also concluded new CUP agreements with six insurers. In FY03, MIGA concluded the largest facultative reinsurance to date, supporting a power project in Bulgaria with € 142.5 million of private insurers' capacity. This was a

TABLE 1   COOPERATION WITH PUBLIC AND PRIVATE INSURERS

MIGA has worked with :		
Private	Bilateral	Multilateral
Lloyd's market	OPIC (USA)	IDB
CHUBB	COFACE (France)	
AIG	GIEK (Norway)	
Munich Re	SACE and Simest (Italy)	
Unistrat	NEXI (Japan)	
Sovereign	CESCE (Spain)	
Zurich	ECGD (UK)	
ACE	FMO (the Netherlands)	
XL	EDC (Canada)	
Citi/Gulf	OeKB (Austria)	
Axis	Funnvera (Finland)	
	SEC (Slovenia)	
	IFTRIC (Israel)	
	COTUNACE (Tunisia)	

particularly significant achievement, as it was syndicated at a time when the private market was reducing tenors and project limits. It clearly demonstrated MIGA's countercyclical role and its ability to lead the private market into projects that it would not have supported at all, or only on less favorable terms.

B. The Future

Over the course of 2002–03, the PRI industry's operating environment has significantly changed—moving from a dynamic and flexible marketplace to a harder and more cautious shadow of itself. The implications of this new environment for the future of the industry and, more generally, the international business community are still unfolding. There is little doubt that political risk concerns are now, more than ever, a top priority in the financial and corporate markets. But can investor needs be satisfied in an era of shortened tenors, reduced coverage capacity, and increased premiums? What can developing countries do about the situation when many promising projects are not moving forward due to investor fears. In particular, what can be done to ensure that critical private sector infrastructure projects in the developing world are adequately funded?

The resilience of the PRI market to temporary adversity should not be underestimated. There are now more than three times the number of knowledgeable underwriters, lawyers, and brokers than a decade ago. There are many more successful "coverage models" to follow, modify, or improve upon. There is also an inherent benefit to a market that has a flexibility stemming from having public, multilateral, and private components. Moreover, these PRI insurers are also more willing than ever to work together.

One could argue that a certain "natural selection" phenomenon is operative in the industry. When clients require short-term coverage in small amounts, the private insurance market is usually ready, willing, and able to meet their needs. On the other hand, when coverage amounts are large and the tenor requirements substantially longer, public and multilateral insurers should be able, *ceteris paribus*, to offer coverage. With each party focusing on its respective competitive advantages and specific segments of the market, private and public sector players should be able to successfully rebuild their businesses and reclaim appropriate roles in the new international financial milieu.

Nevertheless, a crude market-based "Darwinian" approach cannot be the *sole* strategic response to the industry's changed operating environment. Myopic "natural selection" thinking ignores the reality that there is today (and will continue to be tomorrow) a need for public-private partnerships in the new political and economic environment—and that such collaboration is more effective than working in isolation. Indeed, the corollary to the "natural selection" phenomenon is the *natural relationship* and *shared interests* that induces industry participants to work together.

First, public-private collaboration—through products like treaty and facultative reinsurance and the CUP mechanism—works to the benefit of all PRI insurers by increasing coverage capacity for projects and sharing risks among a greater number of insurers. Second, as the relevance of traditional coverage is being increasingly questioned by clients, new product development and efforts to enhance existing products are becoming more and more necessary for addressing investor concerns regarding the value of classic investment insurance. Such initiatives demand an increased level of cooperation and coordination between insurers. Finally, there is an increasing body of evidence that suggests that the PRI market has matured and is already beginning to show signs of segmentation. Given this reality, private, public, and multilateral insurers are viewing each other less as adversaries and more as business *allies* or *partners*, each providing a complementary—but distinct—service to the market.

Hence, it is rational to expect that such partnerships and alliances should increase in the future.

MIGA is one of those insurers that is prepared to play a leadership role in the future—by supporting the industry's need to build and maintain collaborative relationships and by ensuring that a range of valuable insurance services will always remain available to international investors and host countries. In its quest to be a reliable and valued partner, MIGA expects to continue to learn from the experiences of its more experienced Berne Union counterparts in managing claim situations and developing new products. The agency intends to actively cooperate on new business efforts with other investment insurers, particularly new and candidate members of the Berne Union who wish to be fully engaged in MIGA's efforts to develop new solutions for problems in this challenging market. The agency is convinced that the current market environment is particularly ripe for leveraging its resources through increased cooperation with players across the whole spectrum of the PRI industry.

Moreover, having just completed the main phase of its General Capital Increase (which effectively doubled its capital base), the agency has a healthy balance sheet to serve the varying needs of a difficult market. MIGA intends to diversify its portfolio by guaranteeing infrastructure, water, sanitation, and reconstruction projects in underdeveloped regions (generally IDA-eligible, post-conflict, and Southern countries). To these ends, the agency continues to examine and develop coverage for investors facing political risks from subsovereign entities. To ensure that international investors continue to take advantage of the industry and market-specific knowledge of local small business operators and entrepreneurs, MIGA is expanding its SME initiatives. MIGA has already begun to streamline its procedures to facilitate the processing of SME investments, to diversify its portfolio, and to enhance the Agency's long-term financial stability.

Furthermore, in the hope of restoring investor confidence in host countries' ability to attract FDI and large-scale capital-intensive projects, MIGA will increasingly make use of two levers of influence to help stabilize the international investment environment. First, the agency will use its technical assistance capabilities to advise and train host-country officers responsible for various informational, financial, and legal tasks. Second, MIGA's Legal and Claims Department will continue to mediate investment disputes on especially contentious matters before they require formal arbitration or before filing a claim.

Finally, cross-leveraging resources between MIGA and other parts of the World Bank Group will play a critical role in MIGA's efforts to promote investment opportunities in countries that have received little FDI due to recent geopolitical events. MIGA has begun discussions to partner with the IFC for the development of composite products, which would include both insurance and financing components, to meet investors' needs by addressing more comprehensive risk mitigation requirements and to optimize risk-sharing wherever practical.

Any forecast of the PRI industry's future is clouded by a shroud of uncertainty. Nevertheless, a review of past and present experiences has shown that — through collaboration and disciplined response — the private, public, and multilateral sectors of the industry can weather many tempests. MIGA is commited to its mission of facilitating investment flows by working *in conjunction* with its counterparts throughout the industry.

Annex: Representative MIGA-supported Investments

Azerbaijan
In FY03, MIGA provided **Fatoglu Gida Sanayi Ve Ticaret Anonim Sirketi** (Fatoglu Food Industry and Trade Corporation) of Turkey with a guarantee for $529,920 to cover its $588,800 equity investment in **Fatoglu Istehsal Azerbaycan Ltd. Sirketi** (Fatoglu Production Azerbaijan Co. Ltd.), for a period of up to five years, against the risks of transfer restriction, expropriation, and war and civil disturbance. The investment is for the expansion and modernization of a flour mill, which produces flour that is distributed and sold in Azerbaijan and Georgia. Following the expansion, it is estimated that the mill's increased production will account for approximately 10 percent of Azerbaijan's flour supply.

Since its inception in 1999, the project has provided a steady source of local employment. It currently employs over 90 nationals and expects to generate more jobs during the next five years while providing onsite technical and managerial training. In addition, the mill's activities indirectly support approximately 150 jobs through transportation and other related sectors. The project also has upstream benefits for local businesses in the packing and domestic and international shipping industries; approximately 15 percent of the goods and services needed by the project are purchased locally.

The project will not only help develop the emerging agricultural sector, it will also diversify the Azeri economy, which is concentrated in the oil and gas industry. Moreover, it will have a net impact of $1.6 million per year in new taxes and duties, while replacing $6.5 million in imports per year. This is expected to create a positive effect of $500,000 on foreign exchange per year. Fatoglu-Azerbaijan meets three of MIGA's priority concerns: it provides support for SMEs, is a South-South investment, and is located in an IDA eligible country.

Brazil

MIGA has provided **Keppel FELS Energy Pte. Ltd.** of Singapore a $130 million guarantee to cover its investment of over $100 million in **Nordeste Generation Ltda.** (Nordeste) of Brazil in FY02. The coverage is for three years and is against the risks of transfer restriction and expropriation, including the failure by the host government to honor its payment obligation under the Host Government Guarantee to the electrical power supply contract issued in favor of Nordeste. Eighty million dollars of this exposure has been syndicated though MIGA's Cooperative Underwriting Program.

Brazil is in the midst of a severe energy crisis, caused by underinvestment in new generation and transmission capacity and made worse by a series of droughts in recent years, due to dependence on hydro-generating facilities. The state of Bahia, in northeastern Brazil, has been among the most affected by the droughts, which caused serious electricity shortages. This project involves the installation, operation, and maintenance of a barge-mounted emergency power generation facility in Bahia, to address the short-term demand until new, permanent gasfired power projects are brought on line and can put their energy contribution into the national grid. In addition to the benefits to residents in northeastern Brazil, the project is expected to generate significant tax revenue during its three years of operation. The project will employ up to 300 local people for construction and an estimated 160 during operation. Training for the employees will be provided by the sponsor.

MIGA issued a $90 million guarantee in FY01 to **MSF Funding LLC (MSF)** in its first coverage of a capital markets issue, and the first internationally rated securitization of Brazilian loan and lease receivables from the financing of medical equipment—marking a milestone for both MIGA and Brazil. The guarantee covers floating-rate notes issued by MSF Funding LLC, whose parent company, **MSF Holding Ltd.**, provides loan and lease financing for the supply of high technology diagnostic imaging and radiation therapy equipment to hospitals, physician groups, and clinics throughout

Latin America. The notes are based on the company's future leasing revenues and secured by U.S. dollar-denominated financing contracts in Brazil. The guarantee will protect MSF's ability to convert funds generated in local currency into U.S. dollars and to transfer them outside the country, as well as guaranteeing the company against expropriation of its Brazilian bank accounts.

The project aims to address the shortage of adequate spending on health care. MSF is using the financing proceeds to originate new loans and leases in Brazil, where specialized medical equipment is in short supply, and much of what exists is obsolete. The equipment being financed includes magnetic resonance imaging, computed tomography imaging scanners, and other medical devices, which will help improve the quality and cost-efficiency of the country's health care services, particularly for cancer patients. The project is expected to have many other developmental benefits, including the training of local medical staff in the equipment's use and an estimated contribution of $10 million a year in taxes to the Brazilian government.

MIGA proved key to improving the risk profile of the notes and helping the investor secure the financing needed, enabling the issue to be rated above Brazil's local and foreign currency ratings. The Class A Notes received an A2 rating from Moody's Investor Services and an A rating from S&P and Fitch IBCA. The Class B Notes were rated Baa2 and BBB respectively, and the Class C Notes received a BB rating. The guarantee was reinsured with eight Lloyd's of London syndicates and with the Netherlands Development Finance Co. (FMO). FMO is also a shareholder in MSF Holding Ltd., together with IFC, and Philadelphia International Equities.

A MIGA–guaranteed project is also working to upgrade electricity services in power-strapped Brazil, providing safe, legal power connections throughout Rio de Janeiro, including in low-income communities. The $23 million guarantee went to a bank syndicate led by **Citibank N.A.**, covering part of a loan to **Light Serviços de Electricidade S.A.** against transfer restriction and expropriation. The project is expected to improve transmission and distribution by establishing and upgrading power networks and installing transformers and meters.

The project calls for the supply of power to 176,000 additional households and 250 industrial customers. In coordination with the local government and NGOs, Light also has a special program (PRONAI) to upgrade conditions in low-income areas, where safety hazards such as electrocution are rife, and to provide essential services at an affordable cost. The recent power crisis has added a new urgency to the program, which in 2000 reached out to about 150,000 new low-income clients. By 2005, Light expects to be present in 728 slums and 594 low-income communities. For slum residents, the program provides a steady, safe source of power and helps document proof of residence, necessary for getting a telephone and establishing credit. Through the program, Light also works to increase both the quality and quantity of educational programs at the local level, through scholarships, training activities, and the donation of computers and hardware to local schools.

Bulgaria

MIGA recently provided **Bank Austria Creditanstalt AG** with a E23.8 million guarantee for its E25 million shareholder loan to **HVB Bank Bulgaria EAD**. The loan will allow HVB Bulgaria to further expand the financing it provides to Bulgarian companies. MIGA's coverage is for a period of up to eight years and provides protection against the risk of transfer restriction.

The project is consistent with Bulgaria's broader development strategy, supported by the World Bank Group, which focuses on the promotion of competitive private sector–led growth. MIGA's support will help HVB Bulgaria provide additional medium-term financing to businesses, especially small and medium-size enterprises (SMEs). The increased availability of funds with longer tenors is expected to have a positive impact on the financial sector as well and should generate competitive loan pricing and terms for Bulgarian companies in addition to improving SMEs' access to financing.

At year end, HVB Bulgaria will merge with Biochim, Bulgaria's fourth largest bank, which was acquired by Bank Austria Creditanstalt in October 2002. As a subsidiary of the leading Austrian bank, the bank expects to play a leading role in the ongoing process of privatization in Bulgaria, providing know-how, technical solutions, and new products to the market.

In FY02, MIGA provided **AES Horizons, Ltd.**, of the United Kingdom, with a guarantee for $20 million to cover part of a $223 million equity investment in the **Maritza East 1** power project in Bulgaria. The coverage is against expropriation and breach of contract risk, and extends for fifteen years.

The project, MIGA's first in Bulgaria's energy sector, involves the construction of a new 670 MW thermal facility near the country's largest lignite mines, some 250 km southeast of Sofia. This plant is part of Bulgaria's strategy to replace life-expired Soviet-built power plants. The project is one of the first under a new national strategy to make electricity supply more efficient and cost effective by using inexpensive indigenous fuel. The strategy entails not only the break-up of the state's electricity monopoly, but also the gradual replacement of old, costly, and environmentally unsafe plants. The investment follows an international tender carried out in 1998 for a 15-year contract to build-own-operate (BOO) the plant with power sold to the state-owned electricity company. The construction period is expected to be three years.

The project is expected to supply 6 percent of Bulgaria's energy needs by 2007 and to be one of the lowest cost producers in the country—and probably the lowest cost new capacity option. The plant will also be the cleanest coal-fired plant in Bulgaria and will be among the cleanest in Europe. The plant will employ up to 2,500 people during construction and up to 200 during operation. Training will be an integral part of the project. More than $150 million is expected to be spent locally on the procurement of goods.

Ecuador
MIGA achieved several firsts in FY01 with the signing of an $18 million guarantee for the rehabilitation and expansion of water services in Guayaquil, Ecuador. The project represents MIGA's first coverage of a water project and of a performance bond. The guarantee offers protection against the risks of expropriation and war and civil disturbance for an investment by **International Water Services B.V.** of the Netherlands in an Ecuadorian subsidiary. It also covers a performance bond—posted in accordance with the 30-year concession—that guarantees the company's successful management, expansion, and operation of the water services against the risk of wrongful call.

The investment aims to improve the services and operating performance of the existing municipal water utility, especially to poor areas that have little access to potable water and poor sanitary conditions, by reducing the amount of water that is unaccounted for and increasing cash collection. During the first five years of the concession, improvements must be made in the quality of water services, as well as in the number of potable water and sewage connections. Service coverage is expected to increase by 30 to 40 percent. The new project is expected to help improve health and living conditions for the local population, while reducing the cost of water for those who currently rely on other sources of water.

Kenya

In FY02, MIGA has provided **Ormat Holding Corp.** of the Cayman Islands, a wholly owned subsidiary of **Ormat Industries Ltd.** of Israel, with a $70 million guarantee to cover its equity investment and shareholder loan totaling $171 million, in **OrPower 4 Inc.** in Kenya, as well as future loans to the project. The coverage is against the risks of transfer restriction, expropriation, war and civil disturbance, and breach of contract, and is for a period of 14 years. Additionally, MIGA increased coverage on Phase 1 of the plant, insured by MIGA in fiscal year 2000, by $11.5 million.

OrPower 4 Inc. is involved in the design, construction and operation of a 48 MW geothermal power plant, located in the Olkaria geothermal fields, in Kenya's Rift Valley, some 50 kilometers north-west of Nairobi. Geothermal power is a clean, renewable, and low-cost source of energy, and Ormat will bring to the project its experience in this area, as well as state-of-the-art geothermal technology. The plant will add to the capacity already provided by a 12 MW plant built during Phase 1, which MIGA insured in fiscal 2000, and will help alleviate the problem of severe power shortages from which the country suffers. In a country where only about 10 percent of the population has access to electricity, the project will provide power to many first-time users. OrPower 4 will also help reduce Kenya's heavy dependence on hydroelectric power. With some 70 percent of the 1,000 MW installed capacity being hydroelectric, Kenya's national power production was severely curtailed during the three-year drought that ended in 2001. The project will play an important role in achieving greater reliability, security, and stability of power within the national grid, and will reduce the dependence on imported thermal energy, thereby having a positive impact on the balance of payments.

Situated in a rural area with high unemployment and under-employment, the project is expected to employ 44 people for operations and up to 700 full- and part-time workers during the construction. There will be a significant transfer of skills and technology. Training programs will be set up, and will include optimization of operations, plant maintenance, geothermal technique, security, business, and administration. Approximately 80 percent of goods and services will be procured locally. In addition to royalties, the project will pay approximately $27 million in taxes to the government over its lifetime.

Mali

MIGA issued $16.2 million of guarantee coverage to **Société Nationale de Télécommunications du Sénégal** (Sonatel), a Senegalese company, for its $18 million equity investment in **Ikatel SA** of Mali. The 15-year coverage provides protection against the risks of expropriation, war and civil disturbance, and breach of contract. MIGA is also providing $23.4 million of coverage for an eight-month bridge loan of $26 million.

Mali is one of the world's poorest countries, ranked 153 out of 162 countries in the 2001 Human Development Index. A landlocked country, more than half of which is desert, Mali has limited natural resources and tends to rely on two volatile commodities, cotton and gold, for export income. The country's low rate of teledensity has adversely affected economic growth.

The project will help provide various telecommunications services, including fixed lines, wireless, Internet, and satellite communication services, as well as public pay phones. It will also establish the country's first fully digital GSM cellular network, which is expected to improve the quality and efficiency of mobile phones. Ikatel aims to reach 250,000 subscribers through the project over the next nine years. The undertaking is consonant with Mali's development goals, as well as the World Bank Group's Country Assistance Strategy, which advocates increased private sector participation in key sectors, such as telecommunications.

The project represents one of the largest foreign investments in Mali and is expected to offer many development benefits. It will spur the growth of several industries, including small businesses and microenterprises, many of which will provide phone services to those who cannot afford a phone. Consumers will benefit from the diversity of service offerings and lower costs. The project will also generate government revenues in the form of taxes and fees, including a $44 million license fee, which has already been paid. Ikatel plans to directly employ some 200 local staff and should indirectly generate thousands of additional jobs. Other benefits include staff training and a program that involves building affordable housing for employees. The project will also provide new technology to schools, in addition to contributing to local charities and sponsoring regional cultural and sports events.

Mozambique
MIGA has provided the **Sasol Limited Group of South Africa** (Sasol) with guarantees for $27 million to cover $30 million of its investment in **Sasol Petroleum Temane Limitada** (SPT), Mozambique and $45 million to cover $50 million of its investment in the Mozambican branch of the **Republic of Mozambique Pipeline**

Investment Company (Pty) Ltd (ROMPCO), South Africa. Both SPT and ROMPCO will initially be wholly owned subsidiaries of Sasol. The guarantees are for a period of up to 15 years against the risks of: transfer restriction, expropriation, war and civil disturbance, and breach of contract. MIGA's participation was a necessary component for the completion of the deal.

The project involves the development of the Temane and Pande gas fields, the construction of a central processing facility to clean and compress the gas, and the construction of a 865 km cross-border gas pipeline from Temane in Mozambique to Secunda in South Africa. Sasol will also be converting an existing petrochemical plant in South Africa from coal as feedstock to gas.

The project will contribute to developing the Mozambican economy through monetizing its gas reserves—the country will receive significant royalty payments as well as dividends, production bonuses, and corporate taxes in excess of $2 billion over the 25- year lifetime of the project.

Environmentally, the project will contribute to the reduction of harmful emissions by replacing sulphur-rich coal and heavy oils with clean burning natural gas. The project will provide contracting opportunities for both Mozambican and South African companies during the construction phase. The upstream benefits for local enterprises are estimated to be in excess of $1 million per year. The project is expected to create more than 720 job opportunities for local employees during construction. After completion, it is estimated that the CPF and the pipeline will require staff of 25 and 85, respectively. The project will be a substantial addition to Mozambique's infrastructure through the development of roads, water supplies, and the removal of land mines. The Sasol project meets two of MIGA's priority concerns: it is a South-South investment and in an IDA-eligible country. Furthermore, it represents the first cross-border initiative in Sub-Saharan Africa in developing regional natural gas markets.

In FY02, MIGA provided guarantees to **Portus Indico-Sociedade de Serviços Portuarios S.A.** (formerly **DEAIR—Comercio Internacional, Consultoria e Serviços, S.A.**) of Portugal: $459,000 to cover its $510,000 equity investment in, and $6.1 million to cover $6.8 million of shareholder loans, plus interest, to the **Maputo Port Development Company S.A.R.L.** The guarantees are for fifteen years, and are against the risks of transfer restriction, expropriation, and war and civil disturbance.

The project involves the rehabilitation, development, financing, and operation of the Maputo Port under a build-operate-transfer

(BOT) scheme. At its peak, the port's revenues represented 80 percent of Mozambique's balance of trade. Civil war and a general economic decline left the port handling only 2.5 to 3 million tons per annum (tpa), compared to the 12.5 million tpa handled in the late 1960s. By awarding the concession to the private sector in 1997, the government sought to restore port operations to full capacity, lower the cost of port tariffs through improved operating efficiencies, and boost the economy through improved export outlets for the country's traditional products. Given its location, in proximity to three main railway connections, the port provides a very efficient and low-cost outlet for trade not only for Mozambique, but also Zimbabwe, Malawi, Botswana, Swaziland, Zambia, and northern South Africa. These areas are either currently not served, or served through higher cost alternatives in South Africa, which are already operating at capacity.

The port and connecting railway upgrades are expected to raise gross revenues from the current $80 million to $150 million in the short term, indicating a significant increase in traffic volumes. At the same time, direct operating cost will be reduced substantially and translated into lower tariffs for exporters, including operators in neighboring countries. During the three-year construction period, the port will create about 800 additional jobs, all with local contractors. The project will provide its workers with training on new equipment and procedures. The project owners have also pledged to invest $250,000 annually in local community projects during the construction period and $1 million, cumulatively, thereafter. Targeted projects include the creation of new schools in the area, donations to local clinics, and upkeep of local road infrastructure. The project is also expected to contribute $8.8 million in taxes per year to Mozambique, an IDA-eligible country still recovering from the long civil war and recent devastating floods.

Nicaragua
In FY02, MIGA provided **Unión Fenosa Internacional S.A.** (UFI) of Spain with a guarantee for $81.2 million to cover a $90.2 million equity investment in **Empresa Distribuidora de Electricidad del Norte, S. A.** (DISNORTE) and **Empresa Distribuidora de Electricidad del Sur, S. A.** (DISSUR) of Nicaragua. The coverage is for ten years and is against the risks of transfer restriction, expropriation, war and civil disturbance, and breach of contract, including the unfair calling of a performance bond.

Over the past several years, the Nicaraguan government has focused on instituting structural reforms, including privatizing electricity generating and distribution facilities. Following successful completion of the first phase of privatization, UFI was awarded the electricity distribution concession for the western part of the country (divided into north and south), where some four million people reside. The project is expected to result in significant savings due to reduced losses in the distribution system, currently estimated at 30 percent. UFI expects to retain the core employees of DISNORTE and DISSUR, and has promoted the establishment of two new companies, which will provide support services to the project. The project should expand and improve services, allow underserved rural communities new access to electricity, and contribute an estimated $50 million in taxes over the next seven years. The project is participating in a rural electrification program, which also receives financial support from the Swiss government. Additionally, the enterprise is providing scholarships for ten low-income students per year to attend Managua National University's engineering program. Meanwhile, the general economy is expected to reap benefits through improved reliability and quality, as a result of improved management and technology and equipment upgrades.

Notes

1. The figure may not adequately depict the growth of private insurers, as the largest private insurer, Lloyd's, is not a member of the Berne Union. It is estimated that the recent decline of Lloyd's capacity for investment insurance is in the order of 40 to 50 percent.

2. As of June 30, 2002, MIGA's gross and net exposure in Argentina was US$591 million and US$208 million, respectively. As of June 30, 2003, these exposures had declined to US$293 million and US$139 million, respectively. As of that date, MIGA had registered one claim for a project in Argentina that was under review.

3. MIGA's treaty reinsurance allows the agency to cede automatically while it underwrites the project, holds the policy, and takes the credit risk of the reinsurer.

4. Facultative reinsurance enables MIGA to underwrite and manage exposure on a contract-specific basis where reinsurers can perform independent due diligence. In a claim situation, the facultative reinsurers are bound by MIGA's decisions, and MIGA takes the credit risk of the reinsurer.

5. The CUP is an arrangement wherein MIGA is the insurer-of-record, but retains only a portion of the exposure, with the remainder underwritten by one or more private insurers. The CUP agreement is signed by both MIGA and the private insurer, which is administered by MIGA. Although information is shared in the underwriting process, claims are determined on a simultaneous, but separate, basis and recoveries are shared on a *pari passu* basis.

Appendix III

International Political Risk Management: Exploring New Frontiers

Theodore H. Moran, ed.

Published by The World Bank from the second MIGA-Georgetown Symposium, 2000.

This volume can be ordered from The World Bank
P.O. Box 960
Herndon, VA 20172-0960, U.S.A.
Tel. 703-661-1580
800-645-7247
Fax 703-661-1501

Or online at: http://publications.worldbank.org/booksellers

Table of Contents

Preface

More About MIGA

1. MIGA Member Country List
2. Contacts for the Guarantees Department
3. List of Recent MIGA Publications
4. MIGA's Websites

----

1. MIGA Member Country List as of September 30, 2003

Member Countries (163)

Industrialized Countries (22)

Australia, Austria, Belgium, Canada, Denmark, Finland, France, Germany, Greece, Iceland, Ireland, Italy, Japan, Luxembourg, Netherlands, Norway, Portugal, Spain, Sweden, Switzerland, United Kingdom, United States

Developing Countries (141)

Africa
Angola, Benin, Botswana, Burkina Faso, Burundi, Cameroon, Cape Verde, Central African Republic, Chad, Congo (Democratic Republic of), Congo (Republic of), Côte d'Ivoire, Equatorial Guinea, Ethiopia, Eritrea, Gabon, Gambia, Ghana, Guinea, Kenya, Lesotho, Madagascar, Malawi, Mali, Mauritania, Mauritius, Mozambique, Namibia, Nigeria, Rwanda, Senegal, Sierra Leone, Seychelles, South Africa, Sudan, Swaziland, Tanzania, Togo, Uganda, Zambia, Zimbabwe

Asia and the Pacific
Afghanistan, Bangladesh, Cambodia, China, East Timor, Fiji, India, Indonesia, Republic of Korea, Lao People's Democratic Rep., Malaysia, Micronesia, Mongolia, Nepal, Pakistan, Palau, Papua New Guinea, Philippines, Samoa, Singapore, Sri Lanka, Thailand, Vanuatu, Vietnam

Middle East and North Africa
Algeria, Bahrain, Egypt, Israel, Jordan, Kuwait, Lebanon, Libya, Morocco, Oman, Quatar, Saudi Arabia, Syrian Arab Republic, Tunisia, United Arab Emirates, Yemen

Europe and Central Asia
Albania, Armenia, Azerbaijan, Belarus, Bulgaria, Bosnia and Herzegovina, Croatia, Cyprus, Czech Republic, Estonia, FYR Macedonia, Georgia, Hungary, Kazakhstan, Kyrgyz Republic, Latvia, Lithuania, Malta, Moldova, Poland, Romania, Russian Federation, Serbia and Montenegro, Slovak Republic, Slovenia, Tajikistan, Turkey, Turkmenistan, Ukraine, Uzbekistan

Latin America and the Caribbean
Argentina, Bahamas, Barbados, Belize, Bolivia, Brazil, Chile, Colombia, Costa Rica, Dominica, Dominican Republic, Ecuador, El Salvador, Grenada, Guatemala, Guyana, Haiti, Honduras, Jamaica, Nicaragua, Paraguay, Panama, Peru, St. Kitts & Nevis, St. Lucia, St. Vincent, Suriname, Trinidad & Tobago, Uruguay, República Bolinariana de Venezuela

2. Contacts for the Guarantees Department

Vice President

Roger Pruneau
Vice President
202-473-6168
Rpruneau@worldbank.org

Operational Strategy Unit

Peter Jones
Manager
202-458-0443
pjones1@worldbank.org

Syndications/Reinsurance

Marc Roex
Senior Underwriter
202-458-0354
mroex@worldbank.org

Special Projects Group

Monique Koning
Lead Underwriter
202-458-5467
Mkoning@worldbank.org

Infrastructure, Oil & Gas, Mining, and Telecom (Asia/Africa/Middle East)

Philippe Valahu
Manager
656-324-4612
Pvalahu@worldbank.org

Infrastructure, Oil & Gas, Mining, and Telecoms (Latin America/ Europe/Central Asia)

Patricia Veevers-Carter
Manager
202-473-0600
pveeverscarter@worldbank.org

Finance, Agriculture, Manufacturing & Structure (Asia/Africa/Middle East)

Mansour Kane
Manager
202-458-0677
mkane2@worldbank.org

Finance, Agriculture, Manufacturing & Structure (Latin America/ Europe/Central Asia)

Ileana Boza
Manager
202-473-2807
iboza@worldbank.org

Representative Offices

Christophe Bellinger
Director, Paris
33 1 40 69 32 75
Cbellinger@worldbank.org

Philippe Valahu
Manager, Singapore
65 6324 4612
Pvalahu@worldbank.org

Mari Kogiso
Special Representative for Asia
81 3 3597-9100
mkogiso@worldbank.org

Ken Kwaku
Chief Representative, South Africa
27 11 341 9082
Kkwaku@worldbank.org

3. MIGA Publications
All publications can be access or ordered via MIGA's website, www.miga.org

- *MIGA Annual Report 2003*
- *MIGA in Conflict-Affected Countries*
- Corporate Brochure: *Insuring Investments ... Ensuring Opportunities*
- *Investment Information Services Guide*
- *Investment Insurance and Developmental Impact*

- *Investment Guarantee Guide*
- FDI Xchange: *A Customized Information Service Facilitating Foreign Direct Investment in Emerging Markets*
- Factsheets (by Regions): MIGA in Africa, MIGA in Asia, MIGA in Europe and Central Asia, MIGA in Latin America and the Caribbean, MIGA and the United States, MIGA in Middle East and North Africa
- Factsheets (by Sectors): Agribusiness; Telecommunications; Oil and Gas; Mining; Financial; Infrastructure; Manufacturing, Services, and Tourism
- Factsheets (general): MIGA At a Glance, Guarantees Program, Preliminary Application, Capacity-building Services to Investment

4. MIGA's Websites

Visit MIGA's award-winning websites at:

www.miga.org

www.ipanet.org

www.fdixchange.com

www.privatizationlink.com

Index

Marshall Plan, 79–80, 81, 83
Mexico
 FDI to, 33, 103
 underwriting in, 56, 117, 197
MidAmerican Energy Holdings
 Company, 14, 128, 139–40,
 144–45, 148, 179
Middle East, 43, 60, 193
MIGA. *See* Multilateral Investment Guarantee Agency
MMC Enterprise Risk, 53n
mobile plants and equipment,
 37
Moody's Investors Service, 110,
 119
Mozambique and MIGA-
 supported investments,
 212–14
multilateral development
 banks
 *See also specific development
 bank*
 partial risk guaranties, 92
Multilateral Investment Guarantee Agency, 192–216
 See also public providers of
 PRI
 ACE collaboration with,
 45–46, 51–52
 arbitration clause, coverage
 when host government
 refuses to arbitrate under,
 69, 89
 background of, 82, 192
 compared with OPIC, 82
 dispute resolution by,
 200–01, 205
 Guarantees Department contacts, 221–24
 investor country breakdown
 of guarantees, 199–200,
 200fA.5

leveraging resources with
 other World Bank depart-
 ments, 206
 members, 220–21
 preferred status conferred
 by, 126–27
 publications of, 224
 public-private collaboration
 of, 201–6, 203t1
 recent performance of,
 198–201
 regional breakdown of guarantees, 199, 199fA.4,
 200fA.6
 representative investments
 (by country), 206–15
 review of restrictive conditions, 5
 sectoral breakdown of guarantees, 200
 websites of, 224
Munich Re, 48
municipal or provincial governments, effect on political risk, 2, 114

natural catastrophes, exposure
 to, 13, 40
New York City, 46, 58, 75
New York Convention, 69, 88
Nicaragua and MIGA-sup-
 ported investments,
 214–15
Nixon, Richard M., 83
nonhonoring of guaranty coverage, 63, 69, 73, 89, 109,
 117, 118
nonpayment and nondelivery
 coverages, 34, 36, 129

OPIC (Overseas Private Investment Corporation)